THE BLITZ

AN ILLUSTRATED HISTORY

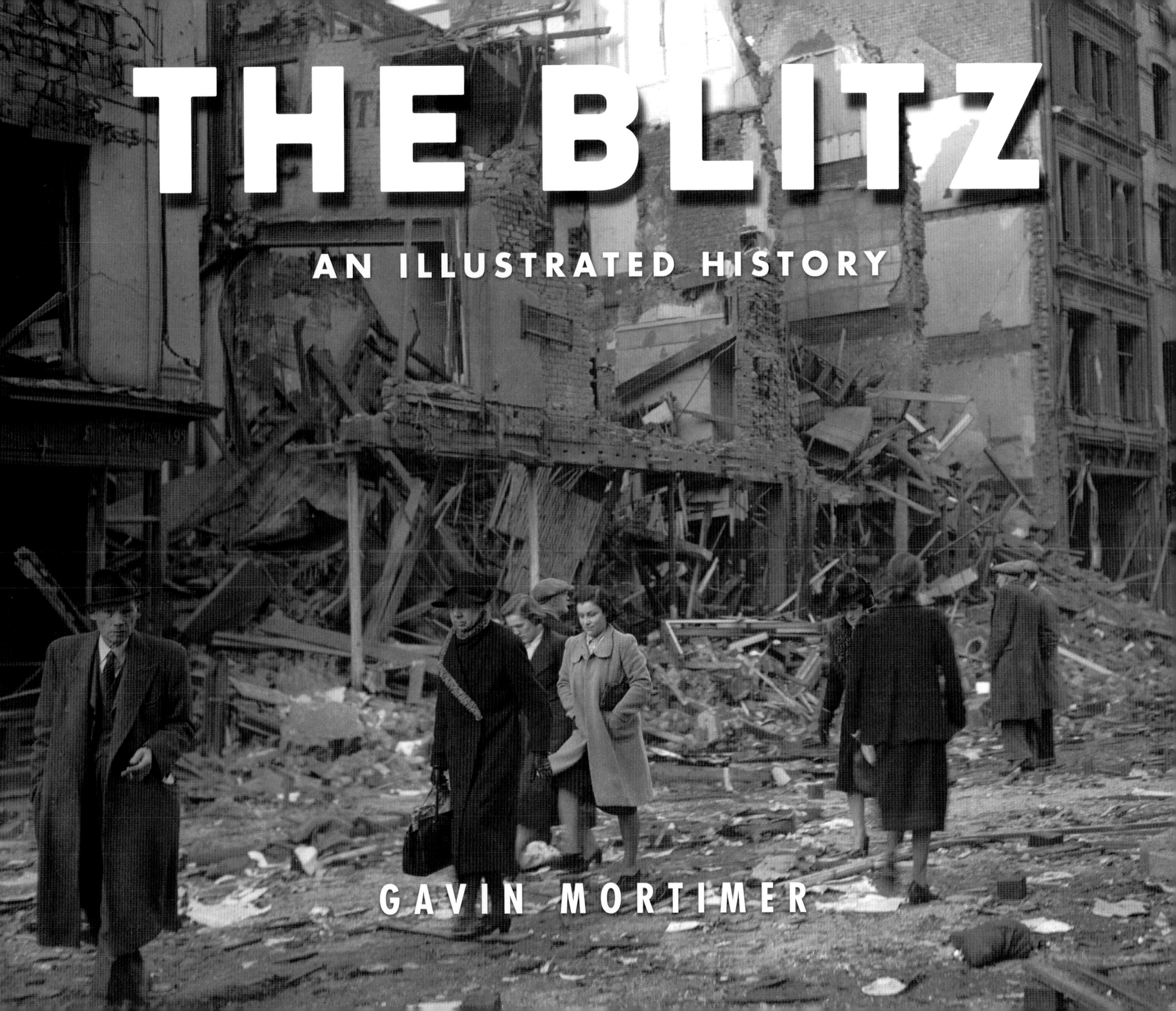

THE BLITZ

AN ILLUSTRATED HISTORY

GAVIN MORTIMER

First published in Great Britain in 2010 by Osprey Publishing,
Midland House, West Way, Botley, Oxford, OX2 0PH, UK
44-02 23rd Street, Suite 219, Long Island City, NY 11101, USA

E-mail: info@ospreypublishing.com

A CIP catalogue record for this book is available from the British Library

ISBN: 978 1 84908 424 6

Page layout by Myriam Bell Design, France
Index by Alan Thatcher
Typeset in Perpetua and Conduit ITC
Originated by PPS Grasmere Ltd, Leeds, UK
Printed in China through Worldprint

10 11 12 13 14 10 9 8 7 6 5 4 3 2 1

Front Cover: London children being rescued after a V-1 landed on their school in July 1944.

Back Cover: Rescuers sift through the rubble of Montford Place in the desperate search for survivors in July 1945.

mirrorpix

Mirrorpix is the photographic archive of the *Daily Mirror*, offering an incredible and unique collection of archive and contemporary images and illustrations spanning more than a century of British and world history.
Since 1903 their photographs have documented the changing face of Britain, capturing the events, movements, conflicts, cultural changes, politics and people who together shaped the story of the twentieth century, right up to the present day.
Their archive contains over 60 million images from world wars to world cups, royal weddings, political scandals, crimes, celebrities behaving badly, social and local history and everything in-between.

www.mirrorpix.com

ACKNOWLEDGEMENTS

I would like to thank all the wonderfully hospitable men and women kind enough to share with me their memories, some funny, many painful, of the Blitz. The Mirrorpix team were a fantastic help during all stages of the book, and have again and again provided valuable assistance and access to their wonderful archives; thank you to them. Thanks should also go to everyone at Osprey, particularly Kate Moore and Emily Holmes.

EDITOR'S NOTE

Unless otherwise indicated all images in this book are drawn from the Mirrorpix archive.

For all those who died, and all those who survived
the terrible years of the Blitz, 1940–45.

CONTENTS

INTRODUCTION

THE CALM BEFORE THE STORM: SEPTEMBER 1939 TO SEPTEMBER 1940

"The Phoney War was a horrible period. We were at war, we were training for war, but there was no war."

Florence Curry, Auxiliary Fire Service

GUERNICA. THE NAME HAUNTED THE BRITISH PEOPLE in the months following the declaration of war with Germany in 1939. Two years earlier, on a sunny April afternoon, as the Spanish market town enjoyed a busy market day, the German Luftwaffe had attacked. Within a couple of hours hundreds lay dead, mute witnesses to Europe's first demonstration of terror bombing.

Now Britain watched and waited in those strange, quiet months that followed 3 September 1939. There were many who could recall the German raids of the First World War, when 5,000 people had been killed or wounded by enemy aircraft and zeppelins, and they wondered how much worse the damage would be when inflicted by the world's most sophisticated air force.

OPPOSITE: The so-called Phoney War left people bored and restless, but at least allowed those children not evacuated from London to play at being air raid wardens. By the end of the summer the streets would no longer be as safe as they once were.

RIGHT: In the 1930s Neville Chamberlain and his government were terrified of the potential damage Hitler's Luftwaffe could inflict on Britain. It was one of the motivating factors for Britain's appeasement policy towards Hitler's Germany. But it was to no avail. With the outbreak of war the British nation braced itself for the inevitable bombing raids that the world had witnessed in Guernica and Rotterdam.

The official estimates lay with the British authorities, and they were extremely frightening. Three hundred tons of bombs had been dropped by Germany on Britain in the First World War. In December 1938 the Lord Chancellor, Frederic Maugham, said in a speech defending the government's appeasement policy that: 'The Germans had it in their power to let loose 3,000 tons of bombs in a single day.' A report published in the same year by the Committee of Imperial Defence estimated that any air attack on Britain – dubbed 'The Knockout Blow' – would begin with 3,500 tons being dropped, followed by 600 tons per day for an unspecified period.

Based on the casualties inflicted on the poor inhabitants of Guernica, the British government planned for 50 casualties per ton of bombs. In other words, when the initial assault came they could expect 175,000 men, women and children to be killed or wounded. The Ministry of Health then indulged in some macabre mathematics and extrapolated the figures to produce a forecast of 600,000 Britons

BELOW LEFT: A group of women paint the kerb white to allow people to find their way through Britain's streets during the blackout hours. Despite the careful preparations a sense of unreality prevailed during the first few months of the war. However, with the desperate retreat following the collapse of France and the first massed German air raids the precautions became all too necessary.

BELOW: This *Daily Mirror* cartoon from 20 August 1940 warned Germany that any attack on London would be like flying into the jaws of hell. By this point the Luftwaffe had already launched their all-out offensive against the RAF with the *Adlerangriff* (Eagle Attack) on 13 August 1940.

OPPOSITE: A gas attack was the greatest fear of the British but fortunately such a horror never came to pass, although drills were frequently carried out.

"The officer in charge of the fire station was a regular and I remember him telling us 'don't complain about sitting around. Get your rest while you can because take my word for it, the bombs will drop one day and when they do, you'll wish you could have a rest then'." Florence Curry, Auxiliary Fire Service, Bow, East London

killed in the first six months of the aerial war, with a further 1,200,000 wounded.

Questions troubled the powers-that-be throughout 1938 and 1939. How would they tend these wounded? Where would they bury the dead? What would they do with those driven insane? How would they deal with the homeless? What could they do to prevent a gas attack?

As well as a call for auxiliary firemen and women, ambulance drivers and special police constables, an air raid wardens' service was formed, called the Air Raid Precaution (ARP), and in 1938 the government distributed a pamphlet asking for the following:

> Men over 30 and women over 18 who by reason of their experience or occupation or their position in social or public life, possess standing or influence in the immediate neighbourhood of their homes. Telephone desirable but not essential.

The 200,000 volunteers who answered their country's call to join the ARP were put to work in the winter of 1938 digging trench shelters in parks, building brick street shelters and sandbagging important buildings. At the same time they underwent first-aid training and learned particularly how to treat victims of a gas attack. Gas masks were distributed to the entire population as was a handbook entitled *Air Raids – What You Must Know, What You Must Do*. Anderson Shelters (named after Sir John Anderson, Lord Privy Seal in charge of Air Raid Precaution and later Home Secretary) were distributed to families, many of whom looked at the six curved sheets of corrugated steel and wondered how on earth they would protect against a high-explosive bomb. Families on an annual income of less than £250 got their shelter free, everyone else was charged £6 14s. They came with a set of instructions explaining how to sink the steel sheets into the ground, bolt them at the top and cover with sandbags and a layer of top soil. Two more panels were fixed at either end, one of which was also a door. Once erected, an Anderson shelter was six feet high, four feet six inches wide, six feet six inches long, and able to house six people.

Meanwhile, the authorities drew up plans for a 'blackout' of towns and cities when the bombing began and also drafted a mass evacuation scheme for the country's city-dwelling children. On Friday 1 September 1939, not long after news reached Britain that Germany had invaded Poland, the country's 1.5 million-strong (of which 400,000 were full-time, earning £3 a week) Civil Defence was mobilised. Along the length and breadth of Britain, men and women left their workplace and reported for duty. Firemen, ambulance drivers, air raid wardens, policemen, none knew exactly what awaited them but they knew that whatever it was, it would be fraught with danger.

The air raid siren first sounded in London on Sunday 3 September, not long after Prime Minister Neville Chamberlain had informed the country that a state of war now existed between Britain and Germany. Winston Churchill recalled later that Chamberlain:

> had scarcely ceased speaking when a strange, prolonged, wailing noise, afterwards to become familiar, broke upon the ear. My wife came into the room braced by the crisis and commented favourably upon the German promptitude and precision.[1]

In fact it was a false alarm sparked by a civilian aircraft from France yet that mattered not to the 650,000 women and children who immediately evacuated London. The siren sounded the next day, Monday, and again on Wednesday 6 September. A squadron of Spitfires was scrambled from its base in Essex to intercept the raiders, as was a squadron of Hurricanes, but there were no Germans to be found. In the nervous confusion two Hurricanes were shot down by the Spitfires over Barking Creek. Everyone was on edge.

But still the Germans didn't come. As autumn turned to winter the British apprehension turned to amusement. '*Blitzkrieg*', they joked to one another, 'more like the "Sitzkrieg"', while others called it the 'Phoney War' or the 'Bore War'. Many of the 400,000 full-time members of the Civil Defence were ridiculed in public with the young fit men who had joined the Auxiliary Fire Service (AFS)

Anderson Shelters were nothing more than sheets of corrugated steel but proved effective if a little uncomfortable. (Topfoto)

coming in for particular abuse. They were derided as 'army dodgers', refused entry to restaurants and subjected to graffiti such as 'Cut price Firemen, £3. Not worth it' being daubed on the walls of their stations. Meanwhile, many of those people evacuated in September began returning home to London, to a city where the theatres and cinemas were reopening and sporting events, shut down upon the outbreak of war, were once again drawing large crowds.

The London-based journalist Molly Panter-Downes wrote an article for the *New Yorker* in the spring of 1940 in which she said so far it had been a 'war of yawns' for the capital's Civil Defence. 'They spend their nights playing cards, taking cat naps and practically yearning for a short air raid', she wrote. A few weeks later the Phoney War ended when Germany swept through the Low Countries and overran France with frightening ease.

Now Britain stood alone against Germany, separated from the might of the Nazi war machine only by the thin ribbon of the English Channel. The new Prime Minister, Winston Churchill, more charismatic and pugnacious than his predecessor, Chamberlain, refused to countenance a peace deal with Hitler and his Third Reich. So on 30 June 1940 Colonel General Jodl, Chief of the Armed Forces Command Staff, published a memorandum entitled *The Continuation of the War Against England*. It included the following:

> There are three possibilities:
>
> Siege. This includes attack by land and sea against all incoming and outgoing traffic. Attack on the English air arm and on the country's war economy and its sources as a whole.
>
> Terror attacks against the English centres of population.
>
> Invasions with the purpose of occupying England.

OPPOSITE: Though women weren't allowed on the front line of firefighting there was no harm in practising.

CHAPTER ONE

HELL FROM ON HIGH: SEPTEMBER 1940

"In England they're filled with curiosity and keep asking 'Why doesn't he come?' Be calm, be calm. He's coming! He's coming!"

Adolf Hitler, addressing a rally in Berlin, 4 September 1940

IN THE FIRST HALF OF JULY Hitler still held out hope that Britain would sue for peace. On 16 July Hitler issued Directive No.16 formally stating his intention to conquer the last outpost of freedom in Western Europe if Churchill refused to heed his call:

> As England, despite the hopelessness of her military situation, has so far shown herself unwilling to come to any compromise, I have therefore decided to begin preparations for, and if necessary to carry out, an invasion of England.

Any successful invasion was dependent on securing air superiority. Reichsmarschall Hermann Göring, the Commander-in-Chief of the Luftwaffe, began to prepare his forces for operations against Great Britain. From the Low Countries he allotted Albert Kesselring's Luftflotte 2; in northern France he earmarked Hugo Sperrle's

OPPOSITE: Early on in the Blitz, many firemen were ill-equipped for the challenges that lay ahead. These three men are on duty without any water-proof clothing.

RIGHT: Buckingham Palace was targeted by the Luftwaffe several times during the first weeks of the Blitz but damage was thankfully slight.

Luftflotte 3 and Hans-Juergen Stumpff's Luftflotte 5 in Scandinavia were readied for action.

Between them the three wings comprised 1,380 bombers, 428 dive-bombers and 1,100 fighters. Arrayed against this considerable force were 48 RAF squadrons of 600 aircraft, from the new and impressive Spitfire fighter to the rather less formidable Defiants.

Throughout July air battles raged over the English Channel and the south coast of England with the Germans initially dominant. On 19 July nine RAF Defiants were ambushed by a patrol of Messerschmitt 109s and six of the British planes were shot down, for the loss of just one German aircraft. The dogfights intensified as the Luftwaffe attacked British shipping and on 2 August Göring felt confident enough to step up his aerial war. Bombing raids would be carried out against military targets on the British mainland to soften up the enemy ahead of Operation *Sealion*, the planned invasion of Britain.

As early as June 1940 there had been light bombing raids on cities such as Stoke and Bristol, but nothing on the scale of those carried out on 11 August. Seventy-five German bombers, escorted by an even larger number of Messerschmitts, attacked the Portland naval base. The following day Portsmouth was hit along with a string of south coast radar stations. However, 13 August was the day – in German eyes at least – that the Battle of Britain truly began, and the Luftwaffe marked the auspicious occasion by attacking Portland again, as well as a factory near Birmingham that made parts for Spitfires and the naval base at Southampton. On the afternoon of Tuesday 13 August, eight-year-old Eric Hill was out shopping with his mother in Southampton when the Germans came.

> We were in the air raid shelter for three, four hours, until we got the All-Clear to come out … when we came out the high street was running with melted margarine and butter because they'd hit the cold storage. And I remember my mother and most of the women, because it was wartime, they were just grabbing handfuls of this butter and trying to ram it into whatever they could so we could have butter or margarine.[1]

DAILY MIRROR, Thursday, Sept. 12, 1940.

Daily Mirror

SEPT 12

No. 11,470 ✦ ONE PENNY

Registered at the G.P.O. as a Newspaper.

HITLER PLAN TO INVADE IS READY

—Premier

THE Prime Minister told the nation in his broadcast last night that the Germans are thoroughly planning a full-scale invasion which may be launched at any time in England, Scotland or Ireland—or all three.

Hundreds of barges and dozens of merchant ships are massed in French, Dutch, Belgian and Norwegian harbours. Troops are waiting.

An invasion attempt could not be long delayed. "Therefore we must regard the next week or so as a very important week, even in our history," said Mr. Churchill. "It ranks with the days of the Armada."

"Every man and woman," said the Prime Minister, "will therefore prepare himself to do his duty, whatever it may be, with special pride and care."

But he also declared that the German effort to secure daylight mastery of the air over England had so far "failed conspicuously." And our air, naval and military strength was greater than ever.

Great Air Battles

Said Mr. Churchill:

"When I said in the Commons the other day that I thought it improbable that the enemy's air attacks in September could be more than three times as great as in August, I was not, of course, referring to the barbarous attacks on the civilian population, but to the great air battles which had been fought out between our fighters and the German Air Force.

"You will understand that whenever the weather is favourable, German bombers, protected by fighters, often three or four hundred at a time, surge over this island, especially Kent, in the hopes of attacking military and other objectives by daylight.

"However, they are met by our fighter squadrons, and nearly always broken up, and their losses average three to one in machines, and six to one in pilots.

"This effort of the Germans to secure daylight mastery of the air over England is, of course, the crux of the whole war. So far it has failed conspicuously.

"We Are Stronger"

"It has cost them very dear, and we have felt stronger, and are actually and relatively a good deal stronger, than when the hard fighting began in July.

"There is no doubt that Hitler is using up his fighter force at a very high rate, and that if he goes on for many more weeks, he will wear down and ruin this vital part of his Air Force.

"That will give us a very great advantage.

"On the other hand, for him to try to invade this country without having secured mastery in the air would be a very hazardous undertaking.

"Nevertheless, all his preparations for invasion on a great scale are steadily going forward.

"Several hundreds of self-propelled barges are moving down the coast of Europe from the German and Dutch harbours to the ports of Northern France, from Dunkirk to Brest and beyond Brest to the French harbours in the Bay of Biscay.

"Besides this, convoys of merchant

Continued on Back Page, Col. 1

92 HUNS DOWN

THE German Air Force lost at least ninety machines in their daylight attacks on London yesterday—then flew into the most terrific A.A. barrage yet when they came over for their night raid on the city.

A circle of heavy A.A. guns wrapped London around a ten-mile radius, and a surprise curtain of death awaited the raiders. At times shells burst at the rate of more than a hundred a minute.

Over a south-east district gunners scored a direct hit on a raider. The machine burst into a thousand blazing fragments which fell to earth like a gigantic firework display.

Another came down in North London, bringing the day's bag to at least ninety-two. The crew were captured.

So clear was the night that the gunners were not assisted for the first few hours of the raid by the searchlights.

The German machines were kept at a tremendously high altitude, but incendiary bombs dropped haphazardly in East London started fresh fires.

Bombs were dropped in south-east districts.

A high explosive bomb crashed on the roof of a London newspaper building, but there were no casualties, two

Continued on Back Page, Col. 3

Missed Goebbels by Ten Feet

During the R.A.F. raid on Berlin on Tuesday night—biggest so far—a 15lb. incendiary bomb fell ten feet from Goebbels's residence and tore a deep hole in the garden, announced the official German news agency.

Salvos of heavy bombs and hundreds of incendiaries fell on Berlin's famous Potsdam station. It quickly caught fire

Admissions of serious damage were made by the Berlin radio last night. Deutschlandsender stated that the R.A.F. tried to destroy all symbols of the Nazi system. They dropped bombs on the Brandenburger Arch, the Physical and Hygienic Institute of Berlin University, the Academy of Art and the Unter den Linden.

*** Story of the raid Page 3

WHAT THE KING SAID . . .

WHEN the King saw the damage inflicted on Buckingham Palace by a time-bomb, "he said much the same as you or I would do if his home had been bombed."

That was how the King's r[illegible] were described to the "Daily Mirror" yesterday by a Palace official.

And a workman said as he helped to repair the damage:

"The King's home has certainly copped a packet. We've been luckier up our way—touch wood!"

Pool Wrecked

The bomb, believed to be a 250-pounder, fell in a Palace garden after the King had visited the ruined houses of his people in London's East End and exploded during a later [illegible]

It wrecked the Princesses' swimming pool, smashing about thirty windows in sitting-rooms and bathrooms and flinging huge pieces of masonry on to the roof.

A lump weighing 1 cwt. was thrown more than 300ft. over the roof of the Palace. It crashed into the court on the other side.

Another landed on the roof and fell [illegible] into the picture gallery.

Pieces of wood still floated yesterday in the water of the green-tiled pool which was built by the King and Queen as a surprise present for the Princesses on their return from Scotland two years ago.

Diving-boards were twisted and half buried. Radiators were jerked from the walls.

Water and gas mains underneath were broken, flooding the engine-room under which the household staff sheltered in safety.

The King and Queen were at Windsor when the bomb fell and there were no casualties.

20 ft. Crater

A sentry and a policeman on duty nearby were safe in their bell shelters.

Yesterday the King and Queen, accompanied by Mr. Churchill, inspected the crater, 10ft. deep and 20ft. wide, and the damaged part of the Palace.

The Queen Visits Bombed Homes.—Story and pictures on pages 6 and 7.

The King and Queen looking round the bomb damage at Buckingham Palace. Note the men at work in the crater. Another Palace picture in middle pages.

EXPLOSIONS SHAKE COAST

Heavy explosions shook the south-east coast yesterday. It is not known whether the explosions were caused by bombs or by shells from German long-range guns

Other explosions were heard along the coast.

Anti-aircraft guns then opened fire on a lone German plane flying at great height which might have been a bomber or a reconnaissance plane "spotting" for German artillery.

For the next six weeks the battle for Britain was fought out in the clear blue skies of southern England. The main Luftwaffe target was RAF Fighter Command, but a myriad of small bombing raids were also launched against other military installations. Often the bombs missed their targets. More than 1,000 civilians were killed by Luftwaffe bombs in August, including 136 children, and that was just a prelude to what lay in store.

Hitler had initially scheduled 10 August as the invasion date. However, bad weather forced its postponement to the 13th and then again when the great British obsession came to its people's rescue. Thereafter, as the Luftwaffe failed to defeat the RAF, despite incurring grievous losses, Hitler began to dither on the date of the invasion. He may have been persuaded by the likes of Admiral Raeder, one of many senior military commanders who doubted the wisdom of a seaborne invasion of Britain, or the Führer may have decided to husband his resources for the conquest of Russia. Whatever the reason, Hitler then turned to the second of General Jodl's propositions for subjugating Britain – terror bombing.

OPPOSITE: The front page of the *Daily Mirror* on 12 September 1940 encapsulated the uncertainty of the time.

LEFT: Firewomen played a crucial, if unseen role, during the Blitz, fielding incident reports and dispatching crews.

BELOW: A little girl rescues her doll's house from her bombed home in Bristol.

GEORGE GREENWELL

THE PHOTOGRAPHER George Greenwell joined the *Daily Mirror* straight from school in 1923. In his 50-year career with the newspaper he made his name in several spheres photographing everything from royalty to ground-breaking surgical procedures. During the Second World War he served his country by volunteering for the London Fire Service but never went out fighting fires without taking his camera with him. This placed him a unique position to create a pictorial record of the nation's capital at war. Apart from the obvious dangers of the fires, falling masonry and the like, Greenwell once had to fight off accusations that he was a spy when two policemen took exception to him photographing the rescue of an injured girl from a bombed out building. When he was taken into protective custody both his fire station chief and his editor told the police, presumably tongue-in-cheek, to keep him there overnight for his own safety. Certainly, he seems to have given no thought to his own personal safety in his desire to capture the perfect image, as indicated by his dramatic account of the Second Great Fire of London on 29 December 1940:

> As I approached Fleet Street from Fire Service Headquarters in Lambeth, fires were raging everywhere. St Bride's, Fleet Street, was a mass of flames. I halted to take two or three shots of the last of this Wren masterpiece and nearly lost my life. Falling masonry just missed me.
>
> I went on to St Paul's Cathedral to find it at the centre of a fantastic fire lit fairyland. Incendiaries were bouncing off window ledges, rooftops, in fact even off our appliances, but, alas, too many had found a more valuable target. Ave Maria Lane was blazing furiously from end to end. St Paul's churchyard was fast becoming an immense conflagration. As I climbed the 300 odd steps to the dome of St Paul's I grinned to myself as I thought of the many bewhiskered professors who, after endless calculations, had decided that St Paul's would fall to the ground after another thousand or so No. 11 buses had passed the building or something like that.
>
> The whole of the Cathedral shivered and swayed as another H.E. fell close.
>
> The stench of explosive and smoke got into one's nostrils. But as I paused for a much-needed rest I saw through a slit window a most amazing spectacle.
>
> All below me was a swaying mass of fire, and the fire officer with me said 'We are certain to go to heaven if cooked on the dome of Paul's'.
>
> We were welcomed on to the balcony, which surrounds the dome with yet another H.E., which had the peculiar effect of appearing to have temporally blown away the great volume of smoke, and there as through a hole in the clouds, was London burning.
>
> It was incredible, yet bewilderingly fascinating.
>
> I could see big fires and smaller fires, and even tiny arch like glares and splutters as more incendiaries rained down upon us.
>
> The St Paul's Fire Watchers were playing a noble part, clambering like monkeys over the roofs and parapets slinging over or covering with sand incendiary bombs, which settled in 'soft spots'.
>
> At one moment the heat was intense. Then it became quite cool.

St Paul's survived the conflagration as did George Greenwell. He was the only photographer to take photos from the dome of St Paul's while all around him London burned. He eventually retired from the *Daily Mirror* in 1973.

TOP: Greenwell took this view from his office at the *Daily Mirror* in Fleet Street during the spring of 1941.

ABOVE: Even the *Mirror*'s photographer wasn't immune to the Luftwaffe bombs, as George Greenwell discovered when he returned to his damaged home (far right) after one raid.

THE TERROR CAMPAIGN

Since Guernica three years earlier, the Nazis had had another opportunity for perfecting the science of terror bombing. They had levelled the Dutch city of Rotterdam the previous May, killing more than 1,000 people in the process. It had brought about the swift capitulation of Holland's main industrial city and Hitler believed a sustained bombardment of London would achieve similar results and finally force the obdurate Churchill to the negotiating table.

Another factor influenced Hitler's decision to switch the focus of the Luftwaffe from destroying the RAF to destroying the British capital. On the night of 24–25 August a handful of German bombers lost their way over blacked-out Britain and accidentally dropped their bombs on London instead of their intended target – the oil terminal at Thameshaven. Churchill ordered reprisals and the next night 81 RAF bombers attacked Berlin. The raid did little damage, materially or otherwise, but Hitler was incensed. For years he and Göring had promised the German people that they were immune from the kind of destruction the Luftwaffe was wreaking on the rest of Europe.

On Wednesday 4 September Hitler addressed a rally in Berlin and assured them they would be avenged, saying:

> In England they're filled with curiosity and keep asking 'Why doesn't he come?' Be calm, be calm. He's coming! He's coming! When the British Air Force drops two or three thousand kilograms of bombs, then we will in one night drop 150, 250, 300, or 400 thousand kilograms. When they declare that they will increase their attacks on our cities, then we will raze their cities.

On 5 September Hitler ordered Göring to begin attacking London and the next day the corpulent figure of the Reichsmarschall arrived in Calais for a front-row seat for what he hoped would be the beginning of the end for Great Britain.

Saturday 7 September in London was, in the words of writer and auxiliary fireman William Sansom, 'one of the fairest days of the century, a day of clear warm air and high blue skies'.[2] Sansom was stationed in Westminster and, like the rest of the capital's firemen and women, had spent the preceding year fighting nothing more fierce than boredom. However, at least they had been trained by the regulars in the techniques of fighting fires and rescuing people, even if they had to wear a uniform of dungarees, rubber boots and a cap

Soldiers discard their tunics as they clean up Chelsea following a Luftwaffe raid.

"When I got home I joined my parents in the cupboard under the stairs. We didn't have an Anderson shelter, my mum didn't think we'd need one because she believed Churchill when he'd said no German bombers would ever reach London." Iris Grant

because there weren't enough double-breasted tunics, rubber leggings and steel helmets to go round.

One of Sansom's auxiliary colleagues, Fred Cockett, had left his job as a catering manager at the House of Commons to become a fireman at Waterloo. He recalled how in the dragging weeks and months of the Phoney War, they had been taught how to rescue someone jumping from a burning building. 'The rescuers had to tuck their chins in and on no account look up. If you did, the jerk as the jumper hit the sheet could whip back your head and break your neck.'[3]

The training had intensified during the late summer of 1940 as the Battle of Britain raged and sporadic attacks were launched by the Luftwaffe against British military targets. However, on the afternoon of 7 September the war seemed a long way away. It was, recalled Sansom, one of those enchanting early autumn days made for 'walking in the park or just sitting at home with the windows open'.

Sixteen-year-old Iris Grant had spent the morning in Welling, in south London, attending a training course to become a dispenser with *Boots* the chemist. She was on the trolley bus back to her home in Plumstead and looking forward to putting her feet up for the rest of the weekend. Her father, who was in his late fifties, was more nervous than most at the prospect of any large-scale German attack on London. Having spent his working life in the Woolwich Arsenal, and living round the corner from the country's largest munitions factory, Charles Grant didn't much fancy being anywhere near the arsenal should it receive a direct hit from a Luftwaffe bomb.

As Londoners made the most of the Indian summer, Göring was also enjoying the sun on his face on Saturday afternoon as he stood on the cliffs of Cap Blanc Nez, just a few miles west of Calais. With him was Albert Kesselring, commander of Luftflotte 2. The previous evening they had issued their force with the operation order for a major strike against target *Loge* – the codeword for the planned attack on London. The order ended with a reminder to all aircrew that:

Shocked, but unscathed, a family is led to safety by an ARP warden following an air raid on London in 1940.

> To achieve the necessary maximum effect it is essential that units fly as a highly concentrated force – during approach, attack and especially on return. The main objective of the operation is to prove that the Luftwaffe can achieve this.

Together Göring and Kesselring watched in appreciative silence as a total of 350 German bombers took off for London, accompanied by an escort of some 600 fighters.

The huge force was picked up by British radar stations at 4pm, as the bombers rendezvoused with their fighter escorts above the French coast. At 4.16pm the tip of the formation crossed the English coast and was spotted by the Observer Corps posts. RAF squadrons were scrambled to meet the invaders as the dense mass advanced from the west, up the Thames Estuary. The outnumbered British fighters succeeded in reaping a heavy toll on the attackers, but such a vast formation was impossible to break up and hundreds of the German bombers maintained their course for the capital.

At 5pm 25-year-old Lillian Patient was closing up the Lyons teashop opposite the Blackwall Tunnel in east London. As a Sally – as all Lyons' waitresses were nicknamed – Lillian had spent the day serving people sodas and shakes, and was about to set out for her home in Walthamstow. She recalled:

> When the sirens went that afternoon, my job was to put up shutters over the front windows of the shop. Looking up in the sky, I saw a formation of German bombers. I left the shutters to put up themselves and made for the staff shelter in the backyard of the shop. The staff were already seated inside and one of them was playing the mouth organ.[4]

To other Londoners who looked skywards the vast flock of German aircraft seemed to blot out the sun. They were two miles high and 20 miles wide, an apocalyptic vista on such a delightful day, accompanied by the 'howling' of the air raid siren. It was Scotland Yard's responsibility to alert each London borough to the impending threat, and from then the borough's job was to sound the alarm as soon as possible. Walter Blanchard who lived in Barking, Essex, was on duty as an air raid messenger at the post commanded by his father when the siren sounded.

Throughout the so-called 'Bore War' many of the 400,000 full-time members of the Civil Defence as well as those young, able-bodied men who joined the Auxiliary Fire Service were ridiculed as 'army dodgers'. No longer labelled 'army dodgers' after the Blitz started, these two auxiliary firemen wear their battle scars with pride.

> He said 'get on your bike, go down to the footbridge, climb up and see if you can see them coming'. I went and looked and for the first time I had a feeling of cold fear. There were, by my count, more than 600 aircraft in the formation of a huge letter 'I'. These were the German bombers coming by daylight.[5]

One of those who had seen the force heading their way from the start was Wing Commander John Hodsoll, Inspector General of Air Raid Precautions, who had tracked the raiders' route from the War Room of the Home Office in Whitehall. Thinking it might be a good idea to see first-hand what he was up against, Hodsoll climbed on to the roof

to watch the raid. 'Huge clouds of black smoke were billowing and spiralling up into the clear blue sky', he later wrote.

> Great spurts of flame were shooting up; there was a dull thud of bombs as they exploded and reverberated in the distance, and an acrid smell of burning was borne in on the wind … the spectacle had an almost eerie fascination which held us spellbound and immobile, and it was some time before I could drag myself away and descend into the street.[6]

The first bombs to fall landed on the docks and Woolwich Arsenal. Iris Grant was still on the trolley bus when she looked out of the window and saw the carnage unfolding before her eyes. 'Someone said "looks like Plumstead" is alight', remembered Iris.

> When I got home I joined my parents in the cupboard under the stairs. We didn't have an Anderson shelter, my mum didn't think we'd need one because she believed Churchill when he'd said no German bombers would ever reach London.[7]

Inside the Woolwich Arsenal an orderly evacuation was taking place, as all the 500 workers knew what would happen if they panicked. One, 20-year-old Joan Witson, recalled how when she went to work in the Danger Sheds, 'a number was painted on our backs [of our overalls] in black paint and we were told that if we ever ran during a raid we would be identified by our number and sacked'. On Saturday 7 September Joan and her workmates cowered in the Woolwich shelter, 'for hours, listening to the terrible noise of the German planes'.

In the first hour of the raid boroughs such as Bermondsey, Poplar and West Ham bore the brunt of the German fury. All of London's principal docks – West India, the Victoria and Albert, and Surrey – went up in flames. In *Front Line,* the official history of the London Fire Brigade during the Second World War, the author described the pyrotechnical pandemonium:

Londoners left homeless by the bombing were initially sent to rest centres.

In the docks themselves strange things were going on. There were pepper fires, loading the surrounding air heavily with stinging particles, so that when the firemen took a deep breath it felt like the burning fire itself. There were rum fires, with torrents of blazing liquid pouring from the warehouse doors and barrels exploding like bombs themselves. There was a paint fire, another cascade of white-hot flame, coating the pumps with varnish that could not be cleaned for weeks. A rubber fire gave forth black clouds of smoke so asphyxiating that it could only be fought from a distance, and was always threatening to choke the attackers. Sugar, it seems, burns well in liquid form as it floats on the water in dockyard basins. Tea makes a blaze that is 'sweet, sickly and very intense'. One man found it odd to be pouring cold water on hot tea leaves. A grain warehouse when burning produced great clouds of black flies that settled in banks upon the walls, whence the firemen washed them off with their jets. There were rats in their hundreds. And the residue of burned wheat was 'a sticky mess that pulls your boots off'.[8]

As the firemen struggled to contain the blazing docks a second wave of German bombers approached from the south. Once again bombs tumbled from the Heinkels and Dorniers, exploding thousands of feet below on the docks and factories lining the Thames, and on the ramshackle houses of the people who worked there. Stepney, in east London, was home to 200,000 people, a melting pot of people of diverse races and religions who somehow managed to live harmoniously despite the cramped conditions. Families as large as 12 people were packed into a single-storey tenement with a similar number on the floor above.

In one such building Bernard Kops cowered against the wall, scared out of his 13-year-old mind at the hell exploding around him. 'That day stands out like a flaming wound in my memory', he wrote in his memoirs 20 years later.

> Imagine a ground floor flat crowded with hysterical women, crying babies and great crashes in the sky and the whole earth shaking ... [then] the men started to play cards and the women tried a little sing-song ... I sat under the table where the men were playing cards, screwing my eyes up and covering my ears.[9]

THE FIRST DAYLIGHT BOMBING RAIDS ON LONDON

THE SOCIETY ARTIST NANCY SPENDER was working as a conductress with the Auxiliary Ambulance Service on the night of 7 September. At the height of the bombardment she was called to an incident in Silvertown, West Ham, (where the Tate and Lyle sugar refinery was located), her account of which was later included in Doreen E. Idle's wartime book *The War Over West Ham*.

> We went off and we weren't allowed any lights at all, and the streets were absolutely pitch black except when we got the full glare of the copper-coloured fire... I've never seen anything like it, you know, right across the sky there was nothing but blazing things and everything going up. As far as we could see everything was on fire – great, red flames were going up and down the brick walls, piles of houses all collapsed or on fire, warehouses like blazing cathedrals standing up and then falling down, bricks going up, bombs coming down, there was a terrific muddle of fire, everything reflected in the water ... well, by now we were in a complete jam, there was nothing but fire-fighting apparatus, ambulances, hosepipes, the whole thing a complete and utter traffic jam, and we just had to take our place in the rather narrow road and wait ... every few minutes one of those blazing piles shot like a fountain into the sky. It reminded me very much of an eighteenth-century print of hot geysers in America, because of the fountains of stuff that jetted up and fell down with a crash. Anyway, we did get through and we got over the bridge and then my driver thought he knew another route ... then we came across another car, an ambulance car, also looking for Oriental Road, and he joined in behind us, and we went on for a bit and then we came to another road, and there wasn't a single house standing – there was nothing, nothing at all except holes. Out of several of these holes little people popped their heads... Anybody hurt? – and not a soul answered. So I said again – anybody hurt? – and still nobody answered, so I went up to one woman and tapped her and said – Is there anybody hurt here? – and she said – over there there's a mother and a two-day-old baby, they've both been dug out, and I think further up there's a boy with a very bad knee, he got dug out, he was buried up to his waist, but I don't know about the others. So I went over to the mother, she didn't speak, and I wrapped her in a blanket and put her on the stretcher... I came back again and collected the boy, with some help, and then we got back to the ambulance with him and after that I just filled the ambulance with as many people as I could cram in, about fifteen or sixteen. Still nobody spoke, it was all the most deathly silence, and I got in beside them this time, not beside the driver, and drew the curtains to shut out the ghastly glow, and deafen the noise a bit, and we drove off.[10]

Smoke rises from behind the dome of St Paul's Cathedral on 7 September following the start of the German operation codenamed *Loge* after the mythical Norse god of fire.

It took an hour or so before the rest of London realised the full extent of what was happening in the east. They'd heard the planes and the bombs but assumed at first it was another raid on a dock or naval base. Gradually it dawned on them that this was it, the long awaited 'knockout blow' that they'd been warned about, and that just a few miles to the east their fellow Londoners were dying in their droves. Auxiliary fireman William Sansom was one of thousands confused to see the sun setting not just in the west, near Putney, but to the east as well, in Stepney, Bow and Poplar. But then, 'when the western skies had already grown dark the fierce red glow in the East struck harshly fast'.

The first wave of German bombers returned to France, refuelled, rearmed, and then took off for another sortie on London. All the while they were pursued by RAF fighters, whose courage was inexhaustible against the aerial armada. Ten German bombers and 22 fighters were shot down, while British casualties were 29 planes downed and 17 pilots killed or badly wounded. 'A German plane crashed close to our house, just at the end of our street', recalled Iris Grant. 'It landed on top of an Anderson shelter killing the woman inside and the pilot. When they pulled out the German they found he was dressed head to foot in clothes bought in Paris.'

Flight Sergeant George Unwin of 19 Squadron was patrolling the skies in search of a suitable target when he spotted, on its way back to France, a twin-engine Dornier light-bomber with a crew of four, including front and rear gunners. Unwin attacked the rear gunner, giving him a short burst from the Spitfire's eight Browning machine guns. Then he closed for the kill, 'firing for quite a long burst, leaning forward to the gunsight which was in the middle of a piece of bullet resistant glass. Suddenly a hole appeared in this glass directly in front of my face. I thought "Good God, I must be dead!"'

A fireman's work was never done during the Blitz. Here a group of firefighters fight a blaze the morning after a London raid.

Unwin wasn't dead, though the bullet had damaged his aircraft, causing an ominous cloud to fill the cockpit. The pilot slid back the hood of the Spitfire and prepared to bail out when 'suddenly I saw that the smoke wasn't black and I could smell that it was glycol. So I strapped myself back in again, left the hood open and started looking for a field to land in.'[11]

It was dark when many of the German bombers returned for their second sortie but they had no trouble finding their target. By midnight the East End of London was an ocean of flames, waves of oranges and reds sweeping all before them. Nine fires were classified 'conflagration', which in the definition of the London Fire Service meant more than 100 pumps were needed to fight each one. There were innumerable 'major fires', necessitating more than 30 pumps and just as many 'serious fires', fireman's vernacular for a fire requiring between 11 and 30 pumps.

Fighting these firestorms were the thousands of men who had volunteered a year or so earlier and spent the ensuing months being ridiculed as 'army dodgers'. In the days that followed 7 September they were rechristened 'heroes with grimy faces', and restaurants that had refused them entry a few months earlier suddenly found them the best table in the house. However, around midnight that Saturday, the vast majority of London's firefighters were experiencing their first blaze. One of the fires in Surrey Docks required 300 pumps, while a further 200 were called to the Woolwich Arsenal to deal with the blazing munitions factory.

For hours the firemen crouched over their hoses, playing water on the fires, ignoring the sounds of falling bombs that reminded one of 'tearing silk'. One remembered looking up into the sky and seeing no longer German bombers but a flock of pigeons. 'They seemed lost, as if they couldn't understand the unnatural dawn. It looked like sunrise all around us. The pigeons seemed white in the glare, birds of peace making a strange contrast with the scene below.'

TOP RIGHT: The clean-up operation continues in Belvedere Road, Waterloo, after one raid.

BOTTOM RIGHT: Exhausted firemen head back to the station after a night on the front line.

The last bombs fell at 4.30am on Sunday. The All-Clear sounded soon after but for the firemen there was to be little respite. The nine conflagrations were still to be brought under control and there were a further 19 major fires and 40 serious fires. The number of smaller fires was practically incalculable. Throughout the Sunday the death toll mounted as rescue teams scoured and searched the shattered buildings. The final tally was 900 with twice as many seriously wounded. The results pleased Göring, who addressed the German people that day: 'This is the historic hour when for the first time our air force delivered its thrust right into the enemy's heart.'

By nightfall on Sunday all nine conflagrations were under control, though the capital's firemen were physically and emotionally spent. Kathleen Clayden, a firewoman in one east London station, had spent the Saturday dispatching pumps down to the docks. Since then she had had little or no news about the fate of the firemen. Towards 5pm on the Sunday they began to arrive back at the station: 'They were soaked to the skin, they smelt terrible and they hadn't even had a cup of tea,' she recalled.

> We made them some sandwiches but they were too tired to even eat. One fireman just sat by the fire and looked at me and said 'I never thought I'd see you again'. I put this man to bed but then after only two or three hours sleep, they were sent out again.[12]

GRIM TRIALS

When the Luftwaffe returned on Sunday night they were less exclusive with their bombs than they had been the day before. Instead of targeting just the docks, they also struck central London. Damage was done at the Royal Courts of Justice on the Strand, in Hyde Park and at the cavalry stables of Chelsea barracks. A railway bridge was hit on Grosvenor Road and a wholesale fruiterers in Covent Garden took a direct hit. It was here that William Sansom first saw another of that

Firemen fight a blaze from below while their colleagues assess the damage in September 1940.

weekend's band of unsung heroes, the men of the Heavy Rescue, hard men with sometimes questionable morals but unquestionable courage.

In pre-war life they had been builders and labourers and now as the bombs fell they used their knowledge of buildings to burrow down inside collapsed buildings and rescue the trapped. If on their way they discovered something worth having, they might pocket it as recompense for the danger. Not money or jewellery but the odd bottle of whisky here, the odd pair of shoes there.

When a building collapsed it did so in one of three ways: it might disintegrate entirely, leaving a smoking mound of timber and masonry; the floor might cave in, forming a V and trapping people at the edges of the floor below; or there might be a curving fall of floors and roofs, one side secure while the other swung downwards. The men of the Heavy Rescue knew all this, and they also knew how to move across debris with extraordinary stealth, conscious that one clumsy move might send a jet of dust into the precious air pocket of a person trapped below.

When they arrived at the wholesalers in Covent Garden they found a building of several storeys in ruins with shocked survivors muttering something about several people still trapped inside. To further impede the rescuers firemen were battling a serious fire at the premises next door and a section of this building threatened to topple onto the wholesalers. Sansom looked on in admiration as:

> in soaking rubble and with the firelight flaring over a street confused with the litter of vegetables and water and hoses and bricks and timber … the rescue workers picked among the brise [sic] blocks of the devastated building and extricated the dead and wounded.

Similar scenes were occurring south of the Thames as the German bombs augmented the fires started the previous day. Down in the docks 14-year-old May Richards was trapped in the family's Anderson shelter by rubble from her bombed out house. For several hours May, her parents and her two brothers lay entombed in their shelter until, finally, they heard the sweet sound of rough Cockney voices up above. One by one May and her family were brought out and carried into the darkened living room of a neighbouring house. Then one of the rescue men reappeared, a worried look on his face and something glistening on his overalls. 'He asked if anyone was injured because he was covered in blood', recalled May. She and the rest of the family shook their heads. A torch was brought and its beam picked out May. 'I was one pool of blood. So the man picked me up in his arms and took me to an ambulance. He was so kind and caring.'[13]

London was in need of a fillip on Monday morning as it woke after a weekend of bombing. One Londoner on her way to work in High Holborn recalled how the 'sight of our firemen will always haunt me. Rolling up their hoses, absolutely exhausted after a night of fighting fires with bombs still raining down, their blackened faces staring out from beneath their helmets.'

Bristolians salvage what they can from their wrecked houses after another heavy raid.

The newspapers did their best to lift the nation's spirits through a mix of patriotism and propaganda. The front page of the *Daily Mirror* proclaimed in bold print that 99 German aircraft had been shot down (in fact none were destroyed during Saturday's night raid) while boasting that all the fires but one were out. It then printed the communiqué issued by the Ministry of Home Security:

> Further particulars can now be given of the heavy attacks directed on London by the enemy during yesterday (Saturday) evening and continued on a smaller scale during the night. Bombing was widespread and in the later part of the attack appeared to be indiscriminate. Damage was severe, but, judged against the backdrop of the war, is not serious.

To balance the vapid official line, the *Mirror* ran some stories of its own, stories guaranteed to stir the jingoistic juices of the British public. There was 18-year-old Basil Bull, a solicitors' clerk, who in an east London district doused two incendiary bombs single-handed and saved a factory in the process; there was the photo showing Londoners clearing up their damaged street under the headline 'They Took It, With Chins Up'; and there was the murderous attack on little Sheila, machine-gunned by a German fighter as she ran for cover in a south coast town (this incident did actually occur on 6 September in Folkestone and the dead girl was nine-year-old Sheila White).

However, it was the *Mirror's* editorial that was to set the tone for the duration of the Blitz. The paper, like its readers, knew that this was just the start. The Germans would be back but in the meantime the *Mirror* had a message for Herr Hitler and his Luftwaffe: 'Terrorism on the maniac model cannot get our people down. The Germans, with their hard soul, will suffer more than we from mass fear.' The paper then urged the RAF to take the fight to Germany because:

Against a burning backdrop two rescuers scamper up a ladder in search of anyone trapped.

the knowledge that we are attacking, and not merely warding off attack, is in itself the best tonic for our workers in the factories, civilians in the bombed cities, and all those devoted men and women who are carrying on in these great trials. Grim trials; or, as Mr Churchill better puts it 'grim and gay'. Those words admirably describe the spirit of our people. Nothing can defeat it.

The Luftwaffe gave their reply that evening when a force of 195 bombers attacked the docks and the East End. The following day, Tuesday 10 September, the same targets received 176 tons of high explosives and 318 incendiary canisters. On the Wednesday 180 bombers hit east London, but at least this time its citizens hunkered in their shelters felt slightly happier. Now the fearful sound of falling bombs was lost against a backdrop of pounding anti-aircraft (AA) guns. For the first few days of the bombing campaign, the gunners had held back on the orders of General Pile, the commanding officer of AA Command, who in turn was under instruction from above. The AA guns were only to open fire if they could positively identify an aircraft as enemy, in case they should inadvertently wing a British fighter. Of the hundreds of bombers who attacked London in the first three raids, just four had been shot down by an AA gun. On the night of 10 September General Pile recalled that it became 'obvious to me, sleeping in my bed, that our system was no good. I became both angry and frightened at the same time, and lay awake the rest of the night thinking how to deal with this business.'[14]

The next day, 11 September, he called a meeting and it was agreed that in future the capital's 200 anti-aircraft guns were to maintain a continuous barrage throughout an enemy air raid at an elevation below which the RAF would not fly. In other words, the RAF would look after the top half of the skies and AA command the bottom half. Pile knew that chances of hitting a German aircraft, particularly at night, would still be slim – a shell fired from an AA gun at an aircraft flying at 17,000 feet took ten seconds to reach its

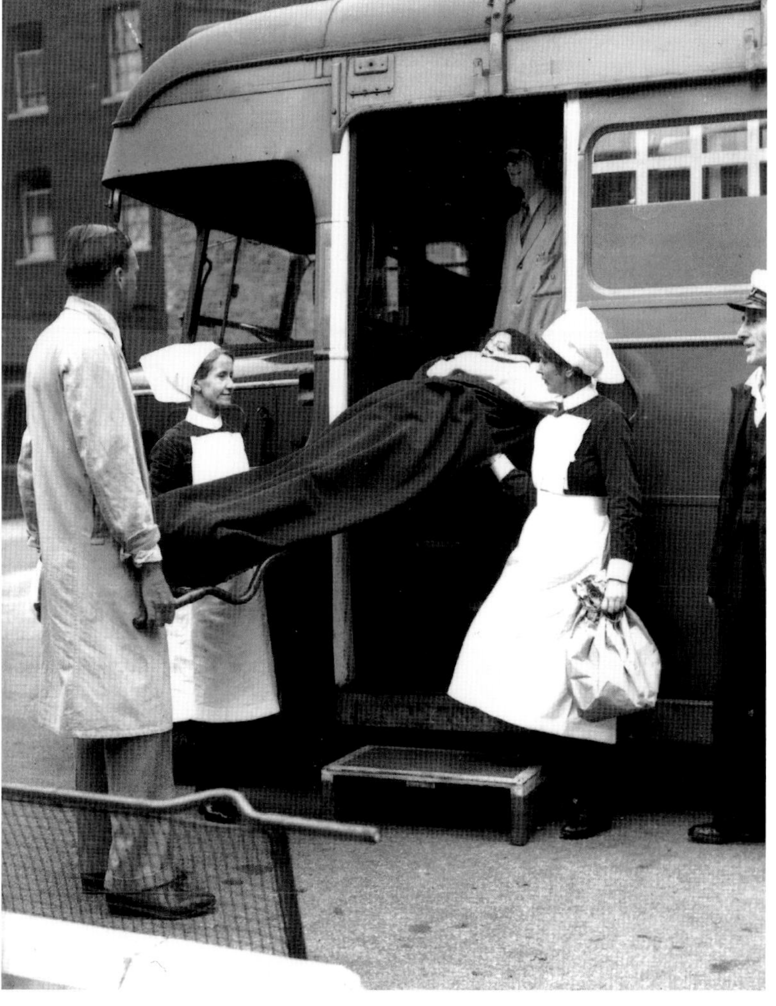

FAR LEFT: Ambulances couldn't cope with the number of injured so this woman is transported by nurses on a Greenline bus.

LEFT: It would be the bus or Tube in future for the owner of this car.

Britain is a nation of tea drinkers. Tea provided comfort to the homeless, quenched the thirst of exhausted firefighters and was often the first thing asked of rescuers by those trapped under wreckage.

target, by which time a plane flying at a speed of 180 miles per hour would have travelled half a mile further on. However, that wasn't the reason for demanding a change in strategy, but Londoners didn't know that. They just wanted to hear the reassuring 'thump-thump' of AA guns. William Gray, a London milkman, put it this way: 'We were always glad to hear our ack-ack opening up. I understand since that they weren't very successful. It was just so we could hear that somebody was hitting back.'[15]

The eruption of the AA barrage on the night of 11 September sent the morale of Londoners soaring. Now they were fighting back. However, not everyone was pleased. General Pile received a letter from one irate suburban councillor 'complaining that the vibration of the guns was cracking the lavatory pans of the council houses'. The general was asked to kindly take his infernal guns elsewhere.

On 12 and 13 September the raids on London were minor, at least compared to the savagery of the preceding days. On the 14th there was a heavy daylight raid which cost the Luftwaffe 14 of its aircraft. On the same day in Germany Admiral Erich Raeder, Commander of the German Navy, informed Hitler at a conference that he favoured the continuation of the Blitz to any all-out seaborne invasion. Most of Raeder's peers were also of the opinion that it was now too late in the season to cross the Channel. The result of the conference was a directive stating that:

> The air attacks against London are to be continued, and the target area is to be expanded against military and other vital installations (e.g. railway stations). Terror attacks against purely residential areas are to be reserved as an ultimate means of pressure, and are therefore not to be employed at present.

BATTLE OF BRITAIN DAY

The following day, Sunday 15th, was the day the Luftwaffe hoped to repeat their success of the previous Saturday. Two hundred bombers, escorted by 700 fighters, took off in the morning expecting little resistance from what they believed was a demoralised RAF. Instead

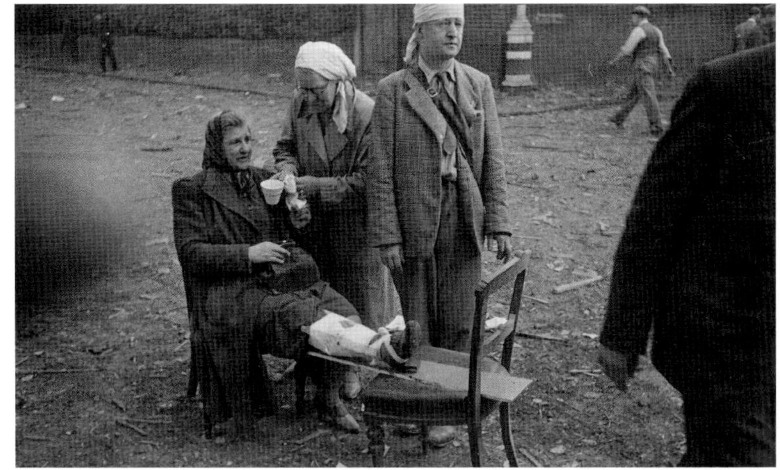

R
S.P.

they were greeted by nine squadrons of British fighters. Despite the massive number of German fighters, the RAF attacked with such ferocity that the bomber fleet was broken up. Those that made it to London were hampered by dense cloud and their bombs fell not in concentrated clusters like eight days previously but scattered over a wide area. With their bombs gone the Germans had to turn and run the gauntlet of the RAF fire once more. Horst Zander, a gunner in a Dornier, had survived one attack on their run in to London and was now hoping his luck would hold on the return trip. 'Our group had become split up', he recalled. 'Every crew sought its own safety in a powered gliding race down over the sea and for home.' Suddenly an RAF fighter appeared from nowhere and raked the Dornier with machine-gun fire. 'The cabin was full of blood. Our pilot was hit,' remembered Zander.

> In the intercom I heard him say feebly 'Heinz Laube, you have to fly us home'. Meanwhile we had reached the North Sea and so had peace in which to change over. The flight mechanic put a first-aid dressing on the badly wounded pilot ... and our observer took over the shot-up machine. Twenty minutes later, the aircraft bucking like a horse, he managed to land us safely.[16]

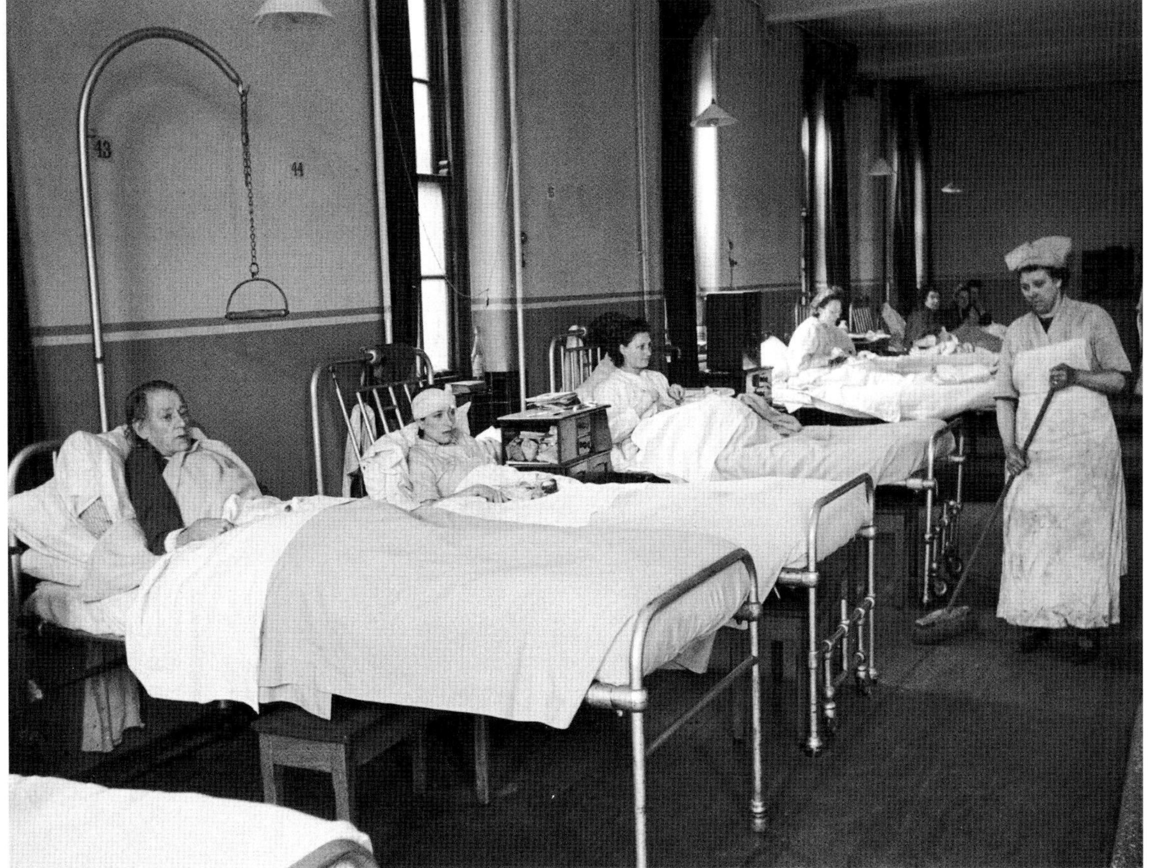

Nearly a quarter of a million Britons suffered wounds of one kind or another during six years of bombing.

As a second wave of German bombers approached London, Winston Churchill arrived at the underground RAF command centre in Uxbridge to watch proceedings unfold in the company of Air Vice-Marshal Park. The Prime Minister sat in silence watching as members of the Women's Auxiliary Air Force (WAAF) plotted the course of the aerial battle being waged above their heads. Soon it became clear that all the available resources of Fighter Command in the south had been scrambled to meet the threat. The first wave of German bombers had been repelled with little damage but what if a second wave should appear? The critical situation was not lost on the Prime Minister. 'What other reserves do we have?' Churchill reportedly asked of Park. 'There are none', came the response.

In fact, a second wave did follow but it was late in arriving because its fighter escort was too busy warding off repeated attacks by the RAF fighters which had already been scrambled. As they proceeded on their course they were attacked repeatedly as more British fighters returned to the fray after refuelling and rearming. In the event the second sortie was as ineffectual as the first, though just as costly in terms of German dead. By the end of the day the Luftwaffe had lost 34 bombers and 26 fighters.

Among that number were the audacious crew of a Dornier who lost their lives attempting to bomb Buckingham Palace. The home of King George VI and Queen Elizabeth had already been targeted by the Luftwaffe in the previous week with three small bombs landing in the quadrangle and chapel on 9 September, and an unexploded bomb piercing the roof above the swimming pool on the west terrace. However, the raider who attacked the Palace this Sunday seemed intent on greater destruction. On the first run the Dornier's bomb landed on the lawn, so he made another pass and this time dropped a delayed action bomb in the Regency bathroom overlooking the west terrace. At this point he was engaged by a Hurricane fighter, the pilot of which later described what happened as the two aircraft exchanged fire:

> I attacked a third time and a member of the crew baled [sic] out. On my fourth attack from the port beam a jar shook my starboard wing as I passed over the E/A [enemy aircraft] and I went into an uncontrollable spin. I think the E/A must have exploded beneath me. I baled [sic] out and as I landed I saw the Dornier hit the ground by Victoria Station ½ mile away.[17]

After landing, the pilot of the Hurricane was surrounded by an angry mob who thought he had come from the Dornier, and it took a few minutes of swift talking to convince them otherwise. The German who had bailed out landed on the roof of a house in Buckingham Gate but died from his injuries.

Two days later, on Tuesday 17 September, Hitler cancelled Operation *Sealion*. Events of 15 September had proved that the Luftwaffe had failed to destroy RAF Fighter Command. Therefore, a new strategy would be implemented. Henceforth, instead of concentrating its attack on military installations and industrial targets through precision daylight raids, the Luftwaffe would start its campaign of terror bombing on London with the aim of breaking the city's collective spirit. These attacks would be carried out at night and not just on the East End. All of London would feel the wrath of the Third Reich.

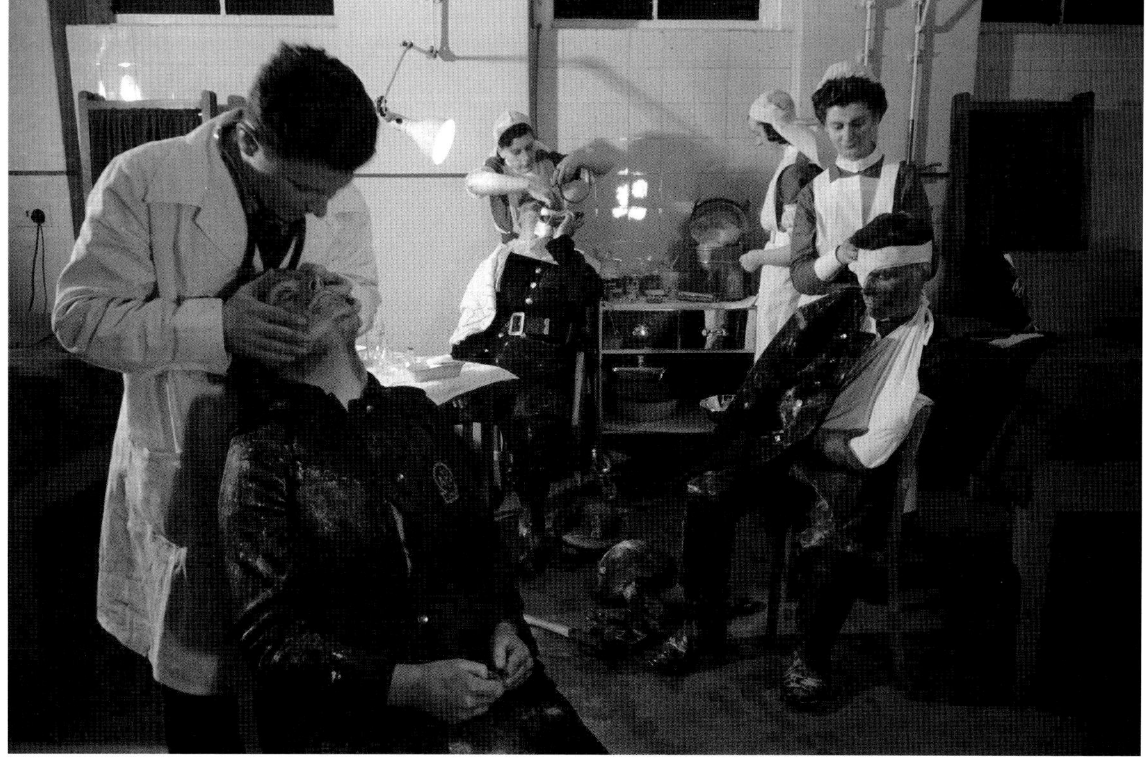

TOP RIGHT: The determination is clear on the faces of these firefighters as they tackle a London blaze.

BOTTOM RIGHT: Firemen's eyes were frequently damaged by burning sparks, as seen in this photo taken after the April 1941 great raids on London.

½ COUPON
NO COUPONS
DANCING
WIDOWS
ONLY
LARGE
TEA
1D

CHAPTER TWO

LONDON CAN TAKE IT! AUTUMN 1940

"Another man, buried for as long as 24 hours, was still alive and only because through the packed rubble there had percolated a small trickle of water from a lavatory pipe above."

William Sansom, Auxiliary Fire Service

THE LUFTWAFFE BOMBED LONDON every night from 17 September to 3 November 1940. One German pilot remarked later that:

> I have no particular memories of individual operations. They were all quite routine, like running a bus service. The London flak defences put on a great show – at night the exploding shells gave the appearance of bubbling pea soup, but very few of our aircraft were hit.[1]

Although the heaviest raids occurred when the moon was full, the Luftwaffe also came when it was pitch dark, guided to their targets by their innovative navigational system – the *Knickebein* (bent leg). In June 1940 Kampfgruppe 100 (KGr 100), the Luftwaffe pathfinders, had been withdrawn from operations in Norway and posted back to

OPPOSITE: A couple of 'cheeky chappies' hold an impromptu 'No Coupon' sale in Oxford Street. Many Londoners relied on a sense of humour to help them survive the darkest moments of the Blitz.

RIGHT: This *Daily Mirror* cartoon aimed to bolster the spirit of the British people as the Luftwaffe stepped up their terror bombing campaign. Even in 1940 the government, the media and the general public were well aware that there was no quick end to the conflict.

Germany to familiarise themselves with the *Knickebein*. British intelligence had heard talk of some navigational ingenuity on the part of the Germans, but, as they told Churchill, all they knew was that the Luftwaffe was:

> preparing a device by means of which they would be able to bomb by day or night whatever the weather. It appeared the Germans had developed a radio beam which, like an invisible searchlight, would guide their bombers with considerable precision to their targets.[2]

The device which KGr 100 was pioneering was the latest variant of the *Knickebein* called the *X-Gerät*. It worked on the principle, first developed by Germany in the 1930s for use in civil aviation, of using radio beams for aircraft directional guidance. At the same time that KGr 100 was getting to grips with the *X-Gerät* in the summer of 1940, all along the northern French coast a string of radio transmitters were erected to facilitate the use of the system and when the transmitters were completed KGr 100 moved to their base at Vannes in Brittany ready for work.

On 14 August, 20 bombers of KGr 100 took off for their inaugural attack on Britain using the *X-Gerät* navigational system. Their target was an armaments factory in the Midlands, and beams from two of the transmitters on the French coast intersected over the factory. When the aircraft were airborne the radio operators switched on their receivers and tuned in to the frequency between 30.0 and 33.3 kilohertz. The steady monotone signal in their headsets broadcast on this frequency indicated they were following the radio beam. If the operator heard dots or dashes the pilot had strayed off the beam. The bombers flew down the beam until the operator heard a warning signal on a second receiver, which was another beam laid across the one they were on. This signal told the crew they were 12 miles from their target. Six miles further on they crossed a second intersecting beam and the

Londoners often woke to strange sights, such as this one, the morning after a heavy raid.

radio operator pressed a button that started a timer with two hands. When they cut across a third beam, three miles from their destination, the operator pressed the timer's button again. One of the hands stopped. The other hand continued until it reached the first and the electric contact released the bombs over the intended target.

Gradually, the British learned about the *Knickebein* and established No. 80 Wing, a special unit designed to counter the threat. Although they considered working on a device to bend the beams off course, sending the German bombers to drop their bombs over uninhabited parts of the country, it was decided there wasn't time. So instead they came up with a project they codenamed *Aspirin*. This was a jamming device that transmitted Morse dashes on the frequencies used by the Luftwaffe bombers so that the operator no longer heard the steady note that told him he was following the correct beam.

However, the jamming system was only partially successful and as September gave way to October it seemed to most of London that the German bombers were having little trouble picking out their city. It wasn't hard: cross the Channel to the Thames Estuary and follow the snaking silver river into the heart of the British capital.

By now the bombs were landing further up the Thames. The Houses of Parliament were hit on 27 September and the following night upmarket properties in Victoria and Pimlico were also damaged. Whitehall caught it too, and a parachute mine fell in Savile

Throughout the dark days of the autumn of 1940 and the spring of 1941 the men who joined the Auxiliary Fire Service were the heroes of the hour. A poignant photograph by Greenwell captures the high price paid by one fireman underneath Waterloo Bridge. Greenwell's original caption read 'He died with his boots on', and he stressed that this image was not a fake.

Row. Yet the mood in the East End was unsettling the Establishment. There was a feeling that not enough was being done to help the homeless, as if the well-to-do didn't care about what happened to the working class. On 4 October John Colville, private secretary to Winston Churchill, paid a visit to Chingford in Essex (the PM's constituency) with Mrs Churchill to tour the worst-hit areas. 'The saddest sight was the homeless refugees in a school', wrote Colville in his diary that night.

An injured man is successfully brought to the surface having survived a Luftwaffe raid on London in October 1940.

One woman, wheeling a baby in a pram, told me she had twice been bombed out of her house and kept on saying disconsolately: 'A load of trouble, a load of trouble'. One woman said: 'It is all very well for them, (looking at us), who have all they want, but we have lost everything.'[3]

15 OCTOBER

Outsiders began to wonder if London could – as the city liked to boast – really 'Take It'. The London correspondent for *Time* magazine didn't appear to think so when he published an article entitled 'The Legacy of Britain'.

On 15 October came the most dramatic raid to date. It began at 8.20pm and went on till 4.40am the following morning. It was eight hours of terror involving 400 bombers flying at altitudes of 16,000 feet. This time they came from all directions: up the Thames Estuary from Holland, across the Kent coast from Belgium and up through Sussex from France. London was lit up by a full moon and the bombers struck with ghastly accuracy.

Among the mainline railway stations badly hit were St Pancras, Waterloo, Marylebone and Victoria. The Battersea Power Station and the Becton gasworks also took a number of hits, as did BBC Headquarters at Portland Place. A bomb landed in Leicester Square, between the venerable Perroquet restaurant and Thurston's famous billiards house. The Drury Lane theatre was scorched by incendiaries and a bomb exploded in the gardens of Dover House, inflicting blast damage on No. 10 Downing Street. Sewers were fractured, gas pipes ruptured and houses shattered. In all, the fire service were called to nearly 1,000 fires and the medical services reported 430 people dead and another 900 seriously wounded.

For the residents of central London the raid of 15 October was every bit as petrifying as 7 September had been for the East End. The Luftwaffe tactics were the same as ever: the pathfinder squadron of KGr 100 dropped the incendiaries, setting the targets on fire, and then, as the firemen rushed to tackle the blaze and residents scrambled for cover, the second wave of bombers approached, unleashing a torrent of high-explosive bombs.

GERMAN BOMBS

A German incendiary bomb (called a *Brandbombe)* weighed about one kilogram and in size and shape resembled the truncheon of a London policeman. It consisted of magnesium with a thermite filling and, as a British Government Home Security handbook issued that autumn noted, it was 'designed to give an intensive combustion at a high temperature by burning the body of electrons which is ignited by the thermite.' The combustion was indeed intensive – a single incendiary bomb burned for 50 seconds at 2,500 degrees Celsius as the thermite priming produced its own oxygen. When this incredible heat had melted and ignited the main magnesium component of the bomb it continued to burn for 20 minutes at temperatures of 1,300 degrees Celsius.

The Germans, as ingenious as ever, soon evolved the incendiary bomb and produced the 'breadbasket'. This was a three-panelled aluminium container measuring 43 inches and painted – like the 36 incendiary bombs it carried – the standard German grey-green. A central rod held the three panels together and the container was fitted with a clockwork mechanism that released the rod five seconds after leaving the aircraft.

Most of the aircraft of KGr 100 – which came to be known as the 'Firestarters' – carried four 'breadbaskets' in each of their eight bomb chutes, giving a total of 1,152 incendiary bombs per plane. When these were dropped they created a 1,750 yard ribbon of flame.

Originally, Britons had been instructed in a Ministry of Home Security handbook to douse fires from incendiary bombs with the hand-held stirrup pump by:

> crawling forward on his stomach with the nozzle in one hand and with his head as close to the floor as possible. This serves to avoid the fumes which rise upwards and enables the face to be protected to a considerable extent from glare and any molten fragments thrown off.

Of course, it wasn't just men who chased incendiaries. It was a favourite pastime of children and of women like Vere Hodgson, who wrote of one such experience in her diary dated 28 September 1940:

> A very exciting night! Four basketfuls of incendiaries dropped all over the house here. We heard them come down like rain. I seized my torch and made for upstairs, not quite sure what it was. Miss M [her flatmate] shouted that thay were burning next door near the house. She tore out of the front door and I followed her. Found her scrambling over the wall. She had gone by mistake to No1 whereas the bombs were at No5. In the darkness I lost her. She shouted to bring the Stirrup Pump. I shouted back: 'Not necessary if the bombs are outside.' I ran back inside for a bucket of sand.[4]

The sand was for the incendiaries, as it was the most effective way of dousing an incendiary bomb. Despite the government's advice about using a stirrup pump it was soon discovered that water was incapable of extinguishing the magnesium. If sand wasn't at hand people used anything that would kill the bomb's oxygen supply: a helmet, a bucket, a chamber pot, a dustbin lid. Across the capital, Londoners ran up and down streets 'doing their bit' for their country by

An incendiary 'breadbasket' illuminates a London street.

'bagging' incendiaries. There were times when air raid wardens had to break up scuffles between groups of youths arguing over whose turn it was to douse a particular incendiary. In time tales of the British bravado reached the Luftwaffe and towards the end of 1940 they began screwing small explosive charges, about one and a quarter inches long, into the tail of some incendiaries. The charge was set to detonate roughly five minutes after the incendiary had started to burn. The charge wasn't designed to kill, merely to maim, and to shower the plucky amateur firefighter with flaming magnesium. London policeman Walter Marshall witnessed a colleague on the receiving end of such a booby-trap:

> Holding a dustbin lid in one hand as a shield and a bucket of sand in the other, he made a pantomime display. It was the first firebomb I'd seen and it exploded as he approached. The explosion hit the dustbin lid and the PC finished up on his behind about ten yards back.[5]

RIGHT: Firemen silhouetted against the fires they fought during the height of the London Blitz.

FAR RIGHT: London was bombed for 57 consecutive days and nights in the autumn of 1940, a ferocious bombing campaign that the world had never previously witnessed.

German high-explosive ordnance ranged from the 50kg bomb to the 1,400kg 'Fritz' bomb to the giant 1,800kg bombs called *Überschwere* by the Germans, and 'Satan' by the Royal Engineer bomb disposal units who sometimes had to defuse the ones that failed to explode.

High-explosive bombs came in two casings, the thin-cased *Sprengbombe-Cylindrisch* (SC) or the thicker-cased *Sprengbombe-Dickwandig* (SD). The SCs were 55 per cent explosives and the staple bomb of the Luftwaffe during the Blitz. Comprising three thin-cased sections, they had a solid nose and an alloy tail. Many SCs had a ring (*Kopfring*) fastened to the nose to stop them from burrowing too deep into the ground on impact. They were intended to cause maximum blast effect and, more often than not, they did just that.

The SDs were 35 per cent explosive and constructed of malleable cast steel that fragmented into lethal shards of shrapnel which tore through the air – and skin – over a radius of 1,100 yards. The deadliest SD bomb was the 'Fritz', a six and a half feet tall harbinger of destruction that weighed 1,400 kilograms and annihilated everything in its immediate path.

Londoners described the sound of a falling bomb in a multitude of ways. To one it was like 'tearing silk', to another it felt as if the bomb was 'pushing the air before it'. The most common verb, however, given to the noise a bomb made as it hurtled earthwards was 'whistling'. This sound was created by the Germans riveting a set of cardboard 'organ pipes' on to the fins of many bombs. It was a simple device but blood-curdling. When the bomb left the aircraft on the start of its 500-mile-per-hour descent, the air rushed through the pipes to create the whistle. It was a noise never to be forgotten by those on the receiving end.

People became adept at listening to the descent of the bomb and knowing where it was going to land. An auxiliary fireman in Hull, Hugh Varah, recalled that:

> As they begin to lose speed, they start to fall earthwards, tracing a large curved trajectory, picking up speed as they fall and the dreadful noise made by the air rushing past the tail fins heralds their coming. That means there's just time to dive for cover. We quickly learned that if the sound was rising in pitch, they were coming our way. But if the note got deeper, they were heading in someone's else's direction.[6]

With no roofs over their heads to keep them warm a group of London children improvise with a brazier and look remarkably cheerful despite the devastation surrounding them.

The official advice to the London Fire Service about what to do if caught in the open by a falling high-explosive bomb advised firefighters to lie flat on their stomachs with their chests raised off the ground to protect their ribs being crushed by the vibration of the detonating bomb. The explosion from a HE bomb, if you were near enough to it, was described by one man as feeling as if there was a troll far below hammering against the surface with a giant sledgehammer.

It was the feeling of helplessness that induced rank terror in many people, the sensation that their fate was out of their hands. Fireman Fred Cockett, who was based at Waterloo, remembered talking to an army friend of his shortly after he had been caught in his first raid while on leave:

"I have no particular memories of individual operations. They were all quite routine, like running a bus service."

Anonymous German bomber pilot

> Despite the fact he'd seen action in France he said nothing had prepared him for the unpleasantness of a heavy air raid. At least in the army he had a rifle, which gave him some feeling of protection and of self-defence. On the streets of London all he could do was pray.

Hugh Varah was intrigued by the reaction of people in Hull to the falling bombs. 'I have seen big men become rooted to the spot, transfixed by terror beyond their control', he recalled.

> I have seen others set off and run blindly in sheer panic, in no particular direction. I have seen people of all ages and [both] sexes cover their heads with a coat in an effort to ward off a bomb. They could not imagine any escape so their minds turned inwards and blotted out any threat of danger.[7]

Then there were the people, often the unlikeliest sort, who appeared merrily indifferent to the brutal bedlam all around. Special Constable Ballard Berkeley, an actor before the war (he found fame in later life playing the dotty Major in *Fawlty Towers*), spent the Blitz on his beat around Haymarket and Piccadilly. During one raid a flaming necklace of incendiary bombs landed on his beat. As Berkeley rushed around dousing the bombs as best he could and ushering people towards the nearest shelter, he recalled the utter contempt for danger displayed by the young paper vendor outside a Lyon's Corner House bellowing 'Star! News! Standard!' 'He just stood there and the bombs came down and he kept selling his papers.' Then another string of incendiaries clattered onto the pavement and Berkeley watched in disbelief as a prostitute came tottering down Coventry Street in impossibly high heels.

> She had an umbrella up and she was singing 'I'm singing in the rain'. The only rain coming down was the incendiary bombs. And I remember thinking … I wish Hitler and Göring could have a look at this. It was quite extraordinary.[8]

As well as the deadly high-explosive bombs and incendiaries the Germans had other types of bomb, such as the oil bomb which, as its name implies, contained nearly 100 pints of oil in a five feet tall canister. Although oil could emit twice as much heat as magnesium it was lighter and often the canisters – which weighed 113 kilograms – failed to penetrate buildings and merely exploded on the roof, releasing a film of oil over an area 65 feet in diameter. As oil burns upwards they were more of an inconvenience for London's firemen than a serious hazard.

The same could not be said of the parachute mine, a weapon that in the eyes of many Londoners was the stomach-churning incarnation of Hitler's campaign of terror bombing. These magnetic mines had first been used by the Nazi war machine in the winter of 1939 for their intended purpose – against British shipping. By the summer of 1940 the Royal Navy had taken steps to deal with the threat so another use was needed for the surplus stock of mines. It was decided to drop the ten-foot mines by parachute on London, though Hitler specified that they should only be used on nights when there was good visibility as they were too expensive to waste on questionable targets.

The first parachute mines (weighing one ton) were delivered onto the heads of Londoners on 7 September and achieved immediate notoriety. At first firemen and air raid wardens had craned their necks for a better look at what was floating towards them. They had presumed it was a pilot – but one of theirs or one of ours? Then they saw it wasn't a man on the end of the canopy but something that resembled a 'tall, blunt-ended pillar box'. When they realised it was a bomb they had only a few seconds to get clear before it hit the ground and exploded with bone-shaking violence. One such mine that had drifted down on a Croydon park at the end of September shattered all the windows on the high street a mile away.

On the night of 15 October several parachute mines fell on Westminster and one in particular stayed in the mind of auxiliary fireman William Sansom. It landed on Alderney Street, between Pimlico and Sloane Square Tube stations, destroying 150 houses and killing 23 people, and creating in the words of Sansom 'a vista of desolation'. He and his fellow rescue workers spent hours recovering the dead and rescuing more than 60 wounded residents. 'Fragments isolate themselves in the memory of what was then too vast a field to visualise as a whole', recalled Sansom later.

> Again the smell of explosive mixture, again the heavy dust hovering for hours, again the discovery that many people were sheltering in empty houses and basements without informing anyone of their whereabouts … of the dead, one man was found in the back kitchen of a house up against the wall and shielding a woman and two children. Another man, buried for as long as 24 hours, was still alive and only because through the packed rubble there had percolated a small trickle of water from a lavatory pipe above.

The day after the raid, on 16 October, John Colville returned to London from a business trip to Cambridge. What he saw stunned him, as he confided to his diary that night:

> Leicester Square is a desert, Pall Mall is badly damaged (the Carlton [club] has collapsed and the Travellers was hit) and a bomb just missed No. 10, doing great damage to the Treasury and wrecking some of the rooms in No.10 itself. Coming into Liverpool Street by train I saw such devastation by the railway line as is impossible to describe. Poor London.

The newspapers tried to balance the destruction wrought on London with accounts of how the RAF had brought down several German bombers. But it was all propaganda. The Luftwaffe lost only one of its planes, a Heinkel bomber unlucky enough to be spotted by the sharp-eyed Defiant pilot from No. 264 squadron. As one German pilot, Erik Sommers, remembered of those early raids over London:

The Blitz at least allowed some dramatic shots of London to be taken, such as this one with St. Paul's prominent.

> All our losses were through mismanagement, bad navigation, bad weather, and by other accidents like wireless failures, bad landings and so on. Sometimes we observed collisions in heavy concentrations of German aircraft. Night fighter opposition was no opposition at all.[9]

THE BEAUFIGHTER

However, all that began to change in October with the introduction of the Beaufighter to replace the obsolescent Blenheim, described by one RAF veteran as 'deadbeat … it leaked like a basket. If you went through a cloud, you were wet.' The Beaufighter was the latest in night fighters. Its maximum speed of 323 miles per hour at 15,000 feet was superior to the Blenheim and the German aircraft that it was intended to destroy, and it had greater firepower than both the Spitfire and the Hurricane. With four 20mm Hispano cannon and six .303-inch machine guns it was a formidable presence in the skies over London. However, what excited the RAF most about the Beaufighter was its airborne interception (AI) radar,

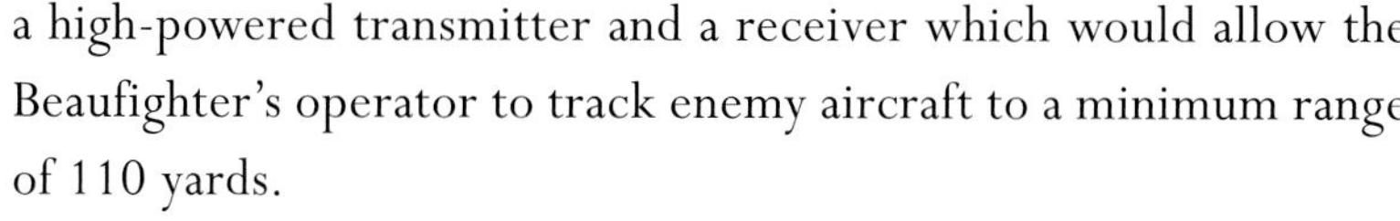

June 5, 1940 THE DAILY MIRROR Page 3

THEY TOOK IT, WITH CHINS UP

After the raid, these street residents rallied and helped each other as best they could. Their homes are wrecked, but not their morale. There's nothing of despair about them—only a fervent hope that we don't bring any more bombs back from Berlin.

HIS FRONT DOOR

When Mr. Ernest Hanbridge went to his East London home after the "All Clear," you see what he found yesterday morning. But it takes a lot to shake an Englishman's composure—so he went in and came out by the "front door."

SET OUT EARLY FOR YOUR TRAIN TODAY

"We shall do our utmost to carry all passengers to work tomorrow, but they are advised to get to their stations early," the Southern Railway stated last night.

Rail damage caused through Saturday night's air raids in the London area was quickly repaired and services showed a marked improvement during the day.

The dislocation in transport was confined mainly to certain areas south and east of London.

Steps were promptly taken to repair damage in the shortest possible time. Alternative routes were put into operation and special bus services were improvised.

Some interruption must still be expected and intending passengers are advised to inquire from their local railway station for information regarding facilities open to them.

Instructions have been issued to the railway and to the L.P.T.B. to allow the widest possible flexibility in the use of season or ordinary tickets by any alternative services.

Every assistance will be given and no unnecessary formality will be allowed to stand in the way of travellers in journeying between their homes and places of work.

ONLY 4 LOST IN HOSTILE

All but four men of the 148 aboard the British destroyer Hostile, sunk by a mine in the Mediterranean on August 23, were rescued by British warships, it was learned authoritatively in Cairo yesterday, states Associated Press.

a high-powered transmitter and a receiver which would allow the Beaufighter's operator to track enemy aircraft to a minimum range of 110 yards.

Lancastrian Richard James had been a gunner on a Blenheim before his squadron, No. 29, took delivery of a fleet of Beaufighters in the autumn of 1940. Gunners were superfluous in the new aircraft as it was the pilot's responsibility to fire the weapons, so instead men such as James became radar operators.

The first time James climbed inside a Beaufighter (through a panel in the bottom of the fuselage that hinged downward) he found it a squeeze. Halfway along the fuselage was his swivel seat, from where he could look through a Perspex dome. The AI radar box looked like a small television screen and was suspended from the low roof just behind the dome. It was a strange-looking contraption with a rubber visor and a set of control knobs. When it was switched on the box's two cathode tubes, one horizontal and the other vertical, became luminous green lines. Then it began to emit a series of radio blips. If there was an aircraft within range an echo bounced back and it appeared on the green lines as a cluster of sparkling lights. This was known as a blip. If the enemy aircraft climbed higher the blip on the vertical tube got bigger so the Beaufighter's radar operator told his pilot to climb. From the blip on the vertical tube it was possible to see if the aircraft was port (left) or starboard (right) and so the operator gave instructions to the pilot and guided him towards their prey until the moment when the blip sat squarely across the tubes. Then the enemy aircraft's bluish exhaust flames would be visible to the pilot. That was the critical moment, the vital, fraught few seconds that troubled every Beaufighter pilot, as Flight-Lieutenant John Cunningham remembered:

> Very often it would be another sector's [British] night fighter or a Wellington bomber. IFF [Identification, Friend or Foe] was nominally fitted but it was totally unreliable. So I would have to get close enough

London 'Took It' though not always without the odd murmur of complaint.

to make a visual identification, which I could do by closing in and getting underneath the aircraft so I could see the plan form of the wing. And while you were underneath, the bomber's gunners were less likely to see you than if you were above them.[10]

Only when the pilot was convinced the aircraft was hostile did he attack.

Within a few months of its introduction the Beaufighter had proved its worth and had shot down dozens of German bombers. Throughout the winter of 1940–41 German crews became increasingly unsettled by the ability of the Beaufighter to seek them thousands of feet up in the charcoal sky. How was it possible they wondered. Desperate to hide details of their AI radar from the Germans, the British came up with a novel way of explaining the success of the Beaufighters' pilots. It was down to carrots. The modest John Cunningham, the deadliest Beaufighter pilot as far as Germans were concerned, was catapulted to fame by the number of enemy aircraft he shot down:

I was given the nickname 'Cat's Eyes' by the Air Ministry to cover up the fact that we were flying aircraft with radar because there was never any mention of radar at that period. So by the time I had two or three successes, the Air Ministry felt that they would have to explain that I had very good vision by night.

They did this by attributing Cunningham's vision to carrots. He ate so many of them that he could see things in the dark that other mere mortals couldn't. Germany, like Britain, had long believed the old wives' tale that a healthy consumption of carrots improved sight, so they fell for it hook, line and sinker. The campaign also helped convince millions of British children to munch on a carrot daily as a replacement for the unobtainable oranges and bananas.

Soldiers from the Royal Pioneer Corps enjoy a well-earned bath after a day spent cleaning up after an air raid.

Daily Mirror

MAY 11

No. 11,364 ONE PENNY
Registered at the G.P.O. as a Newspaper.

ALLIES ADVANCE IN 200 MILE LINE: DUTCH HOLD INVADER

Look Out for Sky Army

Look out for German parachute troops landing in this country. The Home Office issued this request to every citizen last night, with instructions how to act.

Many German invaders have been landed in Belgium and Holland by parachute and in a number of cases they wore uniforms calculated to deceive observers into thinking they were friendly.

The best way in which the ordinary citizen can help the authorities is by keeping watch, and if he sees any such attempt here, by reporting it at once to the nearest police station, giving the most accurate information possible about the place and numbers of men landing.

The police will communicate at once with the appropriate military authorities, who have made arrangements for dealing with any such landing.

If any attempts are made, they would most likely be during the black-out, particularly at dusk or dawn and in open spaces, particularly near aerodromes.

Plans made months ago to deal with the possible landing of German parachute troops in this country were put into force at an hour's notice yesterday.

British troops, equipped with Bren and sub-machine guns, in all the thinly populated areas of Great Britain have been warned to be on the look-out.

French and British troops are advancing on a 200-mile front extending from the North Sea to the Moselle, the official French communique said last night.

"Sharp fighting," the message added, "has taken place in Luxemburg area."

British Headquarters in France announced "Leading elements of the B.E.F. in co-operation with the French Army entered Belgium today. They were accorded a great welcome by the Belgian population."

AFTER a day of fierce fighting, Holland and Belgium announced last night that the German invaders had been held in their 200-mile drive to smash their way to Calais and Dutch and Belgian ports.

In Holland, the Dutch troops, fighting with a desperate determination, destroyed their frontier bridges and engaged the advancing Germans.

"Only at one point, at the sector east of Arnheim, nine miles from the frontier, have the Germans reached the river Yssel," said the Dutch communique last night.

Fight for Rotterdam

The Germans reached the great Dutch port of Rotterdam hidden in barges which sailed up the River Waal. They were cut off in one section of the city. The Dutch set fire to the area, smoked the invaders out, shot and captured them as they ran.

Fighting in Rotterdam streets intensified late last night when the Germans landed reinforcements.

The Dutch moved in reinforcements and dislodged the Germans from the bridge. The Dutch now control all the bridges and fighting was confined to the left bank.

The Belgians announced that their troops had halted the main enemy advance.

At Aachen, German frontier town, the Belgians held up the invaders. At other sectors the Belgians fell back on their previously prepared line of defence.

Luxemburg Overrun

The third object of the German attack, Luxemburg, was overrun.

But driving north, pushing into Belgium and towards Holland, came the British and French Armies.

British planes were bombing and harrying the advancing Germans. R.A.F. machines were bombing Dutch aerodromes captured by the Germans.

"The fight beginning today decides the fate of the German nation for the next thousand years," Hitler announced as he put himself at the head of his troops.

As darkness fell on Europe at war

Continued on Back Page

Dutch Win Back 'Dromes

EVERY aerodrome in Holland seized by the Germans, with the exception of Rotterdam, had been recaptured by the Dutch last night.

This was announced by the Dutch High Command early this morning.

In addition it was stated that the number of German planes shot down over Holland now exceeds 100.

Fourteen undamaged German planes fell into the hands of the Dutch at one of the reconquered aerodromes.

Troop Plane Hits House

A German transport plane carrying nineteen soldiers in Dutch uniforms crashed through the roof of a house last night after being shot down, says a message from The Hague.

Air alarms were sounded there all night at half-hourly intervals.

Earlier R.A.F. machines wrecked many German troop transports on Dutch aerodromes. (Story on back page.)

OUR WAR PREMIER CHURCHILL

MR. WINSTON CHURCHILL became Prime Minister last night.

His appointment and the resignation of Mr. Neville Chamberlain was announced from No. 10, Downing-street in a ten-line notice.

It said:—

"The Right Hon. Neville Chamberlain, M.P., resigned the office of Prime Minister and First Lord of the Treasury this evening, and the Right Hon. Winston Churchill, C.H., M.P., accepted his Majesty's invitation to fill the position.

"The Prime Minister desires that all Ministers should remain at their posts and discharge their functions with full freedom and responsibility while the necessary arrangements for the formation of a new administration are made."

Mr. Chamberlain will, it is expected, become Chancellor of the Exchequer in Mr. Churchill's new Ministry in place of Sir John Simon. Mr. Chamberlain was Chancellor in Mr. Baldwin's Government.

Mr. Churchill was with the King for more than forty minutes immediately after Mr. Chamberlain had tendered his resignation.

Later, broadcasting to the nation, the ex-Premier said Mr. Churchill wished him to be a member of the new War Cabinet.

"I have told him I will gladly assist in that capacity," said Mr. Chamberlain.

It was clear, he went on, that at this critical moment in the war what was needed was the formation of a Government which would include members of the Labour and Liberal Opposition and thus present a united front to the enemy.

He had tried to secure this, but it became clear that such unity could be secured only under another Prime Minister.

"In these circumstances my duty was plain. I sought an audience of the King this evening and tendered him my resignation."

"Hour Has Come"

Speaking with great emotion, Mr. Chamberlain concluded: "The hour has come when we are to be put to the test. The innocent people of Holland and Belgium and France are being tested already.

"You and I must rally behind our new leader, and with our united strength and with unshakable courage work until this wild beast which has sprung out of his lair on us, be finally disarmed and overthrown."

During the day the Cabinet met three times.

The Labour Party National Executive, at their meeting at Bournemouth yesterday, had announced that they would join a new Government under a new Premier.

It was officially announced last night that M. Reynaud, French Premier, had reshuffled his Cabinet, taking into it representatives of all political parties.

Forty or fifty M.P.s yesterday decided to inform the Speaker of their view that the House of Commons should be reassembled immediately.

Recall of Parliament fairly soon is considered certain.

Threat to Bomb More Civilians

Twenty-four civilians have been killed in an attack by Allied aircraft on the open town of Freiburg. That is Berlin's latest lie.

"The German Air Force will now answer back in like manner," say the Nazis, according to Reuter.

"From now on, any further systematic enemy raid on the German population will be returned by a five-fold number of German planes on a British or French town."

More than 100 people have been killed and more than 200 injured in German air raids on open towns in Holland and Belgium. (Story on back page.)

Bombing of Amsterdam Pictures: Page 9

Winston Churchill was a soldier turned reporter who entered parliament in 1900 at the age of 25. During the First World War he served as First Lord of the Admiralty but after the disaster of Gallipolli campaign served in the trenches , and in the 1930s Churchill was one of the first statesmen to warn of the risk of appeasing Nazi Germany. Appointed First Lord of the Admiralty in September 1939, he became Prime Minister in May 1940 when the country lost confidence in Neville Chamberlain. In his first speech as leader on 13 May, Churchill declared that his aim was: 'Victory at all costs – Victory in spite of all terror – Victory, however long and hard the road may be, for without victory there is no survival.' It was this defiance and determination to defeat Hitler that inspired his people during the years that followed. During the Blitz Churchill made numerous visits to bombed out cities and towns following the Luftwaffe raids, just his presence seemed to inspire the public, who rallied against all odds. The photo on the left shows Churchill the day after VE day with Eisenhower, celebrating the Allied victory in Europe.

AIR RAID PRECAUTIONS

MENTION THE WORDS 'Air Raid Warden' to most people and the image that comes to mind is of Warden Hodges (played so beautifully by Bill Pertwee) in the British television comedy series *Dad's Army*. Hodges was a bloody-minded busybody who revelled in the power that came with his position. Without doubt there were some wardens during the Blitz who bore a passing resemblance to Hodges, but for the most part they were dedicated, hard-working and courageous volunteers at the heart of the country's civil defence.

The first Air Raid Precaution (ARP) centres came into being in 1936 and the early volunteers spent most of their time practising their first-aid skills and learning what to do in the event of a gas attack, the overriding fear of the British Government. It wasn't until 1938 that the ARP wardens were put to work preparing for a conventional bombing attack. Across London they dug trenches in parks and squares, and filled sandbags that were used to protect the trench shelters.

With the declaration of war the ARP wardens, many of whom were First World War veterans, patrolled the streets ensuring residents adhered to the blackout regulations. This earned them the reputation as busybodies, but they were simply doing their job. As auxiliary fireman William Sansom wrote in his book *The Blitz*:

> His [the warden's] responsibility knew no concise limit – for he was charged with the general welfare and comfort of the public during and after aerial attack. He had to be patient, understanding and responsible. He had to know much. He had to patrol the streets throughout raids, and without respite of cover between actions. He had to know most thoroughly his post area, and furthermore to have as correct an idea as possible of the habits of shelter of the people who lived there … he became an authority, he had to know.

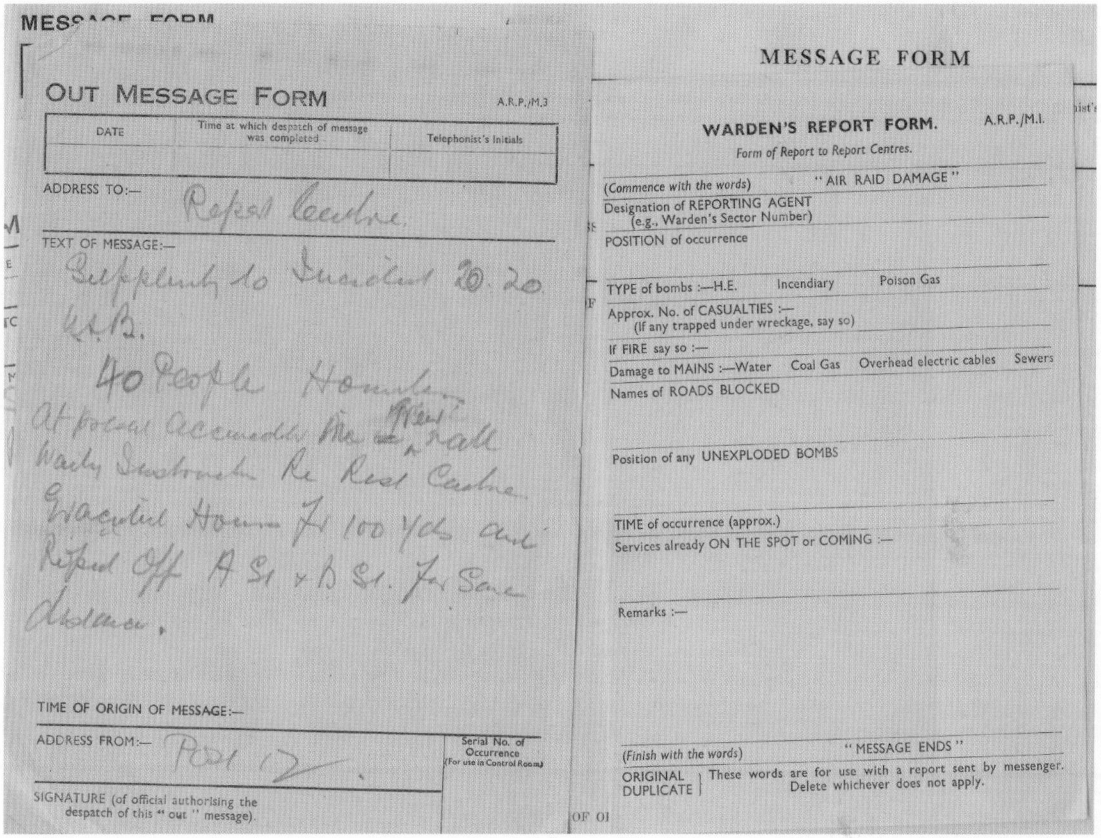

Reporting, recording and logging incidents were important parts of an air raid warden's responsibilities and 'ARP/M1' forms were completed for each incident. Messengers were invaluable in providing communication between wardens and control centres, particularly when telephone lines had been destroyed. These messengers acted as runners, carrying handwritten 'ARP/M3' forms. (Courtesy Peter Doyle)

Women as well as men volunteered as air raid wardens and all wore the barest of uniforms, just a pair of dark blue overalls and a steel helmet with the initials 'ARP' on the front. That was still their attire when the bombs began to drop in September 1940, and suddenly the wardens went from being busybodies to bloody marvels. During an air raid their first task was to report an incident, in which they described to the best of their ability the effects of the bomb. Then they were also responsible for extinguishing incendiary bombs where possible, helping frightened people to the nearest shelter, guiding bombed-out residents to rest centres, tending the wounded until the arrival of the ambulances and assisting rescue teams in freeing the trapped from the rubble of their houses. In many ways it was a thankless task, far less glamorous than the firefighters or the heavy rescue teams, but the air raid wardens were the lifeblood of the Civil Defence. As Sansom put it: 'No more can be said than this – that among all the others, at any type of incident, there was likely to be the shadow of a warden working side by side with the mobilised expert.'

TOP LEFT: Members of the London Fire Service display their medals.

BOTTOM LEFT: District Officer Locke shows his young son the George Medal he won for bravery during the Blitz. The George Cross and the George Medal were instituted on 24 September 1940 by King George VI in order to reward the many acts of civilian courage performed during the Blitz. The George Cross ranks alongside the Victoria Cross, the equivalent military decoration, as the highest award for gallantry.

TOP RIGHT: Weary firemen and women grab a bite to eat as bombs fall on London.

ABOVE: Women from the ATS crew a searchlight belonging to an anti-aircraft battery. The involvement of women in previously male-only roles was crucial to the war effort.

ABOVE: Rescuers prise a young woman free from the remnants of her basement flat following a raid on London.

RIGHT: A couple exchange wedding vows in a London church left airy by the Luftwaffe in October 1940. Continuing ordinary life was a determined act of resistance on the part of Londoners and other bombed-out British citizens.

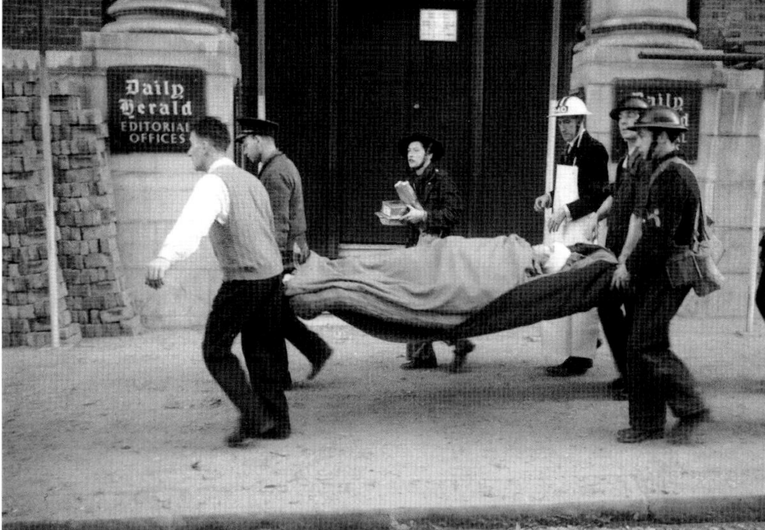

LEFT: Life presumably goes on for this little girl as she washes some clothes in the ruins of her house. However, the fact that she is so spotlessly clean and without injuries means that in all likelihood this image was posed. The reality was not always so photogenic.

TOP: A victim of a daylight raid is transported to hospital after damage caused in Endell Street in Covent Garden in the heart of London.

ABOVE: A woman is helped from her shattered flat in St Pancras by a fireman.

Firemen move a ladder into position as they begin to fight the fires engulfing Covent Garden.

The government even issued a poster telling the nation's youngsters 'Carrots keep you healthy and help you see in the blackout', to promote the humble carrot. Only later did Dore Silverman, who spent the war working in the Ministry of Information, come clean to the public: 'The idea that night fighter pilots ate a lot of carrots to give them better sight in the dark was nonsense. It was a ploy to get people to eat more carrots. They were nutritious and they didn't have to be imported.'[11] The government even produced a cartoon strip character: Doctor Carrot – the Children's Best Friend.

CHAPTER THREE

BUSINESS AS USUAL: NOVEMBER 1940 IN LONDON

"I honestly don't know how we stood it. It was because the English are unimaginative and stolid. Nothing in the air, on the earth and on the water scares them. They get annoyed but never get scared."

John Hughes, Australian War Correspondent

ON SUNDAY 20 OCTOBER a middle-aged woman called Vere Hodgson left her home in Holland Park, west London, to visit the bomb damaged districts of the capital. Hodgson, who owed her first name to her uncle, a marine biologist on Captain Scott's *Discovery* expedition to the Antarctic, was a graduate of Birmingham University. In the 1920s she had taught history in select girls' schools but for the last few years had run a local charity. When she returned from her tour of the city she wrote in her diary:

> Marble Arch looked a bit messed up. Walked from Oxford Circus. Academy Circus has one – and lots of places along there. T.C. [Tottenham Court] road closed and looks pretty derelict. Along New Oxford St. to Holborn ... many shops out of action. At Southampton Row the [Air Raid] Warning went. I persevered along ... High Holborn, heard gunfire, and saw people pointing to the sky and saying 'There they go – they've just turned 'em'. Saw curls of smoke in the sky. Since Holborn seems to have a fascination

OPPOSITE: Bombed out but at least these two Britons have a bottle of beer to cheer them up.

RIGHT: Even Tillz the hen had her own Anderson shelter.

OPPOSITE LEFT: These two photos show the rescue of a woman from her home in City Road in September 1940. Here a man prepares to lift her on to his shoulders before gently descending the ladder with the women on his back.

OPPOSITE RIGHT: This woman appears unconcerned that her street shelter has yet to acquire a roof.

> for them [the Luftwaffe], and I was in an unfamiliar district, I went into a shelter. No one else there. I read the *Observer* until the caretaker arrived. We had a little chat. He said about 15 people came and slept there at night. He considered Holborn had caught it most – barring the East End.

Hodgson had taken refuge in one of the myriad street shelters that were hastily built across London in the spring of 1940. Constructed to hold 50 people, initially these shelters were built of concrete, and when that ran out in due course, the walls were made from bricks. They weren't popular with the average Londoner. 'We called them "splinter shelters"' remembered Joe Richardson, a 16-year-old from Walworth in south London, 'because they were only useful if you were caught out in the open during a raid. You went inside to avoid the bomb splinters. But they were really just a nasty bodge job.'[1] Once the Blitz began, a horrifying design flaw in the shelters soon earned them a more macabre moniker – 'Sandwich Shelters'. If a bomb landed in close proximity to one of the shelters, the blast sucked out the walls and the people inside were sandwiched between the ground and the nine-inch-thick roof made of reinforced concrete.

In addition, the shelters were cold despite the official government advice contained in a leaflet that 'a home-made heater can be made with two large flower pots and a candle'. Also, the fact that there were no toilet facilities in the street shelters made them an unattractive proposition for Londoners, the majority of whom preferred to take their chance at home. In the first three months of the Blitz 60 per cent of the capital's population refused to seek sanctuary in a shelter, adopting the fatalistic philosophy of the soldiers in the First World War: If it's got my number on it…

Certainly, the longer the Blitz continued the more it seemed fate was moving through the capital like an unseen virus, striking down people at random, while leaving others untouched.

During one raid a bomb dropped on Mann Street in Southwark, dislodging the chimney stack of No. 15. The couple inside were sitting at the kitchen table when the chimney crashed through the roof, demolishing the table but leaving them without a scratch. When the Carlton Club was hit during the raid of 15 October a bomb exploded in the library, just after members had filed downstairs to the dining room. Such was the force of the blast, however, that a lamppost outside the club toppled over, killing an off-duty soldier as he ran for shelter.

On another occasion, in Henry Street, Greenwich, a teenage girl was lying in bed listening to the noise of the raid above when she heard something come thudding down the chimney. She shot out of bed and rushed over to the fireplace, to find an unexploded shell from an anti-aircraft gun. On the other hand an acquaintance of Thomas Parkinson wasn't so lucky. 'One young fellow was going out with a nice-looking girlfriend', he recalled.

> He walked her home to her house in Camden Town and he was sitting in the kitchen having a cup of tea with her when an anti-aircraft shell that had gone up and didn't explode, came straight through the house, hit her and killed her stone dead, while he was sitting there.[2]

However, not all Londoners were content to take their chance with fate. Forty per cent of the capital's population preferred to head for a shelter the moment the air raid siren sounded. Of this figure the overwhelming majority (27 per cent) took cover in their Anderson shelters. On its own, the Anderson shelter was uncomfortably functional, but with people spending so much time inside personal touches were soon added. Ruth Tanner, a young girl in Walthamstow during the Blitz, recalled the lengths her father went to in order to make their Anderson shelter habitable.

> It was done properly and had a floor in it. It didn't get water in it and the inside of it was painted a beautiful pink with sawdust thrown all on it to absorb any condensation. Our beds were fixed on the side so that my mum could fold them up and let them down as necessary.[3]

The father of another young London girl, Betty Brown from Chingford in Essex, added a touch of humour to their Anderson shelter. 'Dad built a turreted bit on top, like a castle, and he put a notice over the door saying: "SAIFA ERE". That was the shelter's name – "Safer Here". He thought that was great fun.' However, fate

CITY ROAD

Not only were firefighters on the front line of the Blitz every night tackling the destructive blazes, but their fire stations were also vulnerable to attack. Not much is left of Shaftesbury Avenue Fire Station following a raid by the Luftwaffe on 14 October 1940.

sometimes picked out those in the Anderson Shelters, as Teresa Wilkinson recalled during her days as an air raid warden in West Ham:

> There were four people in one particular house and three of them used the Anderson shelter but one of them – an elderly man – refused point blank to enter the shelter. So he was sleeping in his own bed in the house when a bomb fell on top of the shelter and made an unholy mess, leaving him without his family.[4]

Anderson Shelters were remarkably effective for what they were and they were capable of withstanding the force of a 250kg bomb exploding ten yards away. However, a direct hit would obliterate everyone inside, regardless of whether they covered the roof in soil and a couple of sandbags. For that reason, four per cent of Londoners felt safe only in the depths of the London Underground.

THE UNDERGROUND

The writer Vera Brittain was disconcerted by what she saw one morning in late October 1940 when she arrived at Regent's Park station:

> I find mothers and children already queuing up with cushions and mattresses for their nightly occupation of the Tube, and remember seeing, two days ago, a similar queue outside Golders Green at 11am. Soon, I reflect, London's poorer population, like melancholy troglodytes, will spend its whole life in the Underground, emerging only for half an hour after the morning 'All-Clear' to purchase its loaves and its fish and chips.[5]

Initially, the Government had refused to countenance the idea of allowing people to use the London Underground as a shelter for the reasons articulated by Brittain in her phrase 'melancholy troglodytes'. The last thing Churchill wanted was what he called a 'deep shelter mentality' to take hold of a large swathe of the capital's populace with them living hundreds of feet underground cut off from the real world and not caring about anything other than their own survival. However, short of closing the Underground for the duration of the Blitz there was the little the government could do to prevent people sheltering there. They just bought a ticket for 1½d and went down the escalator.

By 27 September 1940 a London Transport survey estimated that 177,000 people were sheltering in the 79 Underground stations, a tiny fraction of the population and one that never increased thereafter. Faced with this determined, but nonetheless manageable figure, the authorities gave their blessing to the Underground 'troglodytes'.

The London Passenger Transport Board (LPTB) began to allow shelterers into the stations at 4pm, though as Vera Brittain had witnessed at Regent's Park, this didn't prevent the more timorous families queuing up from mid-morning in order to have the best spot on the platform. This was considered to be as far away as possible from the emergency stairs and the temporary toilets (it took a while before lavatory facilities were installed; initially people had to resist the call of nature or use a bucket).

Sleeping in the Tube had other drawbacks apart from the overpowering stench created by 100 or more human beings in a confined space. There were mosquitoes, lice, rats and outbreaks of scabies. It was also hot and stuffy, but nonetheless the atmosphere was one of calm amiability. In his book *The Blitz*, the American-born writer Constantine Fitzgibbon, himself a survivor of the bombing of London, depicted the evening routine of the Tube dweller:

> By seven pm the people on the platforms were settling in. Some of the children were already tucked up for the night. Many people were eating sandwiches, chocolate or fruit, or drinking beer and tea out of thermos flasks. Others were talking and reading. All were surrounded by blankets, pillows and suitcases. There was little laughter and gaiety, but a great deal of talking. Almost no attempt was made to pass the time in an interesting manner. Two groups of people were playing cards: here and there people would be reading magazines in a half-hearted manner: there were almost no books in evidence: most just sat and talked or did nothing at all. At about nine the adults began to settle down for the night, most lying on one blanket, with another over them and a pillow for their heads. Some slept in a sitting position, with their backs to the tunnel walls. It rapidly became impossible to move about for sprawling bodies. One policeman and one shelter marshal, who were on duty, tried to keep a passageway clear.[6]

However, not all the Underground stations were as sombre as the one portrayed in Fitzgibbon's account. At Bethnal Green someone manoeuvred a piano onto the platform and each night there was a sing-song; another station held regular prize raffles and at Swiss Cottage they produced their own newspaper, *The Swiss Cottager*. The redoubtable women of the Women's Voluntary Service (WVS) held

TOP RIGHT: The coffins containing five London firemen killed in the line of duty in October 1940.

BOTTOM RIGHT: Rescuers dig deep into the wreckage of a house in Camden Town in the hope of finding survivors from a raid in October 1940.

Vera Brittain feared that the use of the Underground stations as air raid shelters would lead to poorer inhabitants of London existing like 'melancholy troglodytes'. Churchill too was initially reluctant to allow a 'deep shelter mentality' to take root. However, only 177,000 people were estimated to be using the Underground for shelter by the end of September 1940 and in fact the figure remained fairly consistent for the duration of the war. An idealised image of these communal shelters took root both during and after the war. In reality, initially at least, the overcrowded stations, with little or no sanitary facilities, could be dirty and unpleasant with many people just making do as this East End mother (below left) does with her young daughter sleeping in a fruit box and herself taking shelter on the hard, cold floor. But soon things improved with the Women's Voluntary Service providing tea and sandwiches in many instances, while another photo (below right) clearly shows that impromptu dance and sing-along was one way to pass the time before everyone took their place for another night on the floor of the Underground (opposite).

ALDWYCH

sewing bees and lectures on everything from gardening to cooking, while a troupe of actors toured the Underground stations with a production of *The Bear* by Anton Chekov. Libraries organised the delivery of thousands of books to shelters across the city. Christabel Leighton-Porter, a model for the *Daily Mirror* cartoon character 'Jane', recalled how 'there were people playing accordions and the youngsters could hop on a train and go round the Circle Line and have a wonderful time. I can remember seeing new twin babies down there and really watching them grow up.'[7]

But for many Londoners, cowering deep in the Underground wasn't the done thing. It showed a lack of moral fibre. One young woman described the Tube shelterers as the most demoralising and depressing sight of the Blitz, saying: 'One reads and knows about refugees from other countries, the sort that comes up against it, but you never expected to see your own people doing that.'

The first people began to leave the Tube at around 5am, usually the men who had to go to work. The women and children followed an hour later until by around 7am, as the daily commute commenced, the only sign that hundreds of people had been asleep on the platform a short while earlier was the detritus left behind.

One reason that the Underground's popularity as a place of shelter diminished from the end of September 1940 onwards was a spate of incidents in early October when people realised that fate could reach them even down below the ground. On 12 October an event which William Sansom described as 'one of the unluckiest incidents of the Blitz' occurred when a bomb fell in Trafalgar Square close to the statue of King Charles I. It pierced the surface and exploded in the Underground station below. The concussion of the blast caused the down escalator to collapse on top of several dozen people asleep on the floor at the bottom. Earth and concrete from street level also caved in, adding to the horror of the scene. Rescue workers spent a torturous night digging for survivors as bombs continued to drop close by, and eventually 40 people were brought out alive but seven had died.

The next evening something similar happened at Bounds Green, on the Piccadilly Line in North London, leaving 19 dead, and eight were killed by a bomb that exploded inside Praed Street Station. Then on 14 October a sickening event cost the lives of more than 100 people at Balham Tube station on the southern end of the Northern Line.

Six hundred were packed into the station when the first bombs began to topple from the sky. The Luftwaffe were early that evening. It was only 8pm, so most people were still awake, talking and laughing and singing. A LPTB employee was on the platform chatting to his wife and two children when a terrible explosion rocked the station and the lights went out. For a moment all was silent and then people began to panic. The employee did his best to allay people's fears but then someone shouted 'gas!' Another cried 'water!'

What none of those people, 100 feet below the surface of Balham High Street, knew was that the explosion had severed the web of water mains, telephone wires, sewer lines and gas pipes that ran below street level. It had also caused a large section of the road to collapse, blocking off the exit from the platform up to the booking

The government drew on community spirit to help in the fight against Hitler's Luftwaffe. This community spirit, often termed 'Blitz Spirit' was portrayed in newspaper cartoons throughout the worst of the bombing.

"I used to travel to Bank each day from Streatham by bus and it was very heartening to see the outward expression made by the commercial people. I passed a draper's shop where they had big plate glass windows that had been shattered by a bomb blast and the draper had put up a big notice, saying 'Göring may break our windows but he can't break our hearts'." Joan Varley, Londoner

hall. Within minutes the water was up to the employee's knees as he struggled to open the emergency hatch. People tore frantically at his clothes and hands in their desperation to escape the rising water level. Thanks to the calm courage of the LPTB man nearly 500 people escaped through the hatch, but 111 people failed to make it to safety. One of the rescuers, after he had helped the last of the lucky 500 to the surface, went back to the entrance of the emergency hatch and shone his torch below in the faint hope of finding one or two more:

> I saw a mountain of ballast, sand and water washing through a huge hole at the north end of the platform. The emergency exit [hatch] is very small – you have to stoop to get through it. The water was about two feet deep in the lower booking hall. I crossed it, and went through the emergency exit at an angle, crawling up the ballast. Very noisy it was, with a hissing of gas and water washing down. As it poured through the tunnel it washed past me, like a river, from right to left. It was like the sand and pebbles at Brighton on a very rough day.

MORALE

Remarkably, far from demoralising Londoners such horrific incidents unified them, bringing them closer together. By the end of October, as the middle-class Vere Hodgson discovered when she spent an afternoon in a street shelter chatting away to a working-class warden, the only social division that existed after a month of continual bombing was between those who had remained in the capital, defiant in the face of the bombing, and those who had fled to the safety of the countryside. The latter were derided as meek, while all those who carried on as normal, all those who could 'Take It', experienced a camaraderie the like of which London had never before known. The Blitz, literally and metaphorically, was a great leveller. A person's wealth or accent no longer mattered, strength of character was an individual's most treasured possession and those with it were respected regardless of background.

People began talking to each other, not just in shelters but in queues and on streets and in buses. They swapped bomb stories –

Tooting Fire Station in London was one of many such places destroyed by the Luftwaffe.

The exhilaration of finding a victim alive amidst the rubble. These dramatic photos show the rescue of Mrs Elsie Smith. First emergency workers come across her trapped in her London home, next they check for a pulse, then start to dig down to free the debris from Mrs Smith. Slowly and tenderly the overjoyed Mrs Smith is freed, shaken but alive, and a rescue worker cleans blood and dirt from her face.

close shaves, near misses, freak deaths – and tacitly encouraged one another for the next raid to come. Neighbours helped out with those less fortunate than themselves, lending items that had been destroyed in earlier attacks, and lending their expertise where necessary: repairing a cistern, replacing a window or cooking a meal for a family without gas. In London and in other cities devastated by the Luftwaffe, water carts were sent round in the event of water mains being hit and people queued patiently with their buckets for their turn. People shared taxis on the way home from work, formed firewatching teams to look out for one another's property and established schemes such as the one in East Ham called the Mutual Aid Good Neighbours Association (MAGNA).

However, more often than not acts of compassion and camaraderie were small and spontaneous, such as the one experienced by Joan Varley while travelling home from work on a London bus one evening. It was about 9pm and she was sitting at the back of the top deck, cigarette in hand; the only other passenger was an elderly man at the very front. As they headed down Great Smith in Westminster a stick of bombs fell not far ahead. Then more began to drop. 'The man at the front of the bus walked down the bus and sat next to me and we held hands', recalled Joan. 'Neither of us spoke a word and once we were through the bomb area and were back on to the route, he moved back to the front seat without a word being said.'[8]

It was this sort of stoic solidarity that so impressed outsiders, particularly the foreign correspondents who filed regular reports on the Blitz and the behaviour of Britons. John Hughes was an Australian working for the Press Association. In a letter to his daughter he described the remorselessness of the raids and the carnage they wrought. 'I honestly don't know how we stood it', he told her.

TOP RIGHT: Still in her nightdress, Elsie is carried to a waiting ambulance and then taken on to hospital.

BOTTOM RIGHT: Lucky to be alive: Elsie Smith laughs with joy alongside her husband after her release from hospital.

> It was because the English are unimaginative and stolid. Nothing in the air, on the earth and on the water scares them. They get annoyed but never get scared. I honestly believe that if 100 Nazi paratroopers came down tonight in Piccadilly Circus they would start queuing up to see how our commandos are dealing with them. The Londoner is great on queues. He queues for his bus, his breakfast, lunch and dinner, flicks and for the theatres.[9]

However, not all of London mucked in. Towards the end of the Blitz Dr Haden Guest, member of Parliament for North Islington, asked Herbert Morrison, Minister for Home Security, if he was aware

> that it has become a custom for people with means of transport and wealth to leave the area each night, thereby leaving their houses and business premises unprotected and placing an extra burden upon those who remain who take up the duty of firewatching?

Morrison replied that, regrettably, he was aware of the fact, but when pressed by Guest conceded it was beyond his remit to enforce property owners to remain in their homes each night. 'That', retorted Guest, 'is a scandal'.

Nowhere was it more of a scandal than in Chelsea. By March 1940 the population of the borough had dropped from 57,000 to 36,000 and a third of the rateable properties stood empty. In Belgrave Square, 13 of the 45 houses were put up for sale. This created fierce resentment among those who remained, as the *Westminster and Pimlico News* explained. With the houses empty water rates were unpaid and so the council cut the water supply, thus 'when a fire does occur it's useless for the neighbours to try and get the fire under control because there's lack of water'. The mayor of Westminster, 67-year-old Leonard Eaton-Smith, tried in vain to persuade the rich to attend to their responsibilities but to little avail; by May 1941 only 40

London shops did their best to remain open during the early days of the Blitz despite the inconvenience caused by the Luftwaffe.

per cent of Westminster residents had registered under January's compulsory Firewatching Order. (The greatly respected Eaton-Smith was killed in the early hours of 11 May 1941 when a trench shelter he was visiting on a morale-boosting tour of Westminster received a direct hit during the deadliest raid of the Blitz.)

There were other unpleasant side-effects of the Blitz. There was a small rise in anti-Semitism in parts of London, there was looting (discussed in more detail in chapter six) and the blackout caused bad things to happen. The nationwide blackout was a novel experience for all but the very old, those Britons born in the heyday of the Victorian era who could remember a time before electricity. William Sansom was one of those who found a romanticism in the blackout, revelling in a London devoid of the harsh glare of street lamps and neon signs, writing: 'By moonlight the great buildings assumed a remote and classic magnificence, cold, ancient, lunar palaces carved in bone from the moon.'

The blackout regulations forced householders to keep their windows covered at all times and car drivers to drive without lights. If that wasn't difficult enough for drivers they also had to negotiate their way down roads unlit by street lamps (except on main thoroughfares where a small 'starlight' filtered down) and obey traffic lights that were masked save for a small slit to allow people to see the red, amber and green.

Pedestrians had to find their way using the white lines painted around street lamps and trees and on the corner of some kerbs, guided only by their small torches that had to be pointed downwards at all times. Little wonder that road traffic deaths soared in the months following the declaration of war, prompting some hard-bitten cynics to joke darkly that soon there would be no one left for the Germans to bomb. In December 1939 there were 1,200 deaths on

TOP RIGHT: Rescuers swarm over a flattened property in Invicta Road, Woolwich, London, 14 November 1940.

BOTTOM RIGHT: After a couple of quiet weeks, London was hit hard on 8 December 1940, when several parachute mines were dropped.

Britain's roads (by comparison there were 2,538 fatalities on Britain's roads during the whole of 2007), a horrifying figure that prompted the government to issue posters warning people to 'Look Out in the Black-Out!' Among the advice given underneath was:

> When you first come out into the black-out, stand still for a minute to get your eyes used to the darkness.
>
> Look both ways before stepping off the pavement.
>
> Where there are traffic lights, always cross by them. It is worth going out of your way to do this.

Cars weren't the only hazards during the blackout. The darkness was a haven for prowlers and perverts, as numerous British women soon discovered. Sylvia Clark was on her way home one night from her work in a London Post Office when she received some unwelcome attention as she passed a doorway. 'Before I knew where I was, I had a chap's arm round my neck', she recalled.

> I swung round and I don't swear but I used every foul word I'd ever heard. I said 'If you don't leave me alone, I will scream and scream and somebody will come and help me!' He was rather short and I called him a short-arsed something. His hands dropped and I ran like the wind round the next road to my home.[10]

However, these were exceptions to the rule. Overall Londoners conducted themselves exemplary during the dragging months of late 1940 and early 1941. The mass neurosis that had worried the government in the event of widespread bombing never materialised. In fact, the reverse happened. The experience of being bombed knitted people closer together and made them more purposeful in

---

TOP LEFT: Tailor's dummies burn in a shop window during the 8 December attack on London.

BOTTOM LEFT: The shattered remains of several Anderson Shelters can be seen amid the wreckage after this West Hendon street was hit.

A lone fireman fights a valiant battle from his ladder to quell the inferno at Finsbury Square in Piccadilly, 1940.

everything they did. Absenteeism declined in the workplace because, as Constantine Fitzgibbon wrote: 'People clung to their work as to a stable, understandable link with the realities of the past in the insane and incomprehensible present.'

Incidents of drunkenness fell by 50 per cent and the police arrested fewer people for misdemeanours. There was a thriving black market – particularly for food and cigarettes – but that was insignificant compared to the pre-war doom-mongering when the authorities had feared a breakdown in social order if the population was subjected to terror bombing.

Far from being cowered by the German bombs, many Londoners – particularly the young – found it thrilling, an injection of intensity into what had hitherto been mundane lives. 'The Blitz brought an air of excitement that nobody had experienced in everyday life', reflected Alfred Senchell, a London fireman. 'Everyday life is humdrum; you go to work, you come home. To me, it was out of this world.'[11]

Marie Agazarian, a nurse, remembered how people would arrive for work the morning after a heavy raid 'and start talking and everybody's bomb was a bigger bomb than anyone else's bomb – "Oh, we had a bomb. *So many* people killed!"'[12]

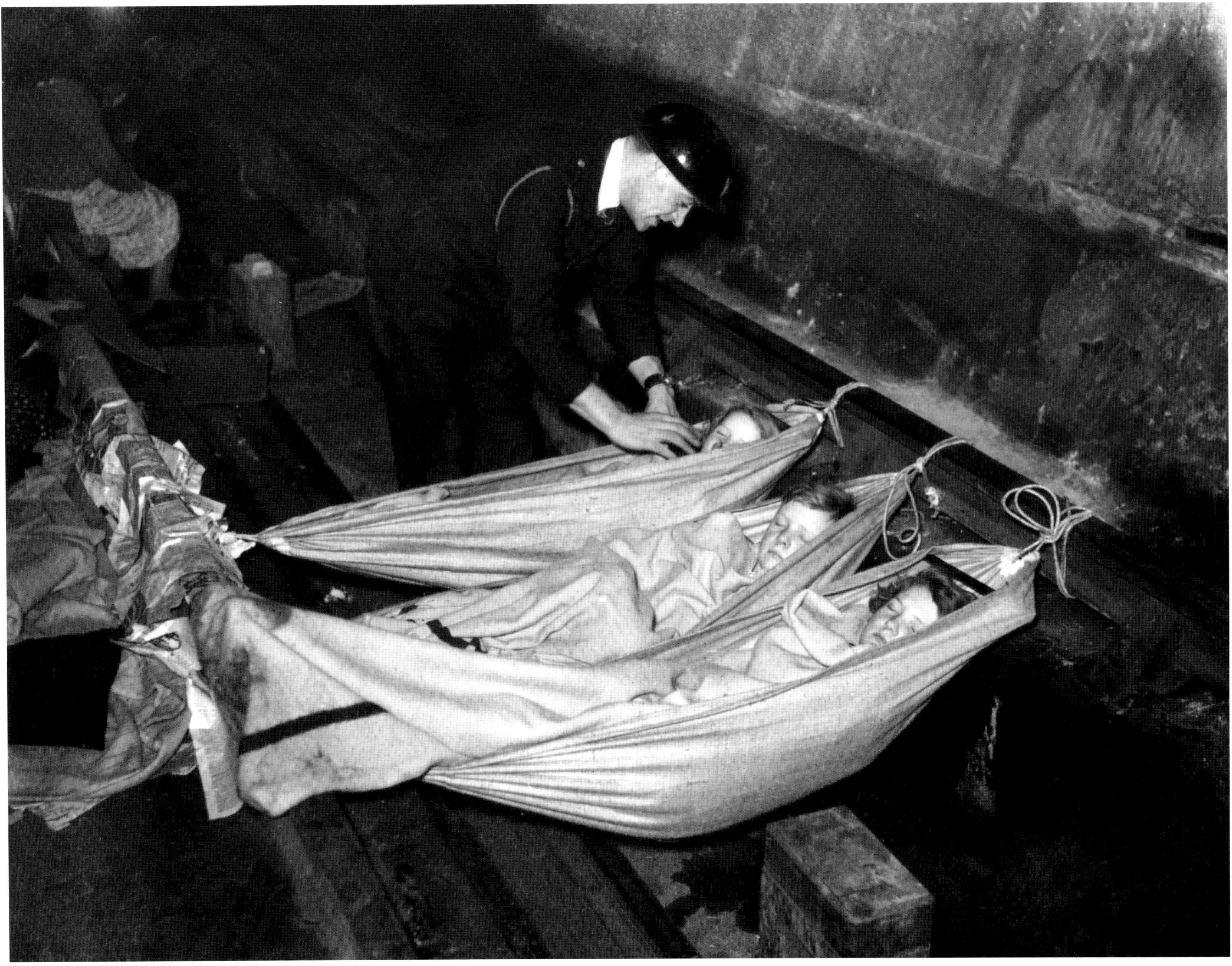

For young women like Florence Curry, a 19-year-old from Stepney in East London, the war allowed her opportunities that she would otherwise never have had. When she left school she had gone to work for a local fruit wholesalers, as her father and brother had done, but the Blitz opened up a new horizon for her. She joined the Auxiliary Fire Service and was posted to the control room of a station in Bow. 'We had some great times when we were off-duty', she recalled. 'We played cricket with the firemen, we had sing-songs in the local pub and sometimes us girls went up into London to go dancing or see a variety show.'

Even those Londoners who suffered directly from the German bombs refused to show anything other than steely defiance, an attitude that coined the phrase 'Business As Usual'. 'I used to travel to Bank [in the City] each day from Streatham by bus', recalled Joan Varley,

> and it was very heartening to see the outward expression made by the commercial people. I passed a draper's shop where they had big plate glass windows that had been shattered by a bomb blast and the draper had put up a big notice, saying 'Göring may break our windows but he can't break our hearts'.[13]

The head of the Luftwaffe would have hated to see such a sign, particularly after his communiqué to his aircrew on 18 October when he had proclaimed with his customary insufferable conceit: 'Your indefatigable, courageous attacks on the head of the British Empire, the City of London with its eight and a half million inhabitants, have reduced the British plutocracy to fear and terror.'

Hatred was the overriding emotion felt by Londoners in October 1940 towards Göring and his Luftwaffe. Any German pilot unfortunate enough to bail out over the capital was often beaten by an angry mob until the police or army arrived to cart him off for interrogation. One young woman, Moyra Macleod, wrote in her diary after one raid: 'I hate Germans and hope we blow the whole bastard lot of them to pieces with their Berlin around their ears.'[14]

James Oates was a young man serving in the Dagenham Home Guard during the raids of 1940 and one day raged in front of his father as he watched the crew of a burning German plane bail out: 'I've got a good mind to get my rifle and shoot the bastards as they come down.' His father, who a quarter of a century earlier had spent his youth in the trenches, reprimanded his son for such thoughts. Never lose your humanity, he told him, or else you have nothing left.[15]

Likewise Bobbie Tanner, the only London firewoman to be awarded the George Medal for gallantry during the Second World War, refused to hate the Germans despite having served in the London docks during the autumn of 1940. 'I had no animosity towards the Germans', she said. 'The pilots were doing their job and ours were doing theirs.'[16]

On 11 May 1941, the morning after London's last and heaviest raid of the Blitz, 30-year-old Gladys Shaw told her Sunday School class to bow their heads in prayer. A few hours earlier the Luftwaffe had killed nearly 1,500 Londoners and left large tracts of the capital a bombed out wasteland, now Shaw asked her young charges to say a prayer for the pilots. 'I tried to make the children know that it was war that was wrong and that the airmen who had done the bombing had mothers too, just like they did.'

OPPOSITE: An air raid warden tucks in three children for the night in the London Underground in October 1940.

MATTOC
SPADE

CHAPTER FOUR

COVENTRATED: THE DEVASTATION OF COVENTRY, 14 NOVEMBER 1940

"We have had it bad in London, Mr Mayor, but I have not seen anything worse than here in Coventry."

King George VI, 16 November 1940

THE LUFTWAFFE DROPPED 5,000 tons of bombs on the British capital during October 1940. A Londoner died for every ton. A further 6,343 people were left seriously wounded, a comparatively small figure indicating that for those unlucky enough to receive a direct hit, shelters – whether they were Andersons or Tube platforms – were by and large doing their job. Nonetheless, Prime Minister Winston Churchill was alarmed enough at the damage being done to the city to write: 'Our outlook at this time was that London, except for its strong buildings, would be gradually and soon reduced to a rubble-heap.'[1]

On Sunday 3 November John Colville, private secretary to Churchill, was one of the many people engaged in discussing what could be done to assist Greece in the likelihood that they would be attacked by Germany. The discussions were prolonged and intense and telegrams flew back and forth between London and Antony

OPPOSITE: Coventry tries its best to go about its business the day after 500 tons of high explosives had been dropped on the city.

RIGHT: What remained of the *Midland Daily Telegraph* building after the destruction of Coventry.

Eden, then in Cairo in his capacity as Secretary of State for War. 'From 9.00pm till 2.00am telegrams to Eden were drafted and redrafted', wrote Colville in his diary, 'and finally in a state of complete exhaustion we all went to bed at 2.00'. Almost as an afterthought he wrote: 'London had its first night free of air-raids for many a long day.'

For those in the front line of the capital's Civil Defence the realisation that London wasn't going to be bombed for the first time since Saturday 7 September was greeted with less restraint.

Westminster fireman William Sansom had heard the howl of the air raid siren at 5.30pm, that sinister prelude to what he assumed would be the 58th consecutive air attack on the city, but then an hour later 'the free liner-like note of the All-Clear siren rang out!' Across London no one stood down from their post, certain that the Germans would appear at some stage, but they never did. The only thing that fell on London that night was the rain. 'No warning at all during the night', wrote Vere Hodgson in her diary on Monday 4 November, adding: 'Marvellous!'

OPPOSITE: A Coventry postman does his best to deliver letters to Smithford Street.

BELOW: Coventry Cathedral on the morning of 15 November 1940.

It was but a temporary respite. Back came the bombers on Monday evening, and again for the next week. On 7 November, Sansom was struck by a curious incident he attended in St Martin's-in-the-Fields when a bomb landed close to the church, causing superficial damage to the building and killing a woman who was carrying her fat cat at the time. The woman was blown to bits but the cat survived, and it was through the name on its collar that the authorities were able to identity the unfortunate woman. The animal, 'held to be largest cat at least in London', became the mascot of Sansom's station and passed the rest of the Blitz in the chief fire officer's favourite armchair.

A week later, Thursday 14 November, London once again received no raiders and the populace enjoyed another night's peace. However, that same night hell was unleashed on Coventry.

London had borne the brunt of the Luftwaffe ferocity for the past two months. Birmingham, Bristol, Southampton and Plymouth had been subjected to small lightning raids throughout October but it was the British capital that was pulverised on a nightly basis. Yet heavy though the destruction was it was becoming apparent to the Germans that, despite Göring's boast to the contrary, the raids were doing little to break the resistance of Londoners. Perhaps if the Luftwaffe had continued to target the impoverished East End, as they had when the attacks started in early September, then they might have achieved their aim of provoking social disorder. 'If only the Germans had had the sense not to bomb west of London Bridge', Clement Attlee told Harold Nicolson around this time, 'there might have been a revolution in this country. As it is, they have smashed about Bond St. and Park Lane and readjusted the balance.'

Despairing of bringing Britain to its knees by singling out London, the German High Command changed strategy and adopted another of General Jodl's directives as published in his memorandum of 30 June 1940. From now on the Luftwaffe would attempt to defeat its enemy by attacking the 'country's war economy and its sources as a whole'.

COVENTRY

The British city chosen to be the first to experience this switch of strategy was Coventry, famous as much for its cathedral as for its factories that manufactured much of the British war machine. Its population worked for, among others, Dunlop, who made gun parts and barrage balloons; Rolls Royce and Vicker Armstrong, aircraft and automobile manufacturers; Humbler and Daimler, renowned for armoured vehicles; and Cash and Courtaulds, where parachutes rolled off the production line.

As early as 1934 the British government had warned Coventry that the city, along with Birmingham, might be a potential target in the event of war with Germany because of its manufacturing capabilities. However, in keeping with the times, the Labour-controlled council was reluctant to believe that another war was heading Europe's way so soon after the cataclysmic events of 1914–18, and so preferred a policy of pacifism to anything that might be construed as war-mongering. Even so, in 1935 an Air Raid Precaution sub-committee was established and Coventry soon had over 400 air raid wardens and 500 volunteer firemen to augment the existing regular service; a tiny figure in comparison to London but just about adequate to meet the needs of a city with a population of approximately 235,000.

Medical staff take the names of Coventry's injured the morning after the raid.

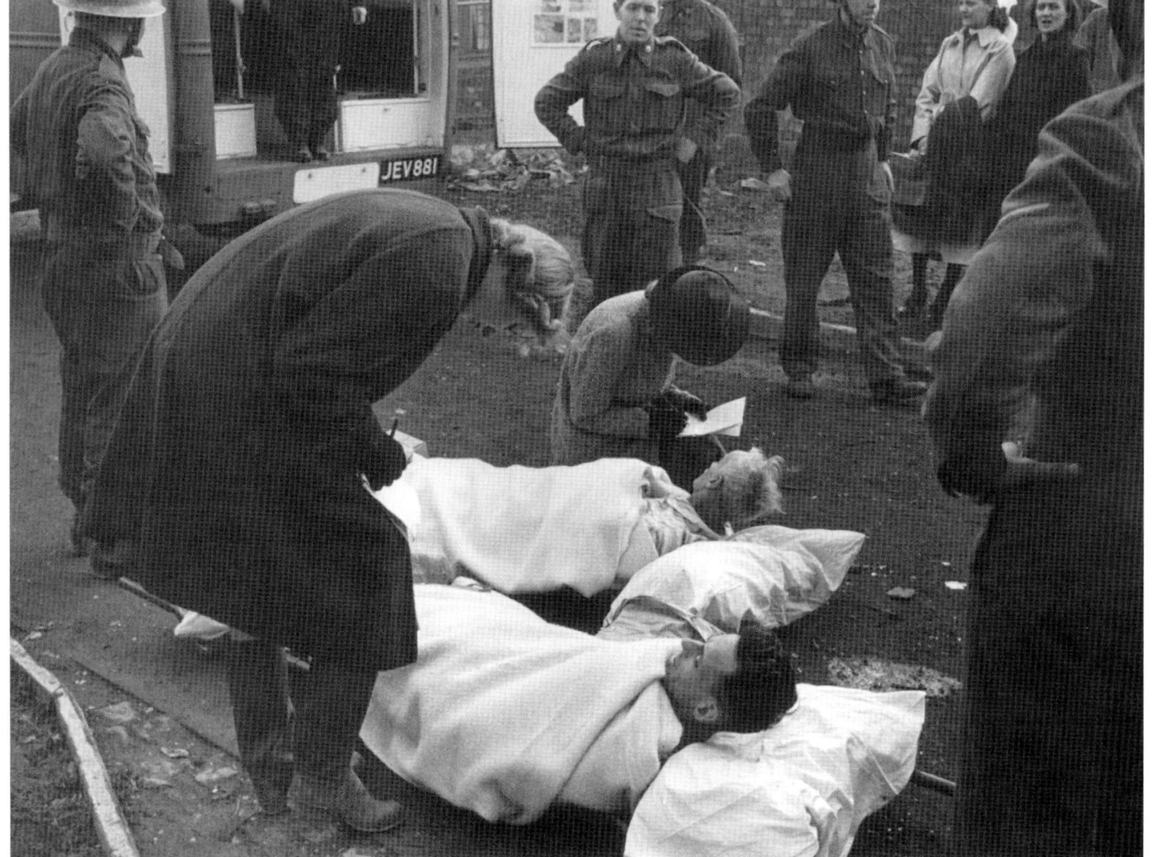

Ironically Coventry's Civil Defence was called into action before their London counterparts when the city was raided for the first time on 19 August 1940. Compared to what lay ahead it was a risible attack, just a lone bomber that dropped 14 bombs on a residential area. The city's paper, the *Midland Daily Telegraph* (in November 1941 the name of the paper was changed to its extant title of *The Coventry Evening Telegraph*), whose offices were based in Vicar Lane, reported that although a few people had lucky escapes no one was killed or wounded by the intruder. 'When you get to my age', a 67-year-old resident of the bombed street told the paper's reporter, 'you take what is coming to you and are glad it is no worse'.

But worse was to follow. In the week after the initial hit-and-run raid on Coventry similar attacks were carried out against Leamington and Nuneaton. Then on 28 August Coventry suffered its first fatalities as a result of German bombs when a larger raid took place. Still ignorant of the ordnance being dropped against them, the *Midland Daily Telegraph*'s diarist described the incendiaries that clattered down first on Coventry's streets as 'parachute flares'. Just as unaware were the residents who rushed out of their houses to stamp out the burning incendiaries. They were still doing so when high explosives straddled the streets. The 56 casualties included 16 dead, among whom was a family of seven whose house took a direct hit.

On 26 September Coventry had its first experience of a daylight bombing raid when shortly before 5.30pm the Standard Motor Works at Canley were attacked by a lone bomber. High-explosive and oil bombs were dropped, causing considerable damage but few serious casualties and no deaths. 'Eye-witnesses were full of praise for the superb airmanship of the raider's pilot', wrote the *Telegraph*'s diarist,

"The Germans can kill our loved ones, but it rests with us whether they shall break our spirit. This raid has brought us together in a common bond. We are now better friends and neighbours than we were… Let us go out and try to live unembittered lives." Bishop of Coventry, Mervyn Haigh, 20 November 1940

> as he made his way through the balloon barrage, banking steeply more than once to avoid not only the cables but also heavy fire from ground defences which opened up before he was more than half way across the city. 'Deserved a medal big as a frying pan', said one.[2]

Then on Saturday 19 October came Coventry's biggest raid to date when between 7.43 and 10.13pm more than 60 high-explosive bombs landed on the city. Twenty four people were killed and twice as many injured during the attack, the worst incident occurring in 'a block of dwellings of a humbler type in Castle Street'. Here 15 people taking refuge in a cellar were killed when the building above was hit and collapsed. There was more bad luck for a family of seven inside their Anderson shelter in the Hen Lane district of the city. A bomb tore through the air annihilating the shelter and all its occupants.

One of the pitiful consequences of the small-scale attacks on Coventry, which continued for the rest of October, was described by the *Telegraph*'s diarist at the end of the month:

> So persistent had air raid become during the last week of this month more than 200 dogs were destroyed at the R.S.P.C.A. headquarters, Coventry, their owners – many of whom had decided to evacuate – having decided not to continue their responsibilities in this direction.

A number of cases of owners not knowing what to do with their 'pal' came to the ears of the *Midland Daily Telegraph* since dogs were not permitted in public air raid shelters.

On 3 November the town of Rugby was attacked and the train station and waterworks received a stick of bombs. However, for the next ten days the bad weather that settled over the Midlands prevented any serious raids by the Luftwaffe. When they did return it was in numbers so great that as a result a new word entered the English language – 'Coventrated' – meaning to destroy by heavy bombardment. (Later in the war, the British gleefully added a second entry along the same lines – 'Hamburgered'.)

Approximately 515 aircraft from Luftflotten 2 and 3 took off from their bases in northern France shortly before 6pm. Fifty of this number broke off to launch a diversionary raid on London while the

Coventry's residential areas suffered as much as its industrial areas during the devastating raids.

rest continued north towards Coventry. That an attack was imminent had been known by the RAF since earlier in the afternoon when it was noted that the German radio beams were intersected over the city. That wasn't unusual; Coventry had been hit several times in the past few months and the Civil Defenders who rushed to their posts in the early evening had no reason to suspect anything too out of the ordinary was about to happen.

At 7.07pm the signal 'Air Raid Message Yellow' was flashed to Coventry, informing that bombers were fast approaching. Three minutes later the message turned to red and the sirens sounded across the city. 'My mother told me to go to the shelter as usual', recalled Thomas Cunningham-Boothe.

> But she and my youngest sister stayed behind because my mother was doing some ironing. But my mother was a very intuitive person and she felt there was danger. She called to my sister and they both went under the stairway where there was a large chest.[3]

Almost as soon as the air raid sirens sounded the first incendiaries were sprinkled across the city, burning brightly with their strange

The King and Queen visit Coventry to show their solidarity after the terrible raid of 14 November. The Queen frequently expressed her gratitude that Buckingham Palace had itself been bombed – the Luftwaffe bombs were indiscriminate in terms of class.

psss-psss-psss sound that some likened to leaves blowing down a street or peas dropping on to a plate. Several landed on the roof of the cathedral and it was while the firewatching teams were busy dealing with those that the high explosives began raining down.

Thomas Cunningham-Boothe was sitting in the family Anderson shelter wondering when his mum and sister were going to join him when he heard a deafening explosion. 'The walls of the house went out, the roof came down and my mother got trapped in the house', he wrote later. 'My sister should have been buried alongside her but she finished up stark naked on the roof of the house. God knows how that happened. She never spoke for four days.' Mrs Cunningham-Boothe crawled out of the wreckage of her house thanks to the artificial leg she'd worn since a baby. With her legs trapped under rubble, she painstakingly removed the harness of her artificial limb and then squirmed free.

By 8pm Coventry's Fire Service had logged 240 fires around the city with one of the fiercest in the cathedral. Half an hour later communication became virtually non-existent as telephone lines burned in the inferno, and the bombs continued to fall with ruthless regularity. One of the German pilots, Guenther Unger, flying a Dornier 17, was in the second wave of bombers to attack the city. 'While we were still over the Channel on the way in we caught sight of a small pin-point of light in front of us, looking rather like a hand torch seen from two hundred yards', he remembered.

> My crew and I speculated as to what it might be – some form of beacon to guide British night fighters, perhaps? As we drew closer to our target the light gradually became larger until suddenly it dawned on us: we were looking at the burning city of Coventry.[4]

Four hundred and forty nine bombers reached the target and dropped 500 tons of high explosives, including 50 1,000kg parachute mines. Some 30,000 incendiaries were also emptied on to the city.

Rescue workers look out from what remains of Coventry.

OPPOSITE: The diarist for the *Midland Daily Telegraph* documented the devastating raid in all its horrendous detail.

The German aircrew, though in their briefing they had been told they were attacking 'an important centre of the enemy armament industry', knew that they were also opening a new front in the war against civilians, one that perhaps would have consequences for their own families in the years to come. 'The usual cheers that greeted a direct hit stuck in our throats', wrote one later. 'The crew just gazed down on the sea of flames in silence. Was this really a military target?'

The bombers arrived over Coventry in 'crocodile' formation, an average of 12 miles between each trailing aircraft and seven miles from the next aircraft on the port or starboard side. Flying at altitudes of between 10,000 and 20,000 feet there was therefore roughly one Luftwaffe bomber to every 330 cubic miles of airspace. For the RAF night fighters, who between them flew around 125 sorties in an attempt to intercept the raiders, it was a night of bitter frustration. Not one enemy aircraft was shot down by an RAF pilot, though two German bombers were destroyed by anti-aircraft fire. One of the luckless British airmen was Peter Townsend, pilot of a Hawker Hurricane in No. 85 squadron, who recalled the misery of that night:

> In their paralytic attempt to defend Coventry and once again London the night defences – fighters and AA – did little to impede the murderous fire attack … to these feeble efforts 85 squadron could make no more than a symbolic contribution. Three or four of us took turns to patrol all through the night. I did a couple of stints of an hour or so, but like the others returned empty-handed.[5]

Also roaming the night sky looking for revenge was Guy Gibson in his Beaufighter with Richard James his radar operator. Yet even with the new-fangled AI radar they had no more luck than Townsend in his Hurricane. 'I was above and saw it [Coventry] burn', said Gibson later, who had been warned before he took off to avoid 50 RAF Hampdens that had been scrambled to deal with the Luftwaffe hordes. 'I never saw a Hampden or a German bomber the whole evening, and this convinced me once and for all that the night sky is very, very big.'[6]

According to the RAF plotters the Coventry Blitz reached its gruesome zenith at 15 minutes to midnight. By then the cathedral was being devoured by flames and hundreds more buildings had simply ceased to exist, as had a heartbreaking number of people. Dilwyn Evans, a Red Cross worker, recalled 'walking past the council housing in the centre. Everything was burning away, debris all around. A lot of people were going about trying to find relatives, friends, goodness knows what.'[7]

There was no let up for several more long, harrowing hours as the Luftwaffe kept coming. The majority of the bombs landed in a relatively small area of the city centred on the Broadgate district, though many landed further afield. In one of the most grisly incidents the residents of a street saw something unfamiliar swing from the sky on the end of a parachute. To Londoners it would have been all too terrifyingly obvious what it was, but Coventry had no prior experience of a 1,000kg parachute mine. A group of curious bystanders stood round wondering what they should do about this ten-foot object. Then it exploded, and a dozen people vanished off the face of the earth.

The All-Clear sounded at 6.16am on Friday 15 November. Dilwyn Evans headed into the city centre to offer succour to the injured and homeless. 'There was smoke everywhere but the fires were burning themselves out', he recalled.

> For about three days we worked night and day. We were absolutely shattered. Having seen a particular person trapped, it was a case of removing the debris by hand … the hardest experience was when we evaluated the condition of a body and realised there was no life but you'd still got to get the body out.

As well as the inestimable human cost of the raid, the sheer scale of destruction to the city's historic buildings was overwhelming. Not only was the cathedral no more but the medieval Palace Yard had gone, as had the 15th-century cottages called Priory Row and St Mary's Guildhall, where Henry VI and Queen Margaret of Anjou had stayed during the Wars of the Roses. When the city's official

Nov. 14–15th. 1940.

The raid which changed the face of central Coventry and caused wholesale havoc throughout the city occurred on this night. It was by far the city's biggest experience of Nazi frightfulness to date, and owing to the terrific destruction caused it had many aspects which could not possibly be repeated. For weeks, the population regarded with horror the amount of deaths and destruction caused, and the almost completely demolished centre of the city remained as a lasting memorial to the fiercest raid experienced to date in this country.– one which gained for the city world-wide sympathy. The semi-destruction of Coventry was quoted in practically every newspaper in the world.

× Later stated to be 200

The raid lasted for 11 hours, from darkness to dawn, (7.10 p.m. to 6.10 a.m.), and was conducted, it is estimated, by at least 500 German 'planes. Not for a moment during the night was the sound of roaring engines absent from the sky, and the ground defences, though terrific at times, were almost powerless to stem the attack. It was announced that two 'planes had been brought down, one of them near Loughborough and the other at Withybrook.

This was wrong

A German communique, issued the following day, claimed that during the attack a total of × 500 tons of bombs was dropped on Coventry, including 30,000 incendiary bombs– ~~a claim that is thought to have been no exaggeration.~~

The raid began with huge showers of incendiaries, which caused fires in all areas of the city, and, although much of the frightfulness that was to come was caused by high explosives of almost every known type, including land mines dropped by parachute, it was fire which caused much of the greatest devastation, particularly in the city centre. For hours on end Broadgate was a fiercely-burning inferno, in which a considerable number of civil defence members lost their lives.

The first estimate of casualties was 1,000 (approximately 200 killed) but that this was a conservative estimate was soon apparent. Ten days after the raid, the death roll was 450 and was still mounting as the bodies of more victims were recovered from debris beneath which they had been trapped. At this time the number of persons injured was about 900.

Thousands of homes in all districts were either badly damaged or wrecked, and one of the major problems of the next few days was the housing of the homeless, most of whom were accommodated temporarily in neighbouring towns and rural areas under an emergency scheme organised by the Ministry of Health, who assumed control of such matters as evacuation.

Despite every effort that was made to check the effects of the raiding 'planes, the Nazi pilots remained in almost undisputed command of the air. Mobile anti-aircraft guns were rushed to all parts of the city to augment the barrage as the raid progressed (among the points from which they were operated being Broadgate and Pool Meadow), but it was of practically no avail. So completely did the raiders control the situation that they were able to shoot down barrage balloons (at least four came down in flames) and carry out dive bombing attacks over the city.

Working under conditions of tremendous difficulty, the whole of the civil defence services covered themselves with glory. Among those who lost their lives were two police officers (P.C's Rollins and Simms), four special constables, a police war historian (and town clerk) Frederick Smith learned from a reporter of the damage that had been inflicted on his city he broke down and wept.

Another victim of the attack was the *Midland Evening Telegraph*, whose offices on Vicar Lane were incinerated by German bombs. When the newspaper's diarist eventually moved into new premises he had much to write about the raid that, in his words, 'changed the face of central Coventry'.

> The raid began with huge showers of incendiaries, which caused fires in all areas of the city, and, although much of the frightfulness that was to come was caused by high explosives of almost every known type, including land mines dropped by parachute, it was fire which caused much of the greatest devastation, particularly in the city centre. For hours on end Broadgate was a fiercely-burning inferno, in which a considerable number of civil defence members lost their lives.
>
> Thousands of homes in all districts were either badly damaged or wrecked, and one of the major problems of the next few days was the housing of the homeless, most of whom were accommodated temporarily in neighbouring towns and rural areas under an emergency scheme organised by the Ministry of Health, who assumed control of such matters as evacuation.
>
> Despite every effort that was made to check the effects of the raiding 'planes, the Nazi pilots remained in almost undisputed command of the air. Mobile anti-aircraft guns were rushed to all parts of the city to augment the barrage as the raid progressed (among the points from which they were operated being Broadgate and Pool Meadow), but it was of practically no avail. So completely did the raiders control the situation that they were able to shoot down barrage balloons (at least four came down in flames) and carry out dive bombing attacks over the city.
>
> The hundreds of fires that were caused were quite beyond the capabilities of the local firefighting resources, and outside help was requisitioned from a large number of towns. Outside help was still being called upon days later, including crews from the London Fire Brigade, South Wales, Lancashire and Yorkshire. A fortnight after the raid some fires in central Coventry were still smouldering beneath the wreckage of the city.
>
> The night's damage was so widespread as to defy any serious attempt at cataloguing within reasonable compass. However, it may be mentioned that the only building still standing and looking more or less as it was prior to the night of November 14th was the National Provincial bank, although the adjacent Lloyds Bank bore little visible signs of damage apart from its roof. The huge Owen Owen building was burned to an empty shell, both sides of the main Broadgate thoroughfare were laid almost flat by the explosive effects of land mines; the greater part of Smithfield Street was a shambles; and half the east side of Hertford Street was also wrecked. The Post Office building was only saved on the following day by a prompt decision to blow up the still blazing Queen's Hotel building and prevent the spread of the fire in that direction.
>
> Other central damage included that which from a sentimental point of view produced a greater effect on the public than almost anything else – the complete destruction of Coventry Cathedral with the exception of the tower and spire.

Two days after the raid the King came to Coventry to see for himself the damage and to show solidarity with his people. With him were Herbert Morrison, the Home Secretary, and Florence Horsbrugh, the parliamentary secretary to the Ministry of Health. By now the full horror of what had happened was sinking in, and the initial feelings of relief – even euphoria at being alive – among the survivors had turned to grief at the realisation that over 500 people were dead (the official number, augmented during the days and weeks that followed as more bodies were unearthed, was given as 568) and a further 1,200 were wounded, 900 seriously. Two and a half thousand homes had been destroyed, 625 shops and 75 business premises likewise. Six hundred soldiers were ferried in to help demolish unsafe buildings. Road and rail services were in chaos, so too the gas, electricity, telephone and water supplies. A mass programme of inoculation was organised to prevent an outbreak of typhoid with 30,000 people vaccinated in three centres.

Dilwyn Evans was in the high street helping to recover a body when he felt a tap on his shoulder. It was the mayor of Coventry (Alderman J. A. Moseley).

> He said 'Excuse me, I've got someone here who would like to have a word with you'. I got up and looked and there was King George VI in full field-marshal's uniform. He just put his hand out and thanked me very much for what we were doing. That repaid me for everything I'd done.

Trailing the King as he toured the desolation was the diarist for the *Midland Evening Telegraph*, who later wrote an account of the visit:

> The tour began with a visit to the ruined cathedral. 'How ghastly' said the King to the Provost. Later he walked through Broadgate shambles, down the almost completely wrecked Smithford Street and later drove out by car to see the work of sheltering and feeding homeless families at St George's Church Hall. En route he saw the heap of rubble which was all that was left of St Nicholas Church as the result of a direct hit by a landmine.
>
> He had lunch by candlelight at the Council House in the Mayor's room (windows boarded up and no electricity) and in the afternoon went for another walking tour in the course of which he chatted to auxiliary firemen still at work in the Priory Street district. He also saw the emergency feeding arrangements for firemen at the Pool Meadow car park.
>
> Before he left the city, the king told the mayor, 'We have had it bad in London, Mr Mayor, but I have not seen anything worse than here in Coventry'.

While Coventry was embarking on a melancholy clean-up operation the rest of the country was learning of the carnage wrought on the city. Vere Hodgson wrote in her diary for 15 November:

> Turned on news at 8am and was alarmed to hear a Midland town had had a bad raid with many casualties. I was terrified it was Brum [Birmingham, where Hodgson was at university]. But at lunch time it was poor Coventry. The cathedral destroyed – a 14.C building. Mother and I walked round it when we visited Coventry last September.

One effect of the Coventry raid was to persuade the British censor to allow its name to be mentioned on the radio and in newspapers, a temporary relaxation of policy. Hitherto the policy, except where London was concerned, was that any place outside the capital to be bombed was referred to merely as a 'south-coast town', 'a Midlands town' or a 'northern city'. It was foolishly fastidious on the part of the Government to try to hide the truth from its people, particularly when millions of people tuned in to hear Lord Haw-Haw (aka William Joyce, the deputy leader of the British Union of Fascists, who fled Britain for Germany in 1937 and subsequently broadcast

Government censors frequently refused to allow bombed locations to be revealed, as was the case with this photo, identified only as a town on 'the south coast'. However, the bombing of Coventry allowed a relaxation of policy.

HARLENE HAIR GROWER & TONIC

Stops FALLING HAIR Increases GROWTH Adds Life & Loveliness to the DULLEST HAIR

HARLENE HAIR GROWER AND TONIC

CREMEX SHAMPOO

UZON BRILLIANTINE

CINEMAS

What does rationing mean to you?

Turog brown bread

SPILLERS LIMITED, CARDIFF

ROSEMARY CLUE TO MURDER Police Say

The Handkerchief

MOTHER OF 11 IS GAOLED

MR. BOOTHBY, M.P.—MOVE FOR NEW INQUIRY COMMITTEE

ROME'S LATEST VISITOR

This Was To Have Been Their Bridal Home

U.S. MOVES TO GIVE US CREDIT

"Britain Bankrupt"

GERMANS CANCEL LEAVE

Town Sang in Six-Hour Blitz

"Coventried"

NO "DANGER PASSED" WHISTLE BY WARDENS

PAT'S SPITFIRE PENNIES ESCAPED IN DIRECT HIT

What Nazis Bombed

300 BAG BY POLES

NO NORWAY REGRETS AT CHOICE OF WAR

AUDLEY END MANSION

CENSORSHIP AND BOMBING RAIDS

THE UNCENSORED REPORTING of the carnage caused in Coventry proved to be the exception to the rule. Less than a fortnight later Bristol was subjected to a prolonged bombardment but the government forbade the media from mentioning the city in its reports of the Blitz. Infuriated, Cecil Harmsworth King, managing director of the *Daily Mirror*, cunningly circumvented what he considered to be tyrannical censorship by prefacing the paper's account of the raid with the publication of the official German description of the attack on Bristol. Winston Churchill was furious, accusing King in a letter of attempting 'to discredit and hamper the Government in a period of extreme danger and difficulty'. King refuted the allegations, saying the Prime Minister was being 'pretty petty'. The *Mirror*'s stance had the required effect, however, with the government informing the media on the evening of 26 November 'that it might at last be stated' which towns and cities had been bombed.

The Daily Mirror, *Tuesday 26 November 1940*

TOWN SANG IN SIX-HOUR BLITZ

'Bristol has been wiped out as a distributing centre and important railway junction. Great stocks of food destined for London were destroyed.' – German Official News Agency

Public shelters ran with community choruses and people caught in churches and chapels sang for six hours as 100 German bombers rained incendiaries and high explosives on a western town – Sunday night's main target for the Luftwaffe. At a hall where a recorder was conducting a service people sat on their seats hour after hour, and went home at the end of the raid unharmed. 'I must say,' said the recorder yesterday, 'that we did not sing only hymns. We even sang "What shall we do with the drunken sailor?"'

Fires were started near a theatre where a concert was being held. A cafe and a clothing store blazed. The roof of the theatre was slightly damaged. For several hours lone raiders arrived almost continuously. A soldier home on leave tried to prevent a fire spreading in a church. When an incendiary fell on the building, he smashed a window with his tin hat, climbed through and extinguished the bomb. But more incendiary bombs fell almost immediately afterwards and the church was seriously damaged. The casualty list, it is believed, will not be so heavy considering the intensity of the raid.

Nazi propaganda on the British airwaves. He was hanged for treason in 1946) gloat of how successful the Luftwaffe had been in raiding Southampton or Bristol or Liverpool.

'I used to listen to William Joyce on the wireless', recalled Leslie Stark from Sussex.

> Sometimes Joyce came out with more things than the BBC. After a big raid he came on the next night and said: 'The glorious Luftwaffe have dropped a number of bombs on oil refineries in Batts Wood, Sussex.' He had everything tapped. He knew exactly where the bombs had been dropped.

The censorship infuriated the British press, the *Daily Mirror* describing the policy in one editorial as 'this strange rule that we ought to get news of our own troubles from Germany'. Evidently the censor's iron hand was at work early on the morning of Friday 15 November, as Hodgson heard news only of the bad raid on a Midlands town; later a name was allowed to be put to the town.

The reason for the greater openness was simple: to pre-empt the German propaganda machine. Better to describe the devastation yourself, the Government reasoned, than let the enemy do it for you. Sure enough, on Friday evening the Germans broadcast a communiqué on the British airwaves detailing how 500 tons of high explosives had been dropped on Coventry the night before, as well as 30,000 incendiary bombs.

The British press responded the following day, Saturday, with their own uncensored accounts of the Coventry Blitz. Clearly the instructions had gone out to editors – describe the devastation in full detail, and work the nation into a collective fury at this wanton destruction.

Accordingly, the front page of the *Mirror* was adorned by a stark photograph showing the dismal remnants of the city's cathedral, underneath which was a graphic account of the aftermath:

> Pathetic streams of refugees, men, women and children, were trekking to the safety of the countryside when darkness fell last night. Every road out of the city, which had had a bomb rained on it at the rate of one a minute, was filled with the same tragic procession.

The *Mirror*'s correspondent described how for seven miles he was swept along on the tide of human flotsam being washed from the city centre. Next to him for part of the way was old Dick Webb, 'his head swathed in bandages, his clothing tattered'. The reporter listened as Webb ridiculed the idea that the attack had been anything other than a desire to kill as many people as possible. 'It is damned nonsense to say that the Germans made any attempt at direct bombing', seethed Webb, 'because as I was walking across the fields a bomb fell twenty yards behind me. It threw me forward and as I got up to run, another one came down just in front of me'.

It wasn't all doom and gloom, however, in the *Mirror* in its edition of 16 November. The paper trumpeted that 19 German aircraft had been downed in the raid on Coventry, bringing the total number for

Construction workers made the most effective rescuers because they best understood a building's structural strengths and weaknesses.

LAST EDITION

The Midland Daily Telegraph

No. 15,426. MIDLAND DAILY TELEGRAPH, FRIDAY, 15 NOVEMBER, 1940

Sheer Strength BEAR BRAND STOCKINGS

Moonlight bombers attack from Norway to Brittany as BERLIN GETS BIGGEST-EVER BOMBING

Coventry bombed: Casualties 1,000

Cathedral and shelters hit

"THE City of Coventry was heavily attacked last night," states a Ministry of Home Security communique issued this afternoon. "The scale of the raids was comparable with those of the largest night attacks on London."

"The enemy were heavily engaged by intensive A.A. fire which kept them at a great height and hindered accurate bombing of industrial targets, but the City itself suffered very seriously."

"PRELIMINARY REPORTS INDICATE THAT THE NUMBER OF CASUALTIES MAY BE IN THE NEIGHBOURHOOD OF A THOUSAND.

"It is feared that extensive damage was done and many buildings destroyed, including the cathedral.

"THE PEOPLE OF COVENTRY BORE THEIR ORDEAL WITH GREAT COURAGE.

"CITY OF THREE SPIRES"

'Coventry pays for Munich' —Nazi radio

Station, railway yards hit

BERLIN last night had its heaviest raid of the war. It lasted from early evening till 1.45 a.m., and resulted in further damage to the Schlesischer station. Fires were started at four other railway centres.

Other raiders were meanwhile attacking industrial targets in other parts of Germany as well as enemy-occupied aerodromes. Ten of our aircraft are missing.

Berlin admits that the raiding force was stronger than ever before, and that "between 10 and 15 planes" reached the capital. An eye-witness account asserts that the raiders flew on undisturbed by searchlights and shells while on the ground transport services were thrown into a state of chaos.

Britain beats the mines

JERVIS BAY SAVED TWO MORE SHIPS

RAIDER SANK ONLY FOUR OF CONVOY

WAVES OF ENEMY PLANES IN DUSK TO DAWN RAID

"THERE will be many stories of heroism to be told when it is possible to collect them," states the official report of last night's air raid on Coventry.

Morrison's praise for Lord Dudley

ITALIAN RETREAT IS ROUT: GREEK DRIVE

120-mile offensive

THE Greek Army is attacking the Italians furiously all along the 120-miles front from the Ionian Sea to the Jugo-Slav border, and says that in the Kalamas sector the Italian retreat has taken on the form of a rout.

ANOTHER TUNE NOW!

First U.S. W. Indies base

RUSSO-JAPANESE AGREEMENT DENIED

R.A.F. DRIVES BACK 50 RAIDERS

TANNIC ACID DANGERS

MOLOTOV BACK HOME

Wedding ring theft

Storm havoc in Brussels

Two-hour gun battle across Channel

AVOID FLU ... VICK

LAST EDITION

The Midland Daily Telegraph

No. 15,427. SATURDAY, 16 NOVEMBER, 1940.

EVERYTHING MUSICAL PURCHASE WITHOUT TAX SCOTCHERS LTD.

Crippled Coventry carries on THE KING'S VISIT TO DAMAGED CITY

Ministry takes over control of Public Services Swift measures to restore normal life

COVENTRY CONTINUED TO-DAY THE TASK OF CLEARING UP THE DEVASTATION CAUSED BY THE NAZI AIR BLITZ WHICH WRECKED PRACTICALLY THE WHOLE OF THE CENTRE OF THE CITY, AND THE GREATER PART OF THE SUBURBS.

HIGH GOVERNMENT OFFICIALS TO-DAY TOOK OVER THE WORK OF RELIEF AND QUICKLY GOT TO THE TASK OF RESTORING ORDER OUT OF ABSOLUTE CHAOS.

Rest Homes Available

The Public Services

COVENTRY "A WARNING TO AMERICA"

BIG R.A.F. RAID ON HAMBURG

Troops quit Le Havre

HIS MAJESTY'S TOUR

Visits stricken areas and expresses deep sympathy with people

THE KING came to Coventry to-day to see the scenes of devastation caused in Thursday night's savage raid on the city. The visit was arranged at less than twelve hours' notice.

'RAID THE BIGGEST ATTACK IN HISTORY OF AIR WAR'—NAZI CLAIM

£10,000 FROM LORD MAYOR'S RELIEF FUND

Malta's canteen fund closes

Heavy attack on London: Two hospitals hit: "Peak" barrage greets Nazis

The King visits Cathedral

R.A.F. WIPE OUT MUSSOLINI'S ALBANIAN H.Q.

Hoover's European aid plan

NO SUPPORT FROM BRITAIN OR U.S.

ACTIVITY SLIGHT IN MIDLANDS

Widow's body found under table

LATE NEWS

Soviet air schools

Covers of the *Midland Daily Telegraph* from 15 and 16 November 1940, covering the devastation and aftermath of the Luftwaffe bombings.

the past seven days to 70. RAF casualties, on the other hand, were just five planes shot down. It was laughable, but it was laudable too, a tonic for a nation wondering where was next after Coventry. The *Mirror*, with its managing director, Cecil Harmsworth King, always with his finger on the nation's pulse, sensed the dread and published a rallying cry in its editorial for the day:

> London has 'taken' its nightly bombing for weeks past; suffering much, but enduring with fortitude. Many other big towns in the Midlands and the North have shared this ordeal. Of these attacks, the one made on Coventry on Thursday night ranks with the severest of those directed against London. We deeply regret the loss of life – inevitably involved in the indiscriminate bombing of a city as large as Coventry. These people have given their lives for the cause. They have not flinched from the trial common to all the civilian population of this country. 'They bore the ordeal with great courage,' says the official announcement. With a courage matching that of the bravest men who have fought for us in wars when civilians were not, as now, in the firing line.

Over the coming days revenge replaced resilience as the motif of the *Mirror.* Cassandra, the paper's popular columnist (in reality, 31-year-old William Neil Connor, of whom Winston Churchill once said 'It is a pity that so able a writer should show himself so dominated by malevolence') warned Germany that in time they too would come to know the terror of indiscriminate bombing and 'we shall see how this new Nazi nightmare society, that has lasted for seven horrible years since Hitler's diseased brain put it into being, can stand up to a nation that is able to hit back and hit back hard'. The paper's resident poet, Patience Strong, published a poem on Monday 18 November entitled *Coventry*:

> The martyred city gashed and scarred
> Her children slain her beauty marred
> Still proudly stands but to the sky
> The very stones for vengeance cry
> As Nations sow so must they reap
> They too for this night's work shall weep
> Such deeds their retribution bring
> God speed the day of reckoning

Within days emergency relief was flooding into Coventry. Forty thousand loaves of bread were dispatched to feed a population still without gas and electricity. Corned beef, every housewife's favourite, also arrived by the lorry-load, as did vegetables and other much-needed commodities. From America came donations of money and clothes to aid the beleaguered city, too many donations in fact, and the British Ambassador in Washington had to diplomatically ask the Americans to temporarily refrain from sending non-essential items as they were taking up too much space in the holds of ships that should have been transporting munitions and manufacturing parts for Britain's war effort.

On 20 November Coventry began to bury its dead. One hundred and seventy two bodies were laid in a mass grave in the London Road cemetery among the yew and cypress trees and bomb craters. The service, first a Roman Catholic ceremony and then a Free Church prayer, was led by the Bishop of Coventry, Mervyn Haigh. When the bishop addressed the huge crowd of mourners a pall of smoke still hung in the cold winter air from a bombed out factory nearby. 'Citizens of Coventry', said the Bishop, in a firm but tender voice,

> No one can voice the sorrow which you share today. First remember that the eyes of millions of people are on us at this time. I wish I could show you some of the letters and messages I have received from people all over the world expressing their regret, sympathy and admiration. The Germans can kill our loved ones, but it rests with us whether they shall break our spirit. This raid has brought us together in a common bond. We are now better friends and neighbours than we were. Let us love and even live in the strength of this new faith. Let us go out and try to live unembittered lives.[8]

CHAPTER FIVE

THE SECOND GREAT FIRE OF LONDON: 29 DECEMBER 1940

"... the thing I shall always remember above all the other things in my life is the monstrous loveliness of that one single view of London on a holiday night – London stabbed with great fires, shaken by explosions, its dark regions along the Thames sparkling with pin points of white-hot bombs..."

Ernie Pyle, American war correspondent

'POOR COVENTRY', ran Vere Hodgson's diary entry on Monday 18 November. 'The more one reads about it the worse it gets.' However, it wasn't just Coventry on the receiving end of the new Luftwaffe strategy. In the second half of November, the Germans visited all four corners of England, causing misery in Birmingham, Liverpool, Plymouth, Sheffield, Portsmouth, Manchester and Bristol. On the last day of the month Southampton endured a seven-hour raid, well remembered by Eric Hill, who was eight years old at the time and living four miles from the city centre:

> The Messerschmitts and Dornier bombers seemed to come right over the estate that I lived on, and turn round, and dive-bomb Southampton. All we could see was the town ablaze – you could just see the glow and we knew that Southampton was really getting hammered.[1]

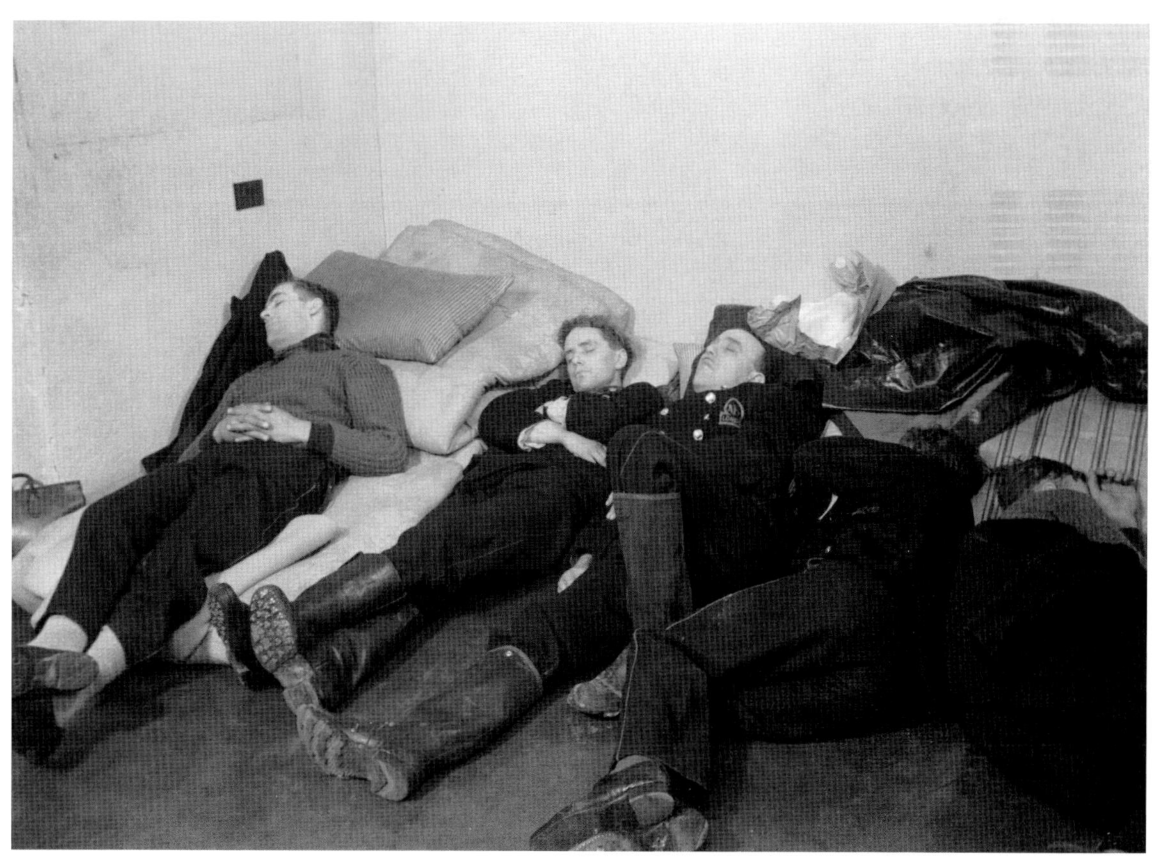

OPPOSITE: Nurses at Westminster Hospital sing carols to the wounded during Christmas 1940.

RIGHT: Firemen get their heads down while they can at Lambeth HQ on the morning of 9 December 1940, prior to the great fires of 29 December.

It was later estimated that 9,000 incendiaries were dropped on the city, starting more than 600 fires and contributing to the deaths of approximately 100 people.

The Luftwaffe's concentration on the rest of the country brought some much-needed respite to London. Despite the city's boast of 'London can Take It', the 57 nights of continuous bombing from 7 September to 3 November had stretched the capital if not to breaking point, then close to it.

Looting was said to be on the increase and Churchill intervened to prevent the prosecution of six firemen for such an offence because he said it would be bad for morale. Rationing was beginning to bite and the war news from overseas in November wasn't encouraging with Hungary, Romania and Slovakia joining the Axis Powers.

The government could suppress the official number of dead and wounded, but they could do nothing about altering the flattened buildings in the city or the flagging spirit of its people. In West Ham, as in other London boroughs, a casualty list was pinned to the outside of the town hall after each raid. Albert Prior, a stretcher bearer with the local Civil Defence unit, wasn't fooled by what he read:

> Many a time, I'd had more casualties through my hands alone than were supposed to have come through the whole of London, but the official figures were designed to keep the morale of the public up. If people had seen the real number of casualties, there'd have been trouble.[2]

In some parts of London there was trouble, according to Arthur Binnie, a second lieutenant in an infantry regiment stationed in the city. 'I regret to say that there were occasions when we had to fix bayonets to prevent people entering bank vaults that were opened by the bombing', he recalled. 'I was getting the feeling that some people wouldn't stand the Blitz for much longer.'

There was a heavy attack on London on 15 November but then for three weeks the city was barely touched, just a few short, sharp raids

London burns on the night of 29 December 1940.

that were negligible in comparison to what had gone before. However, 8 December brought a return to the malevolence of the autumn raids as the Germans launched a large-scale assault on London. 'Last night was very bad indeed', wrote Hodgson in her diary the following day. 'Began soon after 5.30pm … it never ceased until 2.30am. Many bombs came down.'

The raid was notable for the high portion of parachute mines dropped by the Luftwaffe. One landed in the Temple Gardens, part of the Inns of Court by the Embankment, causing widespread damage to the Middle Temple library, where once Dr Johnson and William Thackeray had studied.

Another came down in Langham Place, outside BBC Broadcasting House, at around the time two employees left for the evening, Mr Pocock and Mr Sibbick. The pair fetched their bicycles from the shed in Chapel Mews and then parted company, Sibbick pedalling off towards Oxford Circus contemptuous of the air raid in progress. Pocock, meanwhile, wheeled his bike round to the front of Broadcasting House and asked the two policemen on duty, 23-year-old John Vaughan and a constable Clarke, what they thought would be the safest route home. The policemen responded to the question and also advised Pocock to put on his helmet with the chinstrap round the back of his head. As they were talking Pocock noticed 'a large, dark shiny object approach the lamppost [opposite] and then recede'. In the blackout he assumed it was a taxi trying to park. A second later something that looked like a tarpaulin fell on the same spot. Pocock pointed it out to the policemen, who had their backs to the mysterious object, but when they turned round there was nothing to see but a row of parked cars. They thought it was probably nothing but at Pocock's insistence the three of them went to investigate. Vaughan went first, the other two chatting nonchalantly behind. Suddenly Vaughan turned, shouted something and began to run towards Broadcasting House. Clarke followed but Pocock hesitated, and thinking they were under attack from above, crouched down on the road. Then his world convulsed. 'I had a momentary glimpse of a large ball of blinding, wild, white light and two concentric rings of colour, the inner one lavender and the outer one violet, as I ducked my head', recalled Pocock afterwards. 'The ball seemed to be ten to twenty feet high and was near the lamppost.'

The noise of the explosion Pocock described as a 'colossal growl' and he was hurled across the road by a 'veritable tornado of air blast'. There was a raging pain in his ears from his perforated eardrums and something had ripped into his head, tearing off his helmet. Pocock lay helpless in the gutter, a captive of the force of pressure by the monstrous bomb. 'Just as I felt that I could not hold out much longer', he described,

> I realised that the blast pressure was decreasing and a shower of dust, dirt, and rubble swept past me. Pieces penetrated my face, some skin was blown off and something pierced my thumbnail and my knuckles were cut, causing me involuntarily to let go my hold on the curb. Instantly, although the blast was dying down, I felt myself being slowly

The view looking east from central London as the fire from German incendiary bombs spreads through the city.

"Although it was pitch black everything was silhouetted in red. But the bit that got me was the river. Everything was reflected in that river, and it wasn't a river of water, it was a river of fire, and it was alive. It was a combination of horrendous and beautiful and magnificent." Mary Warschauer, 29 December 1940

> blown across the pavement towards the wall of the building. I tried to hold on but there was nothing to hold on to. Twice I tried to rise but seemed held down. Eventually I staggered to my feet. I looked around and it seemed like a scene from Dante's *Inferno*.[3]

Several people lay dead, including Vaughan and two passing soldiers, while Clarke and many more were badly wounded. Pocock had been so close to the blast that its epicentre had passed over him. He was taken to hospital and later learned that the blast had lasted for a full nine seconds.

Three nights later, 11 December, there was another raid, which encapsulated fortune's cruel vagaries for a number of Londoners. One of the giant 1,800kg 'Satan' bombs was dropped in central London, but instead of landing in a residential area, it fell in the Serpentine in the middle of Hyde Park. A few miles away a smaller bomb came rushing through the air and hit one of two street shelters in Vincent Street, close to Millbank, killing 28 people. Most of those who died shouldn't have been inside: they'd come from the other shelter to break up a fight. Such was the arbitrary nature of the Blitz.

The next ten days were relatively quiet. People hung paper chains in their Anderson Shelters, air raid wardens wore coloured paper hats instead of helmets and the Women's Voluntary Service handed out mince pies at street shelters.

Then on 21 December something odd occurred, a 'mystery' that had still not been explained when William Sansom wrote his memoirs seven years later. Vere Hodgson was aware of it in her house in Holland Park, writing in her diary just a few hours later: 'Something nasty seemed to come down. A new sort of noise.' The next day she wrote that the noise was in fact a German aircraft, laden with bombs, which had crashed on Ebury Bridge two miles away. But then it was found that the twisted scraps of metal scattered in the explosion over a large area weren't in fact from an aircraft but from the windows of the Art Metal Company's premises close to the point of impact of the mysterious explosion.

Eye-witnesses spoke of having seen 'an orange glow in the sky, making a roaring noise, and moving rather slower than an aeroplane' a few seconds before Ebury Street blew apart, sending a four-foot length of railway line flying through the air for 650 yards and scattering bolts from sleepers as far afield as Chelsea. Sansom was one of those first to arrive and he found a 'vast and cold confusion' with scores injured but only three fatalities. Christmas cards littered the desolate landscape and wrapping paper floated on the breeze.

He tried to gently steer an old woman from her eviscerated house but 'she refused to leave the stew, muttering that she had taken a great deal of trouble in preparing it and none of those "yellow Germans", nor anybody was going to stop her from finishing it'. Further down the street Sansom passed a couple sitting in the shell of their house listening to their gramophone, a song called *All Over the Place*.

Civil Defence authorities later concluded that the explosion was caused by a 2,500kg bomb, one of only two dropped on Britain during the war (by comparison the atomic bomb dropped on Hiroshima in 1945, nicknamed 'Little Boy', weighed 4,000kg).

John Colville, private secretary to the Prime Minister, spent Christmas Eve, a Tuesday, in the company of his master as Churchill wrote Christmas cards and organised the sending of gifts. To the King he gave a siren suit and to the Queen a copy of Fowler's *Indispensible Guide to English Usage*. Colville dined in the Central War Room, festooned with Christmas decorations, and wrote in his diary for the day:

> We are not going to bomb Germany tonight, but should they attack us we shall return in great force tomorrow. However, with the aid of bad weather it looks as if the Luftwaffe will get the credit for respecting this *Stille Nacht, heilige Nacht*.

Vere Hodgson escaped to Birmingham for a short break and had goose, followed by a small amount of nuts and chocolate for Christmas dinner. Then she and her friends 'drank to a happier 1941'. John Colville went to the service at Westminster Abbey on Christmas night. Hundreds of people did likewise, arriving 'through the gloom and the blackout, and knelt in the candle-lit knave [sic]'. That evening Colville wrote: 'The unofficial Christmas truce has been kept by both sides. We have not bombed Germany, nor they us.'

The next day, Colville followed Hodgson's example and left the capital for a few days. He chose Yorkshire for a spot of hunting; thousands of other Londoners had also used the festive season to visit family and friends across the country. For weeks the government had been preoccupied with the thought of an understaffed city and encouraged people to remain in London over Christmas. The general instruction if they insisted on going away was to leave office blocks, warehouses and other business premises unlocked, and for goodness sake, organise a firewatching rota over the holiday period. If the Germans launched a heavy raid against an unprepared London, it simply didn't bear thinking about.

As it was, the attack that occurred on the evening of Sunday 29 December wasn't even that heavy compared to previous bombardments.

THE 'CITY' ATTACKED

One hundred and thirty six bombers set out from the airfields of northern France laden with 127 tons of high explosive and 613 canisters of incendiaries, less than a fifth of the ordnance deposited over the capital on the night of 8 December.

The exhilaration of surviving a Luftwaffe raid often made for jokes the morning after.

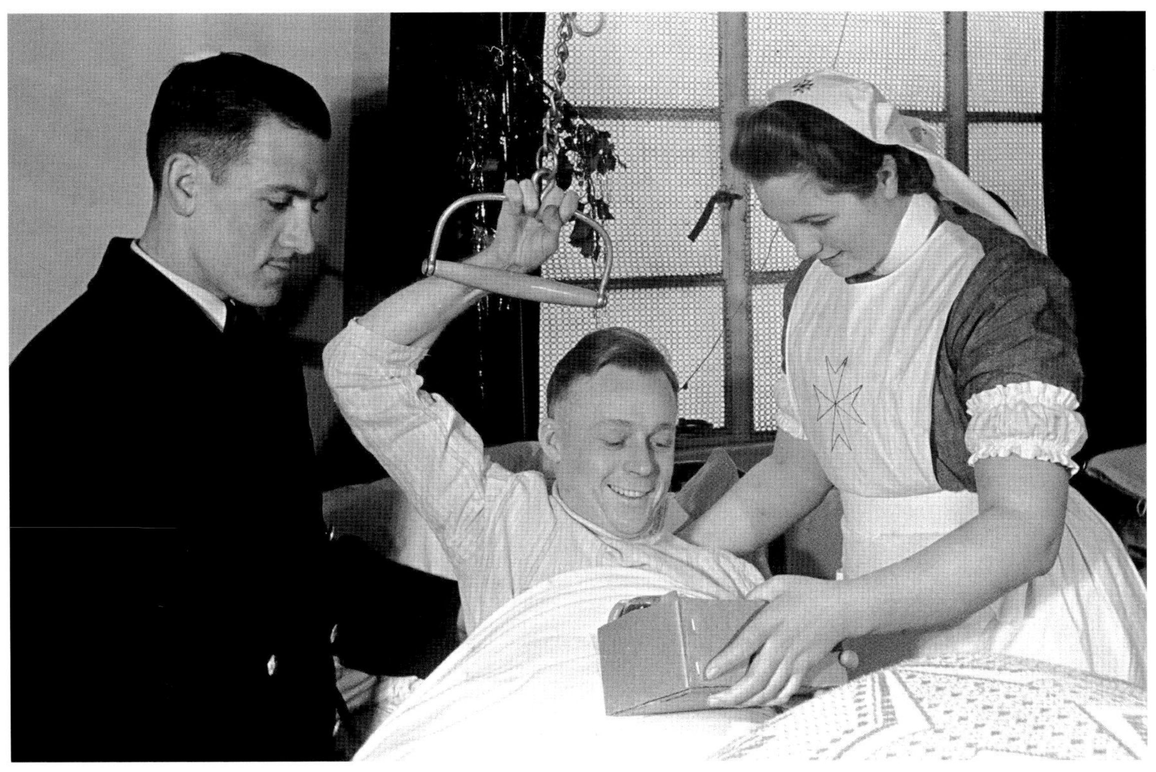

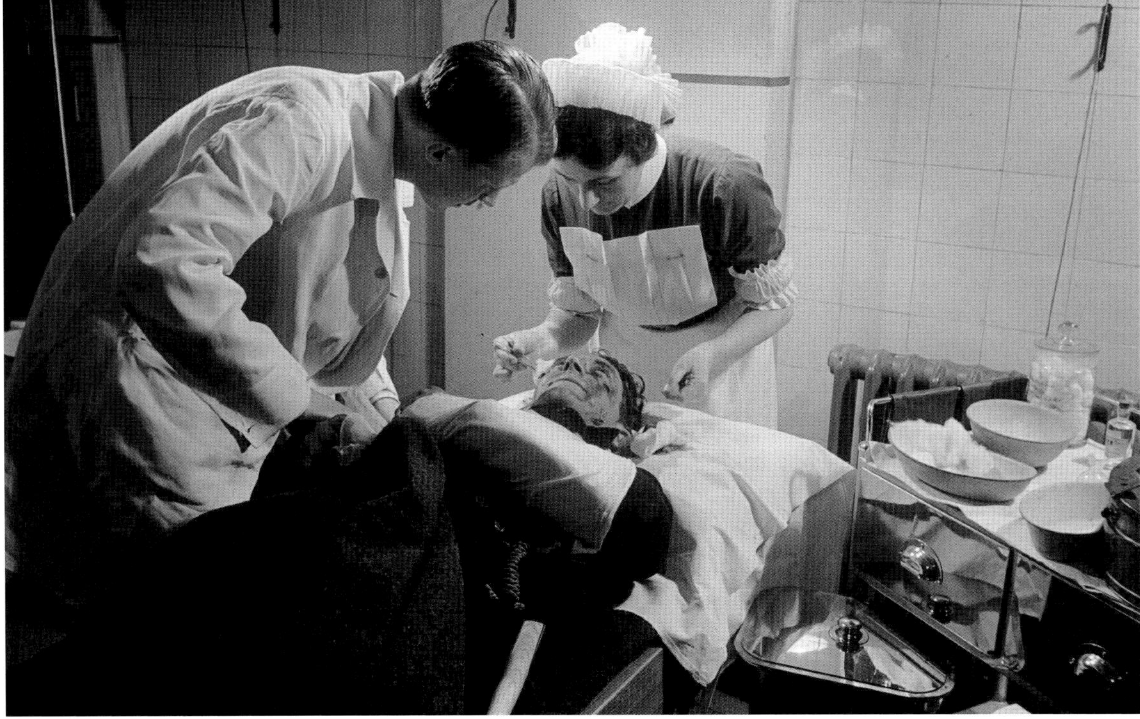

However, the focus of the Luftwaffe this night was the 'City', the core of London a little over one square mile in area, from the Victoria Embankment in the west to Tower Hill in the east and north as far as the borough of Islington. Contained within this area was the capital's financial heartland which, as the Germans were well aware, had closed down for Christmas.

Reserve policeman Walter Marshall was making his way back towards his home in Hoxton Street, Hackney, after spending the afternoon of the 29th in the West End with a friend. 'At about five o'clock it was dark', he later recalled, 'and the first incendiaries started to fall. My mate said "I think London's getting a hiding tonight". He was right.'[4]

As the incendiaries rattled down on pavements, in narrow side streets and on rooftops, their flaring contents were caught by a westerly wind blowing at 50 miles an hour. Soon dozens of buildings were ablaze, not just the modern concrete office blocks, but also the myriad of Victorian structures with slanting roofs of slate or glass, every fireman's nightmare.

Firefighters were quick to arrive but they found countless buildings locked and bolted, from office blocks to public houses to ancient churches. It took precious minutes to batter their way inside the buildings and reach the root of the fire. As they did so they cursed the lack of firewatchers, those people who should have been stationed on the roof of such buildings to deal with incendiary bombs. Instead most were out of town on Christmas visits.

Soon the firemen were tackling the blaze at its source, 'getting at it', to use the vernacular of London's firefighters, as opposed to the custom of the provincial brigades who preferred to remain outside the building in case of falling masonry. However, not long after the fight began disaster struck. The trailer pumps used by the Auxiliary

TOP LEFT: Fireman Watkin receives a Christmas present from the nurses at his London hospital.

BOTTOM LEFT: Burned and bruised, but unbowed, a London fireman is treated at Westminster Hospital.

Fire Service (often pulled by requisitioned London taxis) pumped out water at a rate of approximately 500 gallons per minute. This volume rose to as much as 900 gallons per minute for the heavier appliances used by the regular fire service.

Suddenly the water coming from the pumps slowed from a torrent to a trickle. In some cases it ceased altogether. One fireman described it as watching the water creep back up their hoses. It was discovered that a high-explosive bomb had ruptured the 24-inch emergency pipe that carried water from the Thames under the City to the Grand Junction Canal in Brentford. The main, along with a similar pipe in the West End that pumped water from the Regent's Canal to Shaftesbury Avenue, was capable of reinforcing public mains at a rate of 30,000 gallons of water per minute. With the Thames at a low ebb there was more bad luck when one of the river's fireboats hit a submerged wreck as it came to assist. Another fireboat further down the river was called to help deal with a parachute mine near Tower Bridge. All the firemen could do was look on helplessly as the inferno spread through the condensed buildings of the City, fanned by the strong wind.

For those on the outside looking on, London burning was a spectacular sight. Eighteen-year-old Laurie Roberts, a corporal in the RAF, was travelling back to his base in London having spent Christmas with his family in Farnborough. The glow in the sky was visible long before the train pulled into Waterloo. From Waterloo he walked over the bridge to Trafalgar Square and watched 'the eerie sight' before his eyes.

Mary Warschauer and her boyfriend were on the next bridge but one to the west, Westminster, as the conflagration continued. 'Although it was pitch black everything was silhouetted in red', she recalled. 'But the bit that got me was the river. Everything was reflected in that river, and it wasn't a river of water, it was a river of fire, and it was alive. It was a combination of horrendous and beautiful and magnificent.'[5]

A fire pump could pump out 900 gallons of water per minute but falling bombs often severed water mains leading to chronic shortages.

An American newspaper correspondent enjoying a front row seat during the attack was Ernie Pyle (who won the Pulitzer Prize in 1944, the year before he was killed while covering the US attack on Okinawa). He was in awe of the vista:

> I borrowed a tin hat and went out among the fires. That was exciting too; but the thing I shall always remember above all the other things in my life is the monstrous loveliness of that one single view of London on a holiday night – London stabbed with great fires, shaken by explosions, its dark regions along the Thames sparkling with the pin points of white-hot bombs, all of it roofed over with a ceiling of pink that held bursting shells, balloons, flares and the grind of vicious engines. And in yourself the excitement and anticipation and wonder in your soul that this could be happening at all … these things all went together to make the most hateful, most beautiful single scene I have ever known.[6]

Other more important people were equally transfixed by what they saw. On the roof of the Air Ministry in Whitehall, Arthur Harris, the Deputy Chief of the Air Staff, watched the spectacle alongside a deferential sentry who didn't reply when Harris said: 'The last time London was burnt, if my history is right, was in 1666.' Believing that his superior ought to see what was happening, Harris fetched Air Marshal Charles Portal from his office below. For several minutes the pair stood and observed London incinerate. Then Harris said in a quiet but hard voice: 'Well, they are sowing the wind.'[7]

The firemen trying to contain the fires raging across the City had not given up despite the lack of water. One of them, a man called Sharp, later described to the BBC how he had been battling a blaze near Fleet Street when a gas main exploded spewing chunks of debris high into the air. Then his attention was drawn to one of the few local firewatchers who hadn't shirked his responsibilities over the holiday period, a nameless hero with a bucket of sand his only weapon against

A family enjoy Christmas dinner in their Anderson shelter. (Corbis)

the endless stream of incendiary bombs. Time and again the firewatcher disappeared inside buildings to douse incendiaries until Sharp felt obliged to assist. Together they dashed inside an edifice several storeys high. 'Everything on the ground floor was all right, the air wonderfully cool', Sharp explained on the wireless a few days later.

> Then up stone steps to the second floor, an office. Its windows were uncurtained; the fire glared at us from a few feet away across the road, and a red smoky haze hung over desks and typewriters and files and calendars. The paint round the windows was bubbling, a lot of glass was broken, but nothing was on fire. On the third floor, the managerial floor, linoleum underfoot, mahogany partitions, doors with frosted glass panes. We tried the doors. They were all locked. We went upstairs again, another huge office, and here there was trouble – all the blackout curtains were drawn across the windows and several of them were smouldering. We drew them or pulled them down. The window frames were burning in about a dozen places. Simple to put them out if we had water, but we hadn't any water. There were plenty of buckets of sand about, but sand wasn't any use at the moment, so we emptied the buckets and went upstairs to look for the cistern.[8]

IT REMAINS AS ARGUABLY THE DEFINING PHOTOGRAPH of the Blitz on Britain, the image that symbolised the indomitability of the country and its people. Reproduced throughout the free world in the aftermath of the raid, Herbert Mason's photograph of the dome of St Paul's Cathedral untouched amid a seething mountain of smoke represented a beacon of hope. Mason later left a graphic and gripping account of how he came to capture the extraordinary photograph.

> I remember only too well the night of December 29th, a Sunday night. Shortly after the alert it was obvious that the City was the target for the night. It wasn't long before incendiaries were coming down like rain. Within an hour or so the whole of the City seemed to be lighting up. In the near foreground buildings were blazing furiously and it wasn't long before the Wren Church of St Bride's was a mass of flames. The famous wedding-cake steeple was being licked. In the distance through the smoke you could see the fires increasing, and as the evening wore on an artificial wind sprang through the heat caused by the fires, parted the clouds, the buildings in the foreground collapsed, and there revealed in all its majesty was St Paul's, a hauntingly beautiful picture which no artist could recapture. Down below in the street I went towards Ludgate Hill, which was carpeted in hose pipes, a scampering rat here and there, a reeling bird in the flames. The heat became intense as I approached St Paul's Churchyard. Firemen were fighting a losing battle. Pathetically little water was coming from their hoses. Suddenly a fresh supply would come and a hose running riot would lash out and knock firemen from their feet. The heat was so intense that embers were falling like rain and clattering on your helmet. Cheapside was a mass of flames, leaping from one side of the road to the other. Back at my vantage point on top of the *Daily Mail* building where I was, I could see that this night I was going to obtain the picture which would for ever record the Battle of Britain. After waiting for a few hours the smoke parted like the curtain of a theatre and there before me was this wonderful vista, more like a dream, not frightening – there were very few high explosives. It was obvious that this was going to be the second Great Fire of London. The tragedy of this second great fire of London was the fact that there were so few firewatchers. Single-handed I could have prevented thousands of pounds' worth of damage being done, but the buildings were locked, there was nobody present to force an entry. There were so few people. It was pathetic.[9]

The iconic image of St. Paul's rising through the flames. (Topfoto)

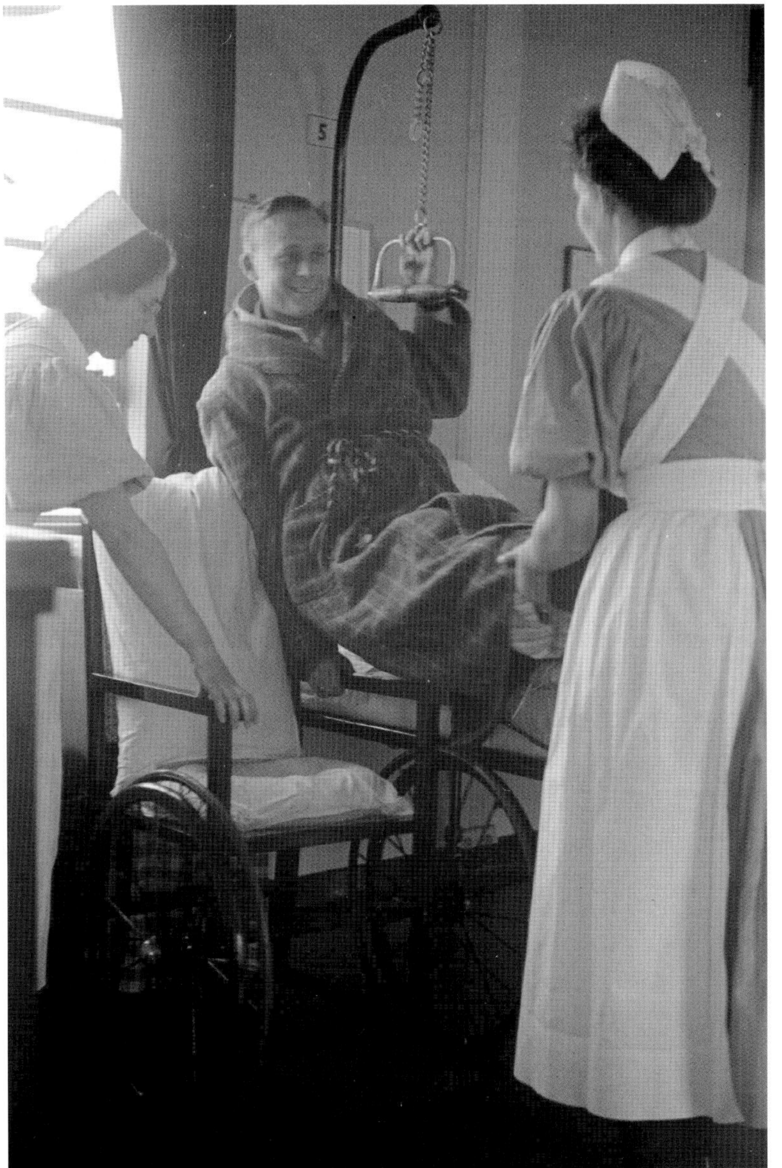

LEFT: A London fireman tries out his wheelchair as he recovers from his injuries.

RIGHT: Bobbie Tanner was the only firewoman to be awarded the George Medal during the Blitz.

The pair made several visits to the cistern, filling their buckets with water and then hurrying down the stairs as fast as they could trying not to let too much water slop over the sides. Then they hurled the water against the burning windows. When the fires were out, they went downstairs, only to discover the floor below, the managerial floor, aflame. Sharp smashed the frosted glass panes and found 'a nice little bonfire was burning on the desk'. Together they started to tackle the blaze but they were being driven back by heat and smoke. 'We were beginning to despair', explained Sharp, 'when – Whoosh! – all the windows blew out and a column of water hit the ceiling, and clouds of black smoke swirled up … the firemen had found time to turn the hose on the building and us.'

The same BBC broadcast bore testimony to the maelstrom that night. Survivors recounted their experiences, the terror of the event engrained in their memories like the smell of smoke in their clothes. One man talked of sparks 'driving down the street like a heavy snowstorm', another of the 'sickening thud as floors and roofs fell' and a third of the 'roaring crash' of masonry. A businessman called Eric Lewis described how he arrived at his office in Basinghall Street desperate to try and salvage what he could. 'All around everywhere was a mass of flames', he said.

And one really felt rather like the sprig of holly on top of a Christmas pudding with the brandy butter blazing all the way around. That was emphasised even more when one looked at the Guildhall, which was one mass of flame. The firemen of top of their ladders were very tiny, and there was very little water available, and with the hoses playing on the fire at the Guildhall it just looked like little boys peeing on an enormous bonfire.[10]

The dust caused by sifting through debris in the search for survivors made rescuers dirty and thirsty. Churchill called the firefighters the 'heroes with grimy faces'.

OPPOSITE: 'Like little boys peeing on an enormous bonfire' was how one eye-witness described the firefighters' brave attempts to douse the inferno of 29 December. Despite their best efforts, the firefighters were unable to prevent the extensive damage caused by the flames.

From a distance they might have looked like boys, but London's firemen acted like men in the face of the wall of flame devouring the City. Sixteen of them lost their lives in the course of the evening, out of a total of 163 people killed. Five hundred more were seriously wounded and the toll to the capital's buildings was equally horrendous. Eight of Christopher Wren's churches were destroyed, including St Bride's in Fleet Street, which had been built in 1672, six years after the First Great Fire of London. Among other important buildings to be damaged in the raid were Guy's Hospital, the GPO headquarters and three telephone exchanges. Thousands of small businesses ceased to be and 50,000 typewriters were lost, a statistical quirk but one that led to much inconvenience in the following months. Yet somehow, amid the death and destruction, the one landmark that remained inviolated was St Paul's Cathedral.

One man told the BBC how:

> for miles around the sky was a bright, orange-red – the balloons in the barrage stood out as clearly as on a sunny day. St Paul's Cathedral was the pivot of the main fire. All around it the flames were leaping up into the sky. And there the Cathedral stood, magnificently firm.[11]

Luck played its part in the cathedral's survival, but so did foresight and fidelity. While other churches and buildings were locked up and abandoned, the cathedral was left open and its dedicated firewatching team was on duty as ever when the Luftwaffe appeared in the early evening. Led by Dr Allen and Mr Linge, the team was composed of clerics, laymen and less pious people, who simply considered it their duty to save the cathedral (a place of worship had been on the site since 604) situated on the highest point of the City.

Twenty eight incendiaries landed on St Paul's during the course of the raid, described by a firewatcher on the roof of the nearby *Daily Telegraph* as a 'veritable cascade', but all but one were swiftly dealt with by the firewatchers. There was a mild panic early on, when the water ran out following the rupture of the emergency main by a high-explosive bomb, but that was when they had cause to bless the prescience of Allen and Linge. Ever since the Blitz had started the pair had built up an emergency water supply in the cathedral, with bath tubs, buckets and barrels placed throughout the cathedral for just such a crisis as they now faced.

The troublesome incendiary had pierced the outer shell of the great dome. Not a problem in itself, but between the outer and inner shell of the dome was a lattice of old beams. If sparks should drop in there the dome would soon go up in flames. Firewatchers rushed towards the dome (112 feet in diameter) and the protruding fizzing incendiary halfway up, and then cheered as the bomb toppled out and clattered down the lead curves to be stamped out on the Stone Gallery.

Stanley Barron, a reporter for the *News Chronicle*, headed towards the City the moment the All-Clear went, terrified of what he might find. 'Great showers of sparks were coming from the burning buildings', he recalled, as he looked up at the cathedral. 'The dome of St Paul's was to be seen against a backdrop of yellow and green and red with great billows of smoke coming across it.'[12] He couldn't believe it had survived, as couldn't an American reporter who, in his premature cable across the Atlantic, included the cathedral as among the victims of the raid.

John Colville's first reaction on hearing news of the raid – quickly labelled the 'Second Great Fire of London' by the newspapers – was to write in his diary that 'the Germans have added to their growing list of atrocities' by desecrating Wren's churches. 'Thank Heavens that Mother and I took the trouble to make a tour of them and admire their beauties one summer's evening two years ago', he added as an afterthought.

While Colville raced back down to London from Yorkshire, the Prime Minister toured the worst hit areas on Monday morning, and 'was cheered by typists, business men and firemen', according to the *Daily Mirror*. One of the exhausted firemen crouched over his hose looked up and through eyes reddened by the smoke, shouted 'Good old Winston!' Churchill smiled at the greeting and replied, 'We'll beat him yet, boys, keep it up!'

On arriving at a corner of a street cordoned off for fear of falling debris, a policeman warned the Prime Minister of the danger but 'he shrugged his shoulders, thanked the officer and walked on'.

TOP LEFT: 30 December 1940 and the dome of St Paul's is intact despite the best efforts of the Luftwaffe.

BOTTOM LEFT: The pumps of the Auxiliary Fire Service being towed past St Paul's, 29 December. The image of St Paul's rising above the destruction became an emotional rallying point for many Londoners.

ABOVE: Firefighters at work in the shadow of St Paul's Cathedral on 29 December.

the City of London two days earlier. Previously, the only requirement of the civilian population was to ensure that factories or offices employing more than 30 people had a team of firewatchers. However, from January 1941 onwards all premises had to be guarded, with the requisite firefighting equipment in place, and to achieve this all males aged between 16 and 60 had to perform 48 hours of firewatching per month (in August 1942 this was expanded to include women aged 25 to 45, and in September 1943 the age for men was raised to 63).

There were other lessons learned from the raid, most notably the interruption of the water supply caused by the fracturing of the emergency main. Hundreds of Emergency Water Supply (EWS) dams were established at strategic points throughout the capital. Some were small and made from canvas, containing 1,000 gallons of water, but others, such as the steel-panelled dam by Spurgeon's Tabernacle in the Elephant and Castle, held 5,000 gallons.

Ground defences were also beefed up with the arrival within AA Command of women from the Auxiliary Territorial Service (ATS), though it was made clear they would not be allowed to fire the anti-aircraft guns.

Another novelty that helped to usher in the start of 1941 was a new type of shelter, one which Churchill had inspected for the first time on 31 December and which allowed him 'to demonstrate his technical knowledge as a builder'. Called the Morrison Shelter (after the Minister of Home Security), it resembled a steel table measuring seven feet by four feet and was nearly three feet from the floor, on which was laid a steel mattress surrounded by wire mesh at the sides. It was designed for use indoors, the hope being that should a house collapse the shelter and those underneath would be unharmed by falling rubble. Morrison Shelters were given away to families earning less than £350 a year and for others cost £7.

On 2 January the *Mirror* reported that the after-effects of the raid four days earlier were still being felt. Scores of buildings had been condemned and army experts were on their way to dynamite them. One edifice already demolished was the church of St Stephen's in Coleman Street, destroyed for the first time in 1666, and now for a second time (it was never rebuilt). Amid the ashes of his church, the reverend F. C. Baker told a reporter: 'I have read much history in my time but I know of no nation so depraved, so hellish and brutal as Germany has proved herself to be. My church is down but my blood is up.'

CHAPTER SIX

BRITAIN GETS BLITZED: JANUARY TO APRIL 1941

"I am full of optimism – don't know if it is ill-placed. But I do not feel we can ever have the Blitz quite so badly on London as last autumn."

Vere Hodgson, diarist, 9 February 1941

THE FIRST MAJOR RAID of 1941 on London occurred on 11 January. Covent Garden market took a battering and the Bow Street Police Station was damaged. At St George's Hospital a bomb fell but failed to detonate. It was one of hundreds, possibly thousands (many of which lie beneath London still) of unexploded bombs that fell in the first few months of the Blitz. After the 11 January attack, the recently formed Bomb Disposal squads were able to move across the city defusing as many of the devices as possible. For a week the Luftwaffe didn't return; then another week passed and there was still no sign of them. February came, but the German bombers didn't. On the 9th of that month, a Sunday, Vere Hodgson spent a peaceful afternoon reading the *Observer* before turning her attention to her diary: 'I am full of optimism – don't know if it is ill-placed. But I do not feel we can ever have the Blitz quite so badly on London as last autumn.'

Hodgson would have been even more buoyant had she been privy to a war directive issued by Hitler three days earlier, on 6 February.

OPPOSITE: Hull resident Miss Kitty Connealey leaves her shattered home to stay with relatives.

RIGHT: Manchester United's Old Trafford stadium was hit during one raid on the city.

Headed 'Directions for Operations against the English War Economy', the directive began with an evaluation of the military operations against Great Britain to date:

(a) Contrary to our former view, the greatest effect of our operations against the English war economy has lain in the high losses in merchant shipping inflicted by our naval and air forces. This effect has been increased by the wrecking of port installations, the destruction of large quantities of supplies and by the diminished use of ships when they are compelled to sail in convoy.

(b) The effect of direct air attacks against the English armament industry is difficult to estimate. But the destruction of many factories and the consequent disorganisation of the armament industry must lead to a considerable fall in production.

(c) The least effect of all (so far as we can see) has been that upon the morale and the will to resist of the English people.

OPPOSITE: Children in Saltburn, North Yorkshire, inspect the damage to their school caused by a German hit and run bomber.

RIGHT: An unexploded bomb rests menacingly outside a London railway station.

Hitler went on to state that clearly 'no decisive success can be expected from terror attacks on residential areas' and as such the prolonged bombardment against London and other British towns and cities had failed to achieve its aim of demoralising the British people. Not that the Nazi leader was too despondent, for by then he had another target in his sights – Russia.

The decision had been taken in December 1940 to launch an attack against Russia the following summer, and beginning in spring the majority of the Luftwaffe squadrons that had been bombing Britain would start moving east in preparation for the assault on Bolshevism, an enemy Hitler loathed far more than the British.

Hitler concluded his directive by instructing the Luftwaffe to continue attacks against Britain for the next three months, focusing more on hitting ports and manufacturing plants than residential areas. In addition, Hitler wanted his air force to assist the German Navy, particularly the U-boats, in targeting British shipping and in effect cutting the country off from the outside world.

However, for the rest of February there was little opportunity for the Luftwaffe to follow their Führer's orders. Britain's allies might have been few and far between at the start of 1941, but one friend she could always rely on was the weather. Thick cloud and constant rain descended across the British Isles for most of the month and only Swansea came under anything that could be called a concerted attack, when the Welsh port was raided on three consecutive nights starting on 19 February.

The first bombs fell at around 7.30pm on the 19th, a Wednesday, and over the 72 hours that followed a total of 30,000 incendiary

OPEN HERE

bombs and 800 high-explosive bombs were dropped on Swansea. Nearly 300 people died and 400 were seriously injured, but one of the lucky ones was Elaine Kidwell, one of the youngest air raid wardens in the country at the time. 'I joined up as a civil defence messenger and when I was 17 years and two months I asked to be an air raid warden even though you had to be 18', she recalled. In the early part of the raid Kidwell was on the roof of Lloyds bank sweeping incendiary bombs into the street below where they were stamped out by fellow wardens.

> [I] suddenly saw a parachute mine drift down a few yards away and it went off, blowing me backwards until I hit a wall. Amazingly, I was all right so I dusted my jacket down and applied my lipstick. My lipstick was like my armour so I felt safer.[1]

Londoners were also feeling safe as February gave way to March. The weather was improving, and so was the war news from abroad. British forces were on top in North Africa, having seized the Libyan port of Benghazi from the Italians, while Italy's military pride was also taking a battering at the hands of the Greeks after Mussolini's soldiers had invaded the previous autumn. The RAF was beginning to strike back at Germany with bombing raids of its own, the largest being a 220-strong force that attacked Hanover on the night of 10 February. There was bleaker news, of course, with the loss of more British shipping, and the announcement that henceforth dinners in restaurants would be limited to one course only, but as William Sansom was to recall: 'With the longest hours of the winter over, with the ominous twilight coming pleasurably later each week, and with the summer ahead, there was a real feeling of respite.'

BOMB DISPOSAL

Some of the chief beneficiaries of the respite were the bomb disposal teams, who set to work defusing the unexploded bombs from earlier raids. The 1,800kg 'Satan' bomb that had plummeted into the Serpentine on 11 December wasn't rendered safe until early March,

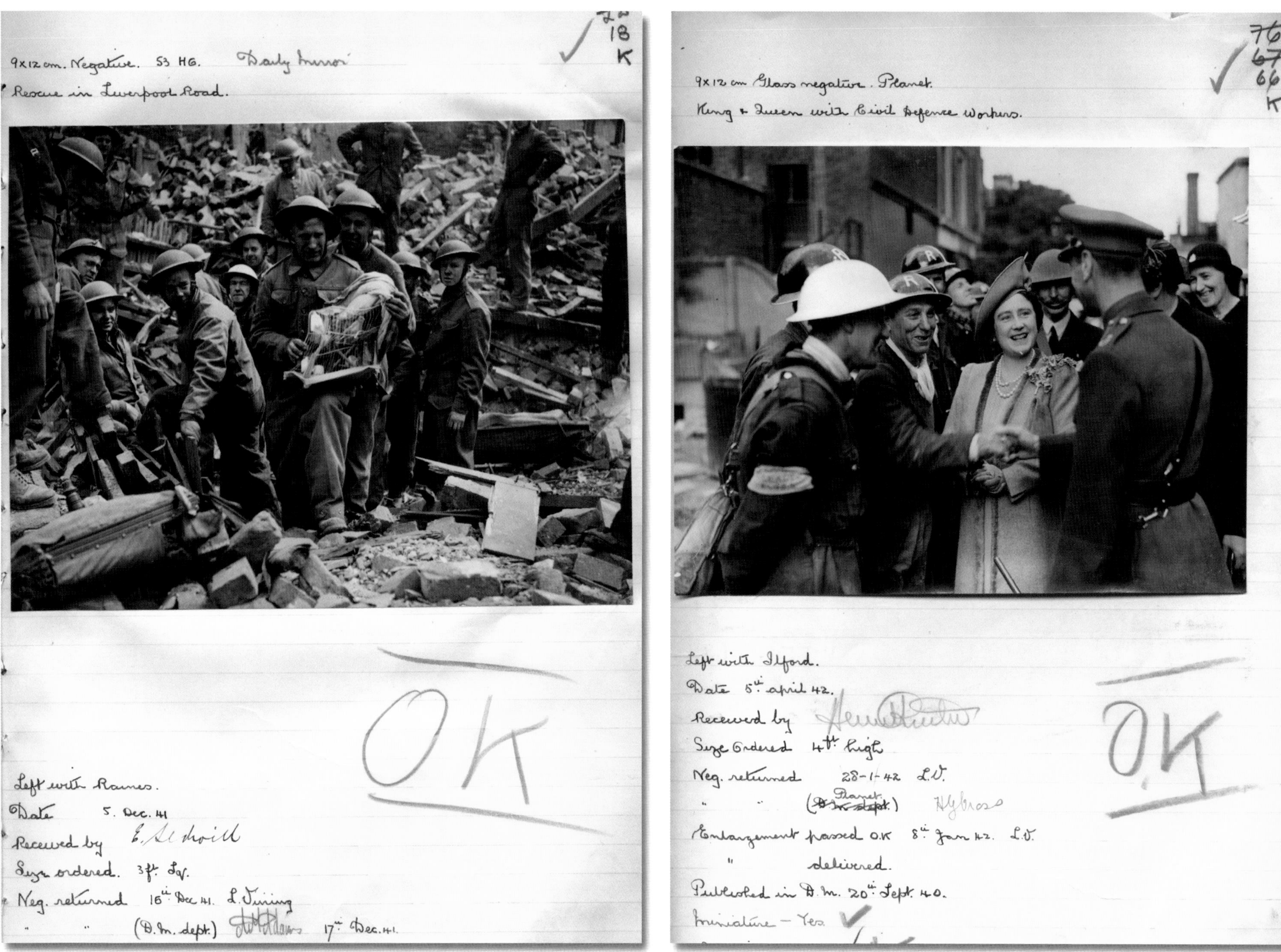

ABOVE AND LEFT: Throughout the war images published in any newspaper were subject to government approval. Here the archives of the *Daily Mirror* show images that have received the 'OK' from the government censor. Clearly, images of the King and Queen visiting cheerful Civil Defence workers, a successful rescue attempt, or families made homeless by bombing raids sharing a meal with neighbours, were considered suitable for public consumption. Images of the dead or mutilated, the horrific realities of a bomb raid, were not.

having caused untold problems by sinking deep into the glutinous bottom of the lake.

Bomb disposal experts were a special breed in 1940, pioneers of a new art few of them knew much about. 'We were told that when bombs dropped they would be lying on the surface', recalled Harry Beckingham, who volunteered for the job in early 1940. 'When the Blitz started we discovered that they didn't lie on the surface but rather 20 feet under.'[2] Most unexploded high-explosive bombs (UXBs) hit the ground at an angle of 80 degrees and continued straight down for around 12 feet during which time the tailpiece and fin were wrenched off before they often jinked sideways or forwards, resulting in their final resting place being as much as ten feet away from a vertical line through the hole of entry.

For a bomb disposal expert the first job on arriving at the scene of a buried UXB was to measure the hole's diameter at a point a few inches below the surface. The hole was normally two inches larger than the bomb that had created it. A hole with a diameter between eight and 12 inches indicated a 50kg bomb; 12 to 18 inches suggested

Londoners in an unidentified residential part of the city survey what remains of their street following the raid of 19 March 1941 when nearly 500 bombers attacked the city.

a 250kg bomb and any hole with a diameter in excess of 18 inches pointed to a 500kg device or bigger. Once they'd measured the hole and estimated the size of their adversary, the engineers began to dig. First they found the fins and tailpiece, which proved what type of bomb it was, then they dug deeper. 'Digging was always the hairiest part of the job', remembered Beckingham,

> because the reason a bomb hadn't exploded was usually because it had been dropped too low from the aircraft to allow time for the charge to pass through the resistor into the firing capacitor. So it hit the ground inert instead of being fully charged. But there was still energy in the bomb and vibrations from people digging might well make it come alive.

Different men had different ways to keep the fear at bay as they dug. 'Too much thinking was unhealthy', recalled Beckingham. 'I just kept to my philosophy that if a bomb went off and I was right on top of it then I wouldn't know anything about it. It would be a nice quick death.' Another bomb disposal expert, Peter Danckwerts, who won a George Cross for his work in defusing dozens of unexploded devices in London, adopted the age-old attitude that it would never happen to him: 'It's really quite impossible to believe, when you're dealing with a great solid object of this sort that it's suddenly going to blow up and disintegrate under your hand', he reflected. 'I think the only way you can be convinced really is by seeing it happen to someone else at close quarters. Indeed, on the whole this kind of job is apt to be rather stimulating.'[3]

As a naval officer, Danckwerts specialised in parachute mines, which had started off as the magnetic mines sewn in British coastal waters by the German Navy. Unlike the smaller high-explosive bombs, the parachute mines that fell and failed to explode lay exposed on the surface of London's streets like upturned pillar boxes (approximately 20 per cent of the 4,000 parachute mines dropped during the Blitz failed to explode because their fuses had not been adequately adapted for use on land). Danckwerts' first job was to locate the small fuse, known as the 'bomb fuse', found on the side of each parachute mine. Normally when a parachute mine hit the ground, this fuse would buzz for 15 seconds and then explode (as in the case of the one that detonated outside BBC Broadcasting House on 8 December), so it was vital, recalled Danckwerts, when dealing with an unexploded parachute mine 'to listen very carefully all the time, and if you heard it buzzing to run like hell, because you might have up to fifteen seconds to get away'. If no buzz was heard then the fuse was unscrewed but not removed, as the Germans had a habit of booby-trapping the fuse so if it was removed entirely it would trigger an explosion. Instead Danckwerts tied a long piece of string to the fuse and then paid it out 55 yards or so to a point where he was under cover. Then he tugged on the string and out came the fuse. Danckwerts was always modest about his work and its concomitant dangers, preferring to lavish praise on his peers who defused smaller unexploded bombs 'which were welded to live rails or inside gasometers'. Nonetheless, in the first month alone of the Blitz on

The city of Birmingham, with its large industries and factories vital to the war effort, was often the target for German bombers, as shown by the damage caused to Market Hall.

London, 183 mines had been defused by men like Danckwerts, though nine had exploded while being made safe.

The challenge of defusing the standard high-explosive bombs dropped by the Germans lay in the variation of fuses used. In the first month of the Blitz most UXBs had an impact fuse numbered 15. Bomb disposal squads soon mastered these by depressing the two spring-loaded plungers with a device called a Crabtree discharger and removing the fuse. 'Then the Germans got more clever', recalled Beckingham, 'and introduced the 17A fuse, which was a delayed action, liable to detonate up to 80 hours later. Worst of all was the antidisturbance 50 fuse.' This fuse was the latest and most lethal of German fuses, requiring less than half an inch to activate the trembler switch. Suddenly life became even more precarious for the bomb disposal experts as they worked, for with such a sensitive fuse even a car passing 55 yards away could set it off.

One of Beckingham's most memorable assignments was to defuse a 250kg UXB that had landed on the tracks outside Victoria Station after one raid. After digging down to the bomb, he scraped away the earth looking for the fuse pocket that would reveal the type of fuse he had to tackle. Sometimes bomb disposal experts found handwritten messages scrawled on the bombs as they looked for the fuse. Danckwerts recalled on one bomb coming across:

> a rude message addressed to Mr Chamberlain chalked on the side, although Mr Chamberlain had been out of office [of Prime Minister] for some months by that time. We found another one which certainly made us pause, because it had a rhyme in German on the side, something to the effect that when you think you've got it, it springs out on you. We didn't like the sound of this at all, and circled round it for quite some time before we tackled it. However, nothing particular happened.

Beckingham found no message on his bomb, just the pocket indicating it was a No. 25 fuse. 'That made life a lot easier than if it had been a 17 or a 50', he said. 'The 25 was an impact fuse, but more advanced than the 15. If you tried using a Crabtree discharger on a 25 you went up with the bomb, but it wasn't as tricky as a delayed action.' Beckingham's bomb measured three feet nine inches in length and 14 inches in diameter. If it had exploded it would have blown him to bits, as unlike the 15 seconds of buzzing on a parachute mine, the impact fuse would have detonated without warning, killing him before his brain had time to register the danger.

Down in his hole, just him and his unexploded bomb, Beckingham put a BD discharger against the cold dark steel. This was a container with a bicycle valve at one end and a tap at the other, and inside was a solution of salt, benzol and methylated spirits. He attached the tap over the bomb's fusehead and began pumping the solution into the fuse. When all the solution was inside the fuse he climbed out of the hole and retired a safe distance where a colleague was waiting with a cup of tea. It took 30 minutes for the solution to short-circuit the fuse. When the time was up, Beckingham walked back along the rails and slipped down into the hole. 'I took out my fuse key, locked it on to the fuse ring, and twisted', he remembered. 'Once the ring was unscrewed I took out the fuse and removed the gaine [a device just over an inch in length that contained a high explosive called Penthrite Wax] so that it was completely safe.'

In total, the men of the Bomb Disposal Units of the Royal Engineers dealt with 50,000 UXBs during and immediately after the war, a small but significant slice of heroism that cost the lives of 490 of their number, approximately one fatality for every 102 bombs defused.

"[I] suddenly saw a parachute mine drift down a few yards away and it went off, blowing me backwards until I hit a wall. Amazingly, I was all right so I dusted my jacket down and applied my lipstick. My lipstick was like my armour so I felt safer." Elaine Kidwell, air raid warden

ATTACKS ACROSS BRITAIN

March 1941 brought with it an improvement in the weather and the German aircrews, frustrated by a month of near inactivity, were soon resuming their savage attacks on Britain.

Portsmouth, Birmingham, Glasgow, Hull, Plymouth, Sheffield and Liverpool were all bombarded. Hitler had revised his directives to the Luftwaffe on 6 February instructing the bombers to focus on the British war machine; nonetheless, the attacks produced many tales of unimaginable horror.

On 12 March Merseyside was subjected to a heavy attack in which 270 incendiary 'breadbaskets' were dropped, along with 350 high-explosive bombs and 60 parachute mines. The docks were ravaged, two ships were sunk, another three holed, flour mills and factories were destroyed and two gas holders at Wallasey were incinerated. On its front page of 19 March the *Daily Mirror* carried a photograph of ten-month-old Irene Marriott, 'buried for three days under the wreckage of her home'. Irene's parents were both killed in the raid – along with over 600 others in the March raids on Liverpool – but she had survived with cuts to her arm and face. 'According to ordinary medical standards she should be dead', said the doctor who treated her. 'Her survival is a miracle.'

Not so fortunate were two children on Humberside when Hull was attacked on 17 March. Auxiliary fireman Hugh Varah was helping remove residents of one bomb-damaged street when his attention was drawn to the whimper of a dog from inside one house. Varah knew such a noise often indicated someone trapped so, taking his torch, he went to investigate. He saw the dog on the ground floor of a damaged house, pawing at a pile of debris. 'I took hold of his collar and pulled him back a little so that I could shine the beam under the timber', he recalled.

DAILY MIRROR, Wednesday, March 19, 1941.

Daily Mirror

MAR 19

No. 11,629 ONE PENNY

Registered at the G.P.O. as a Newspaper.

GIRL WAR WORKERS HAVE STARTED

WOMEN who responded to the appeal of the Minister of Labour for war workers are already at the bench.

Others will start work at the week-end.

Most of the volunteers are married, but many girls of twenty have registered before the compulsion date.

The Ipswich, Suffolk, employment exchange told the *Daily Mirror* that 185 women, most of them married, had responded to the appeal.

"Some of the women are already at work today," an official said, "and many more will be within the next day or two.

"By far the greatest number of applicants were housewives whose husbands are on active service or engaged in other forms of war work."

Ipswich is not alone. Girls of twenty and twenty-one who registered before they need have already been given jobs.

A hundred girls queued .p outside a South London employment exchange.

Hundreds of girls, those who have never gone out to work before and others from "dead" luxury trades, were among those who registered.

Official registration date for the 20 to 21 class is April 19.

This Week-End

Most of the Midland women who registered yesterday will be at work by this week-end.

The manager of one of Birmingham's biggest Labour Exchanges said: "We have had a wonderful response. Most women in the Midlands who have had factory experience have already returned to the bench.

"During next week there will be a big new recruiting campaign for workers in Midland towns.

When the debate on the registration of women for war work takes place in the House of Commons, the Government is likely to agree not to compel girls under twenty to go away from home.

However, providing the conditions were suitable and the parents willing, such girls would not be debarred from working in distant towns.

PUBLIC SCHOOL girls train for war work—page 6.

Band and Dances in Factory

A JAZZ band plays nightly for dancing from midnight to 1 a.m. in a Midlands war factory.

The idea is to be taken up in another factory, where already they have two mid-day concerts a week.

The nightly dance in the one factory was revealed at Coventry Chamber of Commerce yesterday, when a member suggested that it might affect the output.

But the welfare officer in one of the biggest munition factories in the Midlands told the "Daily Mirror" that they had proved that music for the workers encouraged a bigger output. "We are trying to arrange dancing for our workers."

Classical Music

"At present we have concerts each week from 12.50 to 1.25 p.m. On one day E.N.S.A. give a concert and on the other the concert is given by our workers.

"Many of the workers prefer classical music in between their work.

"Recently many of the younger workers asked for a band, so that they can have dances, and I have recommended to our directors that they should have it."

17's MAY JOIN WAAF

"SWEET Seventeens" may now join the Women's Auxiliary Air Force. The lower age limit for recruits, it was announced last night, has been reduced from eighteen to seventeen and a half years in nearly all trades.

Some of the duties for which girls of seventeen and a half may volunteer are: Radio operator, teleprinter operator, clerk, fabric worker, equipment assistant, morse slip reader, cook, sparking plug tester, telephone operator, wireless operator, instrument mechanic.

FARR ROBBED OF £3,000 JEWELLERY

Jewellery worth more than £3,000, belonging to Tommy Farr, the boxer, was stolen during the black-out on Monday night from Lady Natalie Ricketts's house at Surrenden-crescent, on the outskirts of Brighton, which Farr is renting.

The chief piece of jewellery was his platinum ring set with a single diamond valued at £2,000.

Mr. Chamberlain's £84,013

Mr. Neville Chamberlain, it was revealed last night, left £84,013, with net personalty £74,203.

He left a settled legacy of £3,000 to Miss Valerie Cole, his niece, and the remainder to his widow for life.

U.S. WARSHIPS VISIT AUSTRALIA

A U.S. naval squadron will reach Sydney tomorrow and stay two days, it was announced in Canberra yesterday by Mr. A. W. Fadden, Acting Prime Minister.

The squadron .omprises the cruisers Chicago and Portland and the destroyers Clark, Cassin, Conyngham, Downes and Reid.

The visit is described as a training cruise, and the Australian Government regards it as an extraordinarily significant development in the Pacific situation.

Cheering crowds greeted the ships when they called at Auckland, New Zealand, yesterday.—British United Press.

U.S. Search for U-boats Is On—Page 3.

STOLE WAR OFFICE 32-SEATER COACH

Black-out thieves in one night stole a War Department camouflaged thirty-two-seater motor coach in the City of London; forty-three half chests (about forty pounds each) of tea, valued at £350, from a warehouse at Campion's, Green-street, Shenley:

NIGHT FLYER'S D.F.C.

Squadron Leader Michael Frederic Anderson, of the Auxiliary Air Force, No. 604 Squadron, whose father lives at Hitchin, Herts, has been awarded the *D.F.C.* During the last four months, says the announcement, he has carried out numerous night operational flights, destroying a Heinkel 111 and probably a Junkers 88, and has destroyed another enemy plane by day.

THREE MORE U-BOATS SUNK, SAYS PREMIER

"I have just received news of the certain destruction of three U-boats. Not since October 13, 1939, have I been cheered by news of such a delectable triple event."

Mr. Churchill said this in London yesterday.

He was proposing the health, at a Pilgrims' luncheon, of the new U.S. Ambassador, Mr. J. G. Winant, whose speech is reported in page 6.

Sinks Nazi Supply Ship

A 5,000-ton German supply ship, heavily laden, was torpedoed and sunk by a bomber of the Coastal Command in moonlight early yesterday.

A heavy explosion was followed by flames, debris was flung into the air and the ship sank rapidly by the bows.

BURIED 3 DAYS—LIVES

Ten-months-old Irene Marriott was buried for three days under the wreckage of her home—destroyed in a Merseyside raid—and survived.

Her parents were killed and it was the body of her father which protected the baby from some of the debris.

The picture below shows Irene in hospital. Her arm is in splints. Her head, which was badly cut, is bandaged. But her cheeks are still rosy.

"According to ordinary medical standards she should be dead," say the doctors. "Her survival is a miracle."

When Irene gets well an aunt will adopt her.

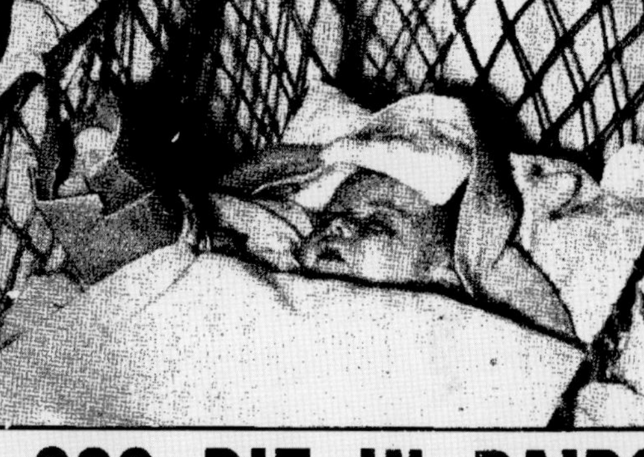

1,000 DIE IN RAIDS

A THOUSAND people were killed and 1,300 seriously injured in last week's raids on Merseyside and Clydeside. Each area was raided twice on successive nights—Merseyside on Wednesday and Thursday and the Clyde area on Thursday and Friday.

An Air Ministry and Ministry of Home Security communique issued last night says latest reports indicate that on Merseyside 500 people were killed and 500 seriously injured, while in the Clyde area about 500 were killed and 800 seriously injured.

Activity on Clydeside is now getting back to normal.

Women and children have been taken to safe areas. Some workers are sleeping in shelters to be near their work.

Although many homes in one town were damaged, hundreds of them will be made habitable in ten days.

"First-aid" repairs are being made to the least damaged houses and soldiers are demolishing dangerous buildings.

ALL TO BEAT INVASION

"STAND firm. Carry on. Beat the invader." With this slogan the Minister of Home Security ended a broadcast last night.

He said that the Government leaflet of advice about invasion would be distributed soon and families should sit around the fire and study it point by point.

"It is not called, 'How to look after your wife, your family or yourself in an invasion,' said the Minister. "It is called, 'Beating the Invader.' If the Germans land here the only thing that matters is to beat them before they can do serious harm. It lies with the civil population.

"If you are doing anything important for the war effort, you will get to your work and do it for all you're worth, every day and all day. The cows have to be milked, Hitler or no Hitler.

"I want to say one special word to the men and women of the civil defence service. If the time comes when it is the duty of other people to get into their houses and stop there, you know that there is no lying low for you."

Cover from the *Daily Mirror*, 19 March 1941, detailing the story of Irene Marriott, as well as other stories of the day.

> At first I couldn't see anything but then I saw what I took to be a piece of rag. I moved the light to one side and saw a child's arm and I realised that the rag was part of her dress. I tore frantically at the timbers and crawled to where the child was. I pushed my arm beneath her and cradled her in my arms. Then I realised that she was holding the hand of another child. That's as far as my memory will allow me to go.[4]

Varah's mind blanked out the next few harrowing minutes. He emerged from the house 'carrying the decapitated body of a little boy over my shoulder and the lifeless form of a little girl under my right arm'. His fellow rescue workers rushed to help their shocked colleague and a policeman gently prised the dead girl from Varah's grip, but only 'on the understanding that they did not wake her as she was asleep'.[5]

London had experienced many similar stunning incidents in the first few months of the Blitz, but since the attack of 11 January there had been eight weeks of tranquil bliss. Londoners called it the 'Lull'. Slowly frayed nerves began to knit themselves back together and the sound of birdsong in early spring was a balm to those people who had come to dread the howl of the air raid siren. However, on 8 March the Luftwaffe reacquainted the capital with terror.

Life had been slowly returning to normal in the interim. Thousands of children had returned to London from the countryside whence they had fled six months earlier, and theatres and cinemas were playing to packed houses, even if their hours were a little different from those of the pre-war years. The curtain went up at theatres around 6pm most nights, coming down no later than 8.30pm, allowing performers and their paying public time to return home. Cinemas opened a little while longer, till 10pm in some cases,

TOP LEFT: The respite in 1941 allowed many buildings rendered unsafe by the bombing to be demolished, as was the case with this house in Birmingham.

BOTTOM LEFT: The King inspects the crew of a Birmingham fire station. Derided during the early part of the war, firefighters found that official visits such as this, as well as the gallantry medals introduced by the King, were a huge morale boost for weary crews.

as it was assumed most people who went to picture houses lived locally.

Dance clubs were also enjoying a surge in popularity and one of the most popular was the Cafe de Paris in Piccadilly, sandwiched between the Rialto Cinema and the Lyons' Corner House in Coventry Street. It was filling up fast by 9pm on Saturday 8 March, dashing young military officers stepping aside at the entrance to allow their lady friends to descend the long flight of stairs that led to the basement cafe, a bearpit in medieval London.

The guests who arrived felt safe in the Cafe, despite the bombs that had already started to fall. After all, the establishment advertised itself as the safest place to dance and dine in London, and once inside all one heard was the hip jazz of Ken 'Snakehips' Johnson and his Caribbean dance band.

There was no moon on 8 March but the German navigators had little trouble following the Thames and unloading their bombs on the blacked-out city. They met with rapid success.

The North Lodge of Buckingham Palace was hit, as was the Tate Gallery – though the bomb failed to explode – and Garland's Hotel in Suffolk Street, just round the corner from the Cafe de Paris, was soon aflame.

Guests at the Cafe were welcomed by the head barman, an American by the name of Henry McElhone, and once they had their drinks they could sit at a table or lean against the railings of the bar's balcony and look down on another, deeper level, where the restaurant and dance floor were located. When it was their turn to eat, or dance, they descended via a double curved stairway.

The superstitious in London were said to steer clear of the Cafe de Paris because the restaurant-cum-dance floor was modelled on the style of the Titanic's ballroom, even down to the same colours of furnishing and glass.

On the evening of Saturday 8 March the Cafe had its usual fill of the great and the good and the glamorous, prominent among whom

Sunlight pierces the skeleton of this devastated building in Swansea in February 1941.

ROYAL MAIL
EPO 326

was Lady Betty Baldwin, daughter of Stanley Baldwin the former Prime Minister, who was with a group of friends enjoying a night away from her work with the ambulance service. A man called Simons, a successful businessman, had popped in for a drink after finishing his shift as an air raid warden. On the dance floor the accents were as cosmopolitan as the uniforms: British, Dutch, Belgian, French, Australian, American and Canadian. They drank and danced, and then died as two 50kg bombs came whistling out of the darkness, straight down the ventilation shaft of the building immediately above, and on to the cafe below. One bomb failed to detonate. The other exploded on the dance floor among the men and women swinging to the music of Snakehips Johnson. One of those dancing was Ruth Wittman and her husband. 'The place was packed and I stopped right in front of "Snakehips" when something told me to get off the dance floor', she recalled. Wittman and her husband walked over to a table. 'As we sat down, the bomb fell right in front of the band, literally where I'd been standing. "Snakehips" lost his head, I was blown back and I was struck across my nose and eyes.'[6]

Another woman, a Canadian called Mrs Blair-Hickman, described the moment the bomb exploded as 'like swimming through cotton wool, if you can imagine such a thing. I didn't lose consciousness, I don't think I could have done. I remember everything that happened and when I came to I was sitting on somebody ... it turned out to be an officer wearing a kilt.'[7] Blair-Hickman's leg was broken and her face bleeding, but she was alive. However, 34 other people hadn't been so fortunate. Irene Ballyn had been on the upper level of the cafe when the bomb exploded, leaning against the balcony sipping a glass of champagne. When she came to a man leant over her and gave her a glass of sal volatile to drink. As she did so she heard the sound of groans, low cries and whimpering.

The sight that greeted reserve policeman Ballard Berkeley when he arrived was one he never forgot. The once exclusive club resembled an abattoir. 'The explosion within this confined space was tremendous', he recalled.

> It blew legs off people, heads off people and it exploded their lungs so that when I went into this place, I saw people sitting at tables quite naturally – dead. Dressed beautifully without a mark on them. Dead. It was like looking at waxworks. It was a horrifying sight. I remember speaking to a sergeant friend of mine who looked terrible. He said he had tripped over something and when he bent down to pick it up, it was a girl's head. And then he saw her sitting at her table without a head. And he was sick.[8]

Slivers of horror from the night remained embedded in survivors' memories for years after. Some never forgot the yellow powder from the unexploded bomb that lay over everything like a spectral dust; others remembered the acrid smell as they stumbled to safety; for a few it was the sight of people looking like pin cushions, hundreds of

OPPOSITE: Parachute mines struck fear into the hearts of Londoners and the damage caused by this one in Red Lion Square shows why.

BELOW: Wales suffered with attacks on both Swansea and Cardiff, where this photo was taken.

TOP LEFT: This UXB exploded in a London street while a bomb disposal unit was working to defuse it on the morning of 9 March 1941.

BOTTOM LEFT: The weather kept the Luftwaffe at bay in early 1941, allowing the London Fire Service to blow off steam in a rugby match against Beaumont College.

ABOVE: Firemen tackle an inferno at the Lipton's Tea Warehouse in Shoreditch on the night of 11 January 1941.

ABOVE: A firefighter fights a lonely battle up high during the raid of 11 January 1941.

TOP RIGHT AND RIGHT: Three auxiliary firemen killed in early 1941 are laid to rest in a Wembley cemetery. In total more than 300 firefighters were killed in London during the Blitz of 1940–44.

shards of glass from the restaurant's mirrors protruding from their bodies. The common recollection of the night, however, was of the appearance of evil not long after the first rescue services had arrived. Mrs Blair-Hickman was still lying semi-conscious on top of the dead kilted soldier when:

> I saw somebody creeping around in a vague sort of dreamlike way, and this man came up, and he felt around. He felt my hand, which was lying relaxed – I really was feeling most odd – and I found, I realised later, that what he'd done was take a ring off my finger. He must have done that to quite a lot of other people.

'One hears a lot about the bravery and the good things that happened during the war', reflected Berkeley,

> but there were also some very nasty people and some very nasty things happened. Some of the looters in the Cafe de Paris cut off the people's fingers to get the rings. That, to me, was the most awful thing. It was impossible with the dead, the injured, the firemen and wardens and police everywhere, it was impossible to know who was who and it was very easy to cut away a finger here, snap off a necklace there.[9]

ABOVE: The shattered remnants of the Cafe de Paris dance floor taken from a vantage point on the stairs leading to the balcony.

OPPOSITE: Children dance to the sound of a barrel organ in one of London's bombed streets in February 1941.

Looting was the cancer of the Blitz. Britons could stoically accept the German bombs but to know there were those elements among your own people who would exploit your misfortune by robbing you was hard to accept.

No one much minded about the Heavy Rescue teams and fire crews who sometimes took a case of whisky from a burning store to slake their thirst – that was considered liberating more than looting. It was the callous thieving they despised most. It was common for damaged houses to have their gas and electricity meters ransacked within hours of being bombed, while another favourite target was First World War medals, proudly on display on a wall or in a cabinet case. A week after Coventry was bombed a 28-year-old engineer called Chrich was sentenced to three months' hard labour for stealing a church register dated 1760 from the ruins of Coventry Cathedral. However, the looting continued. Three auxiliary firemen drafted in from outside the city were found guilty of pilfering from a shop and each sentenced to six months' imprisonment. Finally, Coventry's magistrates reached the end of their tether and 'warned that they would deal with anyone coming before them on this charge with the greatest severity'. In other words, the next person found guilty of looting would be flogged.

Often the gangs were run by a Fagin figure, ordering young urchins to do his dirty work. Lambeth juvenile court had to deal with a teenage girl caught removing clothes from a dead woman, and a five-year-old boy who'd stolen five shillings from a gas meter. A gang of firewatchers in the Elephant and Castle, led by a former wrestler, patrolled up and down the Walworth Road and when the coast was clear, one would hurl a brick through a shop window and then his accomplices nipped in and helped themselves.

FLAT TO LET
PORTER
TO be LET
GRIFFIN F.S.I.
HARRODS LTD

The charge against looting was led by the newspapers. At the end of November the *Daily Mirror* began a campaign called 'Hang A Looter'.

> Hang a looter and stop this filthy crime. Fines and imprisonment have done nothing to stop the ghouls who rob even bodies lying in the ruins of little homes. Looting is in fact on the increase. There have been more than 450 cases in London alone during the past ten weeks ... the heaviest penalty so far has been five years' penal servitude. It has not stopped looting. But the law, under the Defence regulations, can sentence to death. The country demands that this crime be stamped out... To cover themselves the thieves often mingle with a rescue squad, pretending to help so that they can get nearer to their prey. A.R.P workers have had to interrupt their work to make sure the beasts are not among them. Judges and magistrates have hinted that a death sentence will have to be passed ... impose it now before looting increases still more.

No one was hanged for looting during the war.

OPPOSITE: The Albert Bridge road in London fell victim to a hit-and-run raider.

TOP RIGHT: Firemen put on a water show for visiting dignitaries at Hyde Park in February 1941.

BOTTOM RIGHT: A grateful woman hands a cup of tea to a fireman after a night spent fighting fires in Camberwell, south London, on 8 March 1940.

CHAPTER SEVEN

NO MERCY FOR MERSEYSIDE: MAY 1941

"A nightmare of droning bombers, exploding bombs and gunfire..."

Anthony Cruikshank, survivor of the raids on Liverpool, May 1941

BY APRIL 1941 German forces were heading east in readiness for the invasion of Russia, but the Luftwaffe hadn't yet finished with Britain. After the carnage at the Cafe de Paris, there was another heavy raid on the capital on 19 March when 479 bombers dropped 467 tons of high explosives and 3,347 incendiaries over London. Then there was nothing for nearly a month. Instead, the Nazis turned their attention to other parts of the United Kingdom. There was little strategic value to these raids – Hitler had long since abandoned his plan to invade Britain – rather they were intended to conceal the relocation of vast numbers of his forces from western to eastern Europe.

Scotland was targeted on the nights of 13 and 14 March. On the first night, 240 bombers rained bombs on the shipyards and armaments factories of Clydebank during a nine-hour raid. The Polish

OPPOSITE: A community destroyed. One man surveys the wreckage all around him in Bridlington.

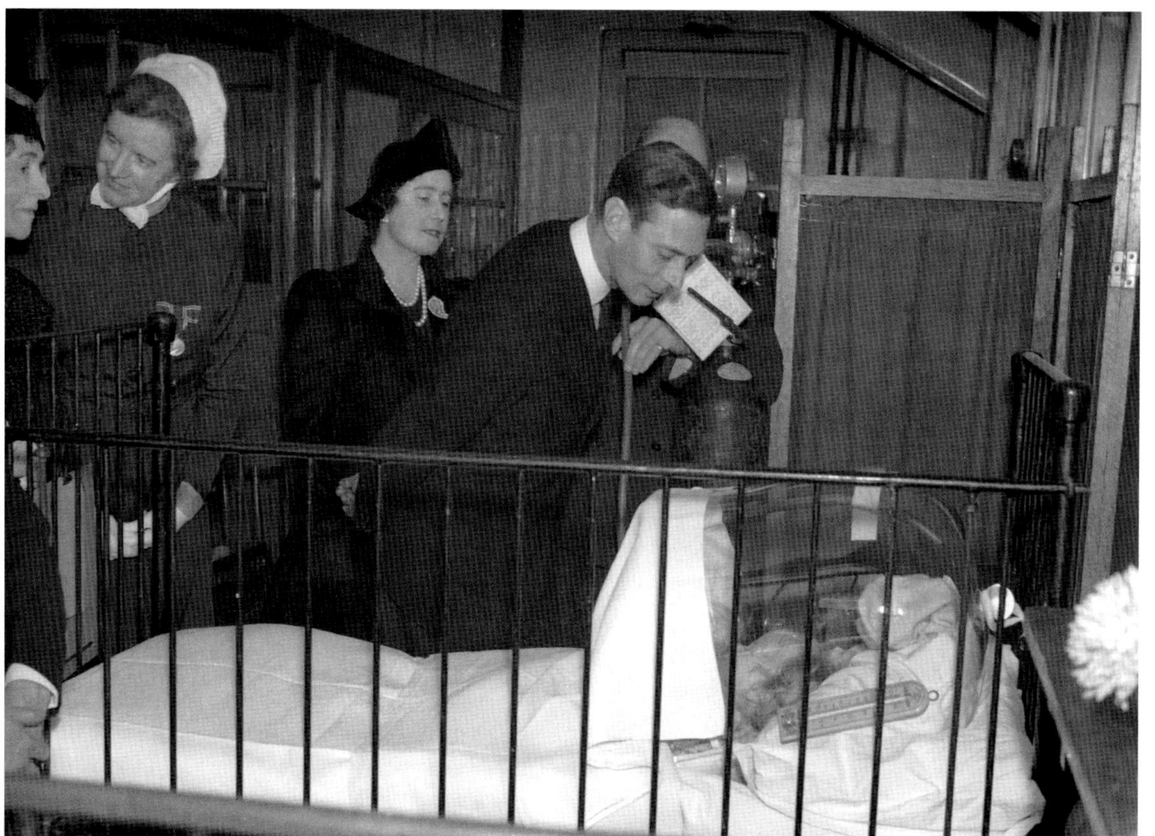

RIGHT: The King and Queen made many morale-boosting visits to cities devastated by the Blitz; this photo shows them visiting a small injured child in hospital.

Norwich was one of the cities targeted by the Luftwaffe. In many cases it would take years, if not decades, to completely recover from the devastation wrought on Britain's cities.

destroyer ORP *Piorun* was being repaired in one of the docks as the Luftwaffe arrived and her guns joined in the barrage against the raiders. It had little effect, in either preventing damage on the ground or weakening the resolution of the German aircrew. They returned the next night and added to the carnage of the day before. The official German communiqué announcing the attack on Scotland said the intensity of the raid 'put Coventry in the shade'.

In total 528 civilians were killed during the two days of bombardments and a further 600 were seriously wounded. Thousands more were left homeless, a great many of whom were shipyard workers and their families, and others involved in important war work. The tightly packed tenement buildings on the Clyde made the job of rescue teams looking for survivors amid the rubble particularly arduous, but they continued their searches undaunted. Most of the bodies they pulled out in the days that followed the Blitz were lifeless, but then on 21 March something extraordinary happened. As one rescue team burrowed deep down inside a collapsed tenement they heard a faint voice. It belonged to Frederick Clarke, a 32-year-old reserve policeman, who had spent the last eight days trapped under the rubble. He reached out a hand to his rescuer and whispered his name, then said he believed at least one more person was still alive close by. As the rescuers continued their search a female medic crawled through the wreckage and gave Clarke an injection. 'That wasn't bad, was it?' she asked him. 'No, not so bad', replied Clarke with a weak smile. For more than an hour, in the most trying of circumstances, the Heavy Rescue team tried to free Clarke from his tomb. At one point his foot became trapped and one of the men was heard to mutter that he doubted if he could survive much longer. 'No, I'm not away', said Clarke, forcefully, 'I'm all right'. Eventually Clarke was brought to the surface, only to die on his way to hospital.[1]

However, Clarke's conviction that there were others also trapped proved correct. Not long after he had been found, 22-year-old John Cormack was discovered still lying in the bed he'd been in when the raiders had struck eight days earlier. He asked for a cup of tea and the message was relayed to the surface. Within minutes Cormack was sitting up in bed drinking a cup of tea under hundreds of tons of rubble, and once free the young man celebrated by smoking a cigarette in the ambulance that took him to hospital. He made a full recovery.

The *Clydebank Press* encapsulated the swirling emotions of its people when it ran an article written by a witness to the raid:

> Lives were being wantonly sacrificed in this mad, insensate lust to kill and destroy, and hearts and high hopes were being ruthlessly shattered. With a heavy heart I turned away with my mother and sister on either side of me, to seek a shelter from the hail of death that descended from the sky. Somehow, in a providential manner, we came through the ordeal waiting and watching for the dawn amid the thunderous reports, the crashes and heavy explosions and the blazing, crackling buildings ...

> the cold, red dawn saw parts of Clydeside a smouldering mass of ruins and heaped-up masonry and debris where death hovered, a place of stunned, questioning people, homeless and penniless, dimly trying to fathom the meaning of it all. The once proud, prosperous homes were laid low, families killed or ruined, careers senselessly shattered, toil, blood, tears, the destiny of the people.

The next target for the German bombers was Plymouth, attacked on 20 March, and the following month Ulster had its first experience of terror bombing. James Craig, the first Prime Minister of Northern Ireland, had always been sceptical that Ulster would ever be visited by the Luftwaffe. Right up to his death in November 1940 he believed Hitler attached little strategic importance to the Province. It was a view shared by many in the Northern Ireland establishment. Lady Londonderry had written to her husband in London earlier in the war: 'All sorts of rot going on here. Air raid warnings and black-outs! As if anyone cared or wished to bomb Belfast.'

Even after John Andrews had succeeded Craig as Prime Minister, Ulster was slow in preparing itself for the possibility of being attacked. At the start of 1941 public air raid shelters were few and the Belfast Corporation stood accused in some quarters of lacking the urgency to support its Civil Defence. After the bombing of Clydebank some within the Government expressed their fear that Belfast was in grave danger. On 24 March John McDermott, Minister for Security, wrote to Andrews outlining his concern: 'Up to now we have escaped attack. So had Clydeside until recently. Clydeside got its Blitz during the period of the last moon... The period of the next moon from say the 7th to the 16th of April may well bring our turn.'

Then on the night of 7 April the Germans did come, destroying the Harland and Wolfe factory that made aircraft parts, and also firebombing the docks and timber yards. That was just a taste of what was to come. Eight days later, the day after Easter Monday, the Luftwaffe returned and this time they were less meticulous in their bombing. Residential areas in the north of Belfast were inundated with bombs (including 76 parachute mines) and large swathes of the Lower Shankhill and Antrim Road were wasted.

Liverpool was bombed continuously, culminating in the terrible attacks of May 1941.

As fires raged across the city the water ran dry after a rupture of the mains by a high-explosive bomb. When the supply was restored Belfast's firemen struggled to contain the inferno. Crews rushed in from other parts of the Province and at 4.30am a telegram was sent to Éamon de Valera in Dublin requesting the assistance of Eire's firefighters. The Taoiseach agreed and dispatched 13 fire engines to Belfast to help restore order.

By the time the last of the fires were out, Belfast was a charred and blackened mess. More than 35,000 houses had been damaged or destroyed, as had 11 churches and two hospitals. The human cost was more ghastly. Nine hundred people had been killed and nearly twice as many wounded. Compared to other cases, the attack on Belfast had been nothing exceptional – 200 tons of high explosive and

Plymouth burns after the vicious raids of April 1941 that cost nearly 300 lives.

96,000 incendiary bombs – but most of the city's inhabitants had never before been bombed, and they hadn't been adequately informed as to what to do or where to go in the event of a raid. Even if they had sought the sanctuary of a shelter, there weren't enough to accommodate Belfast's population.

'Many Dead in Ulster Blitz', ran the headline in the *Daily Mirror* on 17 April and underneath the paper described the attack as 'vicious and indiscriminate'. On the same day that the *Mirror's* report on the devastation in Ulster appeared, the Luftwaffe set out to inflict similar despair on the people of Portsmouth. Yet between them the 230 German bombers succeeded in dropping only eight bombs on the south coast city – thanks to an ingenious deception plan by British defence forces codenamed *Starfish*.

SOUTH COAST ATTACKS

The *Starfish* scheme was initiated in late 1940 by No. 80 Wing of the RAF, the unit responsible for countering Germany's devices such as the *Knickebein* radar beam. As well as attempts to jam the beam, No. 80 also came up with the idea of creating decoy fires that, from thousands of feet up, would resemble burning towns. The fires would be sited in an uninhabited area approximately four or five miles away from the intended target (the RAF knew the targets in advance because the German radio transmitters switched on their beams a few hours before a raid and where they intersected would be that night's objective) and would be ignited by remote control from a secure post half a mile away. In addition, the *Starfish* fires would only be started once the first incendiaries had been dropped on the real target, so the onus was on firefighters to douse the first fires as quickly as possible.

Portsmouth's *Starfish* site was Sinah Common on Hayling Island, a couple of miles east of the city, an ideal location for the audacious decoy plan. On the night of 17 April the weather was also ideal, a thick sea mist that made precision bombing hard for the Luftwaffe bomb aimers. When they saw the raging fires beneath them they jettisoned their bombs without delay, unwittingly blasting Sinah Common to kingdom come. One hundred and seventy high-explosive bombs landed on the dunes and grasslands, along with 32 parachute mines and thousands of incendiary bombs. Yet the only human in close proximity was the fearless *Starfish* operator responsible for igniting the decoy fires. He remained in telephone contact with his superior at No. 80 Wing HQ throughout the ordeal, seemingly unperturbed by the pyrotechnics around him. 'During the attack I rang the *Starfish* operator at Hayling Island and asked him how things were going', recalled Squadron Leader John Whitehead, one of No. 80 Wing's senior officers. '"Oh fine," he answered, and held out the receiver so that I could hear the crump-crump-crump of bombs going off. I said to him "Now, you look after yourself", and he replied, "Oh, it's all right, I've got my tin hat on"'.

There was no such good fortune for another south coast city, Plymouth, when the Luftwaffe struck them the following week. Plymouth had already been savaged in March, when 292 people were

"The once proud, prosperous homes were laid low, families killed or ruined, careers senselessly shattered, toil, blood, tears, the destiny of the people." Clydebank Press

killed during two consecutive nights of attack. Australian Prime Minister Robert Gordon Menzies was staying in the city at the time and he saw for himself the bloodshed. The most distressing sight was at the City Hospital Maternity Ward, the victim of a direct hit that killed four nurses and 19 patients, all aged three or under. The youngest was Harold Santilla, who died with his mother just one week after she had given him life.

Unlike the misty evening of 17 April that had helped save Portsmouth, the evening of Monday 21 April was clear and cloudless. The first of the 120 bombers began dropping their bombs a little after 8.30pm, with the Devonport district of the city bearing the brunt of the six-hour attack. Nearly 100 sailors were killed when the naval barracks took a direct hit but dozens of civilians were also killed and a school was flattened.

Two Clydeside boys push their bikes through the charred wreckage of their street.

The next night the Luftwaffe called again, and this time they were less picky about where they dropped their bombs. A telephone exchange was hit, so too was the city's museum and a Catholic Church. An air shelter at Portland Square was also hit and 72 people inside were killed.

To the city's dismay the Germans returned for a third successive night, hurling incendiaries across a large area, and on Thursday 24th Plymouth suffered its fourth night of attacks.

The weekend saw a brief respite, but the raids recommenced on the Monday and lasted until the Wednesday. The worst incident was the deaths of 43 sailors aboard HMS *Raleigh*, at anchor in the docks, though the Devonport High School for Girls was also destroyed as were 100,000 books in the Plymouth Central Library.

One of the first outsiders to enter Plymouth after its week-long Blitz was Quentin Reynolds, a 39-year-old American war reporter, who had witnessed the fall of France and the ravaging

One US reporter, Quentin Reynolds, described the damage done to Plymouth as surpassing that inflicted on London and Coventry.

of London. 'I had seen Coventry and Southampton and Liverpool', he wrote, 'and had, of course, lived in London during all of 1940 and 1941 blitzes, but nothing I had seen prepared me for the sight of Plymouth after it had been bombed five nights in one week.'[2]

Reynolds toured the city, seeing for himself the annihilation, and then sat down to describe to his American readers the terrible scenes.

> Plymouth was never a large city. At the time it received what was intended to have been its death blow, it had a population of about 204,000. This included the suburb of Devonport. In Britain Plymouth has always been known as the city of Sir Francis Drake, not because he was born there, but because he sailed from Plymouth so often when he went to fight the Spaniards. A huge statue of Drake stands overlooking the sea, on the Hoe, a large limestone plateau 120 feet above the water. There were no factories, virtually no industry, in Plymouth, outside of the docks, and the city was more than 90 per cent residential. That is what gave the city its clean, tidy look; that and the fact that most of the houses were built of native limestone. Plymouth was a city of shrines. Down in the town proper there were 25 ancient churches, each steeped in tradition … within an hour many tangible evidences of the past glories of Plymouth were wiped out by the invader. Two hundred bombers, each carrying at least 1,000 pounds of explosives, flew over the city dropping death and destruction from the skies. Plymouth was ablaze.

Reynolds lingered in Plymouth a few days, marvelling at the clean-up operation and proud to hear that many of the food supplies arriving from London were financed by American generosity. He was also heartened by the reaction of the city's mayor Waldorf Astor, and his wife Nancy (both American-born), for the way in which they helped get Plymouth back on its feet. The mayor oversaw the distribution of food and clothing to the homeless from 30 centres he had rapidly established, while Nancy Astor took charge of evacuating the city's children in case the Germans were tempted to return in May. Then they both arranged for a morale-boosting concert and dance to be held on the Hoe, the finale of which was a song written and sung by a group of Welsh sailors. Reynolds was among the 3,000 people who cheered and clapped the final verse of the song:

> We'll be coming back to Plymouth by and by
> When old Adolf's in the sweet by and by
> When we've made a mess of Göring and Goebbels is in mourning
> We'll be coming back to Plymouth by and by
> We'll cheer our Winston Churchill by and by
> When he makes our skies more clear by and by
> We will welcome Franklin Roosevelt and thank him for his help;
> To smash the blinkin' Nazis from the sky.

LIVERPOOL

Unlike many other British cities and towns bombed in the spring of 1941, Merseyside was already a veteran of the Blitz. The Germans knew that Liverpool was second only to London in importance for the British war effort. Its port was of great significance, welcoming

BELOW: Bristol was one of the cities under constant attack throughout the Blitz. Here survivors of a recent attack gingerly pick their way through the remains of their former homes. Little if anything survived a direct attack such as this.

OPPOSITE: More than 1,700 people were killed on Merseyside during the May 1941 attacks. Here Liverpudlians survey the damage to the city's tram lines.

RIGHT: Residents of Plymouth scan the lists of the dead for names of loved ones. (Getty Images)

vital supply convoys from North America and providing a haven for the Royal Navy vessels that hunted the German U-boats. With its large dockyards and numerous munitions factories, Merseysiders were proud of the part their city played in helping Britain's fight against the Nazis.

Merseyside had first been raided in August the previous year when Prenton in Birkenhead was attacked. Wallasey and Liverpool were targeted in the same month and on 19 August 22 prisoners in Walton jail were killed by a bomb blast.

Attacks continued throughout the autumn, the heaviest raid coming on 28 November when 200 people were killed, including 169 who died when a shelter they were in under the Junior Technical School in Durning Road was hit by a parachute mine. Winston Churchill described the loss as possibly 'the worst single incident' of the Blitz.

BEAUFIGHTER VERSUS BOMBERS

By the spring of 1941 the RAF was enjoying far greater success in shooting down German bombers than it had at the start of Blitz. The new Beaufighters, with their AI radar, proved effective in detecting the enemy intruders in the night sky, while Spitfires and Hurricanes were deployed in 'layers', in other words patrolling the sky at pre-arranged altitudes, rather than haphazardly. When Merseyside was attacked on 12 March, the RAF shot down eight Luftwaffe bombers and the anti-aircraft crews claimed another three. The strike-rate continued through April, and during the Liverpool Blitz of early May, Flight-Lieutenant Guy Gibson and his radar operator Richard James enjoyed one particularly fruitful night in their Beaufighter. Gibson later left an account of the incident that was published after he was killed in action in 1944:

> 'Hullo, all Bad Hat [the squadron call sign used by the ground controller] aircraft. Bandits going for Liverpool – rough course three-four-zero. Stand by.'
>
> Still no orders; round and round I went, getting almost dizzy. It was a lovely night, clear as a bell and just a small new moon. Ideal. But we must wait. Wait for orders. I pictured the controller sitting at his desk a hundred miles away. On his table all the green ships were moving north, amongst them a few red flags; that was us. He must have been harassed at all the activity, hoping that he was doing the right thing. Suddenly:
>
> 'Tally-ho, tally-ho.' This was Bad Hat 34, a new fellow called Lance Martin.
>
> 'O.K., 34, good luck. Listen out.'
>
> Silence in the air for ten minutes. Then:
>
> 'Hullo, Control. 34 calling. It was a Wimpy [RAF slang for a Wellington bomber], blast it. I nearly cracked him down.'
>
> Another problem for the Controller. What was a Wellington doing here? Was it a friendly or was it one of ours flown by a German crew? What was he going to do? What must he say?
>
> 'Hullo, 34, identify and challenge.'
>
> 'O.K., Control. I have: it's friendly.'
>
> 'O.K., Listen out.'
>
> ... The air was full of radio background 'mush' and now and again came an odd order from below. An unreal scene, a scene engineered by science. This was twentieth century war. The war of electricity.
>
> ... It was then that I saw it. A black shadow with flames spitting out of the twin exhausts. He wasn't coming directly towards me, but rather more from left to right. For a minute I felt rather like one does when driving a car. You see another chap coming towards you and you hoot your horn wildly to tell him to keep to his right side. A funny feeling of alarm and I felt my thumb tighten against the gun button as if to do the same, but there wasn't much time. A hard kick on the rudder bar brought the Beau into the right position, and I squinted through the ringsight. One ring deflection. No, give it two. I didn't know much about this deflection business, anyway. 'Look out, Jimmy', I found myself whispering, thinking for a second that the bandit might hear me, rather as one does, or might do, if you were slinking up on a sentry from behind.
>
> Then my four cannons and six machine guns blazed into the night. The effect was startling. An enormous explosion rent the air and it became, quite suddenly, as light as day. For a moment I was rather stunned by what happened as I watched my victim fall quickly towards the earth. We were away out to sea. No one had bailed out. Even if they had the sea was pretty cold.
>
> I felt pleased and worried at the same time. Pleased to have shot down something; worried because I didn't know what it was. James was more excited than I and kept yelling at me from the back. Then a sort of anti-climax came over us both, and we wanted to land quickly and tell the boys all about it.[3]

Before returning to base, Gibson and James encountered a second German bomber, which they shot down in flames.

Today Gibson is best remembered for his role in the Dambusters Raid, his inspiring leadership, skilful flying and dedication to duty in this and over a hundred other bombing raids resulted in the award of the Victoria Cross, Britain's highest award for gallantry. Squadron Leader Guy Gibson was just 26 at the time of his death.

The Beaufighter was one of Britain's greatest tools against the Luftwaffe night bombings.

An open air service for the congregation of Norwich Cathedral courtesy of the Luftwaffe.

Rescuers search the second floor of a house in Shoreditch, 1941.

20 December heralded what were dubbed the Christmas Raids, a bleak four days that cost the lives of 365 people, including 74 who died when the shelter they were in took a direct hit.

Liverpool then experienced a lull similar to that experienced by Londoners, though the Luftwaffe returned in force on the night of 12 March in a raid that claimed the lives of 174 people in Wallasey. Winston Churchill called on Liverpool the following month, another of his flying visits to a bombed out British city. John Colville, his private secretary, had accompanied the Prime Minister a fortnight earlier to Bristol, which was just recovering from the latest of series of heavy raids in a short period. 'The people looked bewildered but, as at Swansea [which they'd also toured after a raid], were brave and were thrilled by the sight of Winston who drove about sitting on the hood of an open car and waving his hat.'

On 1 May, six days after Churchill's trip to Liverpool, the city had other visitors, these ones far less welcome. For the next six days the Luftwaffe poured incendiaries and high-explosive bombs on the heads of Merseysiders. In total 1,741 people were killed and 1,150 seriously wounded.

The bloodiest night of the week-long Blitz was Saturday 3 May when the SS *Malakand*, a 7,000-ton cargo liner in Huskisson Dock No. 2, was hit. On the ship were 1,000 tons of bombs and shells destined for the British forces in the Middle East. They exploded with a terrifying roar, ripping the vessel to shreds and sending shards of her shattered hull as far as two miles away. Miraculously, only four people were killed in the disaster.

There were also tales of great personal tragedy that night and few were as grievous as the blow that befell Anthony Cruikshank. He had spent Saturday evening at the cinema, watching James Cagney in *Torrid Zone*, before returning home and climbing into bed. A little

TOP LEFT: The occupants of this Anderson shelter, shown in the foreground surrounded by squares of turf, stood no chance when the Germans destroyed it during a raid on Clydeside.

BOTTOM LEFT: Norwich was hit hard, with historic buildings that had stood for several centuries reduced to rubble.

before midnight the air raid siren sounded, so Cruikshank reported for firewatching duty at St John's Church in Fountains Road. He later recalled the night as being a 'nightmare of droning bombers, exploding bombs and gunfire'.[4]

A stick of incendiaries that fell on the church in the early hours of Sunday 4 May were quickly doused by Cruikshank and his team. That was the most eventful moment of the night for him. However, he was concerned by the inferno he saw a few hundred yards to the west, in the Kirkdale district of the city, close to the docks. Two of his brothers and their families lived over there. He set off around 5am to visit his brother James and his family, picking his way 'cautiously through lots of debris and rubble until I came to his street, where I was met by an eerie silence. Where his house should have been there was nothing but crumbled brickwork. I saw a pair of shoes sticking out, which I knew were his.'

Cruikshank rushed over the Stanley hospital to be greeted with the gruesome sight of row upon row of corpses, among which were his 29-year-old brother and his eight-year-old nephew, John. He also discovered that his other brother's house had been destroyed and his 26-year-old sister-in-law had been killed.

A few hours later Cruikshank attended Mass in St John's, one of the few churches unmolested by the Luftwaffe bombs. The raiders had gone but suddenly the calm of the church was shattered by a deafening explosion of a delayed action bomb nearby. People began screaming and running for cover. 'Stay where you are', shouted the priest. 'Nothing can harm you. You are in God's House.'

Over the coming days a forlorn trail of homeless people snaked out of the city along the Walton Road towards the rural areas of Aintree and Fazakerly, their meagre belongings loaded into carts, trolleys and prams. The last bombs fell on Wednesday 7 May when, reflected Cruikshank, 'the traumatised people of Liverpool were dangerously near to capitulation'.

Having withstood the dropping of 2,315 high-explosive bombs, 120 land mines and hundreds of thousands of incendiaries, Merseysiders had reached their breaking point, but then the attacks stopped. Instead the Luftwaffe switched their attention south, to London, and one last final raid on the British capital before they moved east towards Russia.

CATE

CHAPTER EIGHT

HELLFIRE: 10 MAY 1941

"This war is too important to be fought by generals – it is being fought by the people."

Quentin Reynolds, American war correspondent and London resident, May 1941

ON 2 APRIL 1941 the Independent Labour politician Willie Gallacher clashed with Colonel Llewellin, the Parliamentary Secretary to the Ministry of Aircraft Production in the House of Commons. Gallacher asked the latter if he was aware that in its edition of 20 March the *Daily Mail* had invited its readers to send donations to the 'Bomb Berlin Fund' of the Ministry and if he was aware, could the honourable gentleman confirm that such a fund existed 'for the indiscriminate reprisal bombing of civilians'. There was no such fund, Llewellin assured Gallacher, though he was pleased to add that the ministry was 'ready to receive and is continuously receiving gifts for the purchase of war materials, including bombs, and I think that the House can rely on the RAF duly to deliver any bombs so provided'.

Gallacher didn't appreciate the levity of Llewellin's response. Rather, wasn't the minster 'concerned about an important daily paper publishing such a statement as that the Ministry has a "Bomb Berlin Fund"? Would it not be something which every Member would use against Germany if there was a "Bomb London Fund" or a "Bomb Glasgow Fund" in Germany? Why is the *Daily Mail* allowed to publish such a statement?' Colonel Llewellin considered Gallacher's question too conciliatory towards the Germans and closed the debate with a terse rejoinder: 'There is no: "Bomb Berlin Fund",' he reiterated, 'but I must say that it rather encourages people in this country, especially in London, to hear that Berlin has been bombed.'[1]

The following week the RAF did indeed bomb Berlin, which the *Mail* and some, though not all, Londoners enjoyed. 'There was some expectation that revenge would be sought on the capital itself', recalled auxiliary fireman William Sansom, 'on a purely eye-for-an-eye passion declared vehemently over the German radio'.

LONDON HIT AGAIN

On Wednesday 16 April Germany took its revenge. A massive force of nearly 700 bombers pounded the capital, dropping 890 tons of high explosives and 4,200 canisters of incendiaries. Three days later they were back in even bigger numbers and 1,026 tons of explosives exploded around the ears of Londoners. One thousand people died on 'The Wednesday', as the first raid came to be known, a further 1,200 on 'The Saturday'.

For a city that had become accustomed to tranquillity after the turmoil of the previous autumn, the sudden return to random death

OPPOSITE: 'Business as usual' as Londoners head to the office the day after the heavy raid of 16 April 1941.

Albert, Prince Regent, doffs his hat on the night of 16 April 1941 as around him Holborn burns and weary firemen move on to the next deadly blaze.

Nurses look out from the shattered remains of their London hospital following the raids of April 1941.

Pimlico burns after taking several direct hits during the devastating raid of Wednesday 16 April 1941.

Sometimes the best efforts of London's firefighters were useless, as in the case of this inferno in Southwark on 16 April 1941.

"I walked around the still burning streets of London on Sunday morning. The streets were filled with grim-faced, sullen-looking men and women. They were through taking it. They wanted to give it."

Quentin Reynolds, 11 May 1940

and destruction caused more unease than those earlier relentless raids that had at least allowed them to follow a routine, something so important for most human beings. On the morning of the first raid, the Wednesday, Vere Hodgson had been telling her diary about the sweetness of her primroses; a day later she mournfully catalogued the devastation caused to her neighbourhood and ended with a reflection: 'Sometimes I think it will end for me like that girl in Liverpool who wrote a diary. The Blitz was going well overhead, and she sat writing about it … the diary was eventually found – she never was.'

The 'Saturday Raid' of 19 April 1941 cost the lives of 1,200 Londoners.

Nowhere in the capital was more unlucky on the Wednesday than Sutherland Terrace in Pimlico. A stick of high explosives had fallen on the street early on in the raid, causing severe damage to property and people, and while rescue workers beavered away to bring out the living from the rubble, further calamity descended silently from the sky. First they spotted the evil gleam of the mine's parachute as it came in from south of the Thames. At first they reckoned it was going to land further north, but then its trajectory slowed and down it came on Sutherland Terrace. 'It was just as though a huge orange flare had gone up under your feet', a stretcher bearer later told Sansom. 'A hell of a bang. Then it was like a sandpapered ramrod down your throat, and your lungs puffing out like a pouter pigeon. Then dead, dead silence. Then, as though some time afterwards, a slow shower of bricks from everywhere.'

One man simply disappeared. One minute he had been in Sutherland Terrace, the next he was nowhere to be found, obliterated into a million little pieces, or so his comrades presumed. Three days later he was found in Hanwell hospital, sitting up in bed and cheerfully recounting how, when he'd come to, he found he'd been blown a quarter of a mile by the force of the blast, with nothing more serious than a broken heel and a dozen stitches to a scalp wound.

Those rescue workers who arrived at Sutherland Terrace after the landmine had dropped likened the scene to the killing fields of Flanders in the First World War. There were dead and mutilated bodies wherever they looked. The front page of the *Daily Mirror* on Friday 18th bore testimony to the human cost of the raid, a photograph of a dead fireman under the stark headline 'Duty Done'.

Westminster was spared the worst of the Saturday raid. Instead it was east and south London that suffered, and parachute mines were once again in plentiful supply. In East Ham Tony Cox, a young boy,

St Paul's Cathedral certainly appeared to have a divine protector during the Blitz. Not only had it escaped serious damage during the firestorm raid of 29 December 1940, but twice the cathedral was hit by high-explosive bombs that failed to explode. The first fell on 12 September 1940 in Dean's Yard, lodging itself 30 feet beneath ground, and was painstakingly defused by Lieutenant Robert Davies and Sapper George Cameron Wylie, both of whom were awarded the George Cross for bravery. The second bomb to land on St Paul's did so on 16 April 1941 and was found by the Right Reverend Walter Robert Matthews, the Dean of the Cathedral, who left an account of the event:

> Shortly after 4am I discovered a sea-mine enveloped in a green silk parachute at the north-east corner of the Cathedral. It was about 8 feet high and lay close to the site of St Paul's Cross. I was somewhat dazed by the events of the night and did not realise at once what the shrouded object might be. It crossed my mind that the silk might have been blown out of some warehouse. I went up to the place and drew aside the silk covering. It then appeared that the object beneath it was a shining steel sea-mine. It was like an inverted, elongated pear in shape and had rows of 'horns' at the top and bottom. It had dropped perpendicularly, and most fortunately had remained in that posture. I was afraid that I might cause the mine to topple over if I dragged the covering silk and remained still and perplexed for some little time, holding the silk in my hands. I then returned to the Crypt and told Canon Alexander what I had found. After that, accompanied by Mr Tanner, the Dean's verger, I went to the police station at Snow Hill. After some delay we saw the police officer in charge, who reported the mine to the Admiralty. He sent a constable back with me to make his report. When we arrived at the Cheapside gate to the churchyard I unlocked it and was putting the keys back into my pocket when the constable, somewhat agitated, said: 'I should leave the keys and your helmet here, if I were you, sir, these things go off, they say, if any steel is brought near them.' I told him I had almost touched it when I first saw it. I then took him towards the Cathedral and, having peered at the object through the shrubs, he said he had seen enough and departed. Later a naval officer with two ratings arrived. I took them to the mine and they proceeded to deal with the 'horns'. Ultimately the mine was removed – alas! with the beautiful silk parachute. I heard later that while the last horn was being rendered safe a fire engine was driven, contrary to police instruction, at full speed from Cheapside to Cannon Street. This caused the mechanism to start into action and there was great danger that the mine would explode after all. Shortly, however, the ticking stopped and the last horn was removed.[2]

St Paul's rises defiantly above the ruins of the neighbouring streets despite the ferocity of the April and May raids.

The area around St Paul's Cathedral was heavily bombed on 10 May 1941 but the famous landmark once again came through safely.

headed to the Anderson shelter his family shared with their neighbours. On this night it was just him and his mum, as his dad was on duty with the fire service and the neighbours had remained indoors. The initial excitement of the Blitz had worn off for Cox, and he no longer collected bomb shrapnel or other souvenirs of war. He just wanted the raids to stop. As he and his mum sat in the shelter listening to the ungodly din above them, everything seemed to go quiet. 'There was just one bomber flying overhead', recalled Cox.

> As the hush intensified a flapping noise became apparent. I had no doubt it was a parachute mine. I threw myself to the floor of the shelter as my mother got to her knees, saying 'Oh God' repeatedly. Suddenly everything seemed to heave upwards and then drop down.[3]

Like the stretcher bearer in Sutherland Terrace, Cox heard silence in the immediate aftermath of the mine's explosion and then the heavy rain of falling debris. Cox emerged from the shelter into a great cloud of dust. Slates cascaded from rooftops and for a moment he thought he and his mum were the only people left alive in London. Gradually other people staggered through the artificial fog, numb and dazed, hardly daring to believe they'd survived.

There was another small era of peace for the capital following the attacks of April, and while Liverpool burned, Londoners boated on the Serpentine, strolled across Hyde Park or dozed in an armchair enjoying the warm May sunshine. Then on Thursday 8 May the RAF bombed Hamburg and Bremen and London shivered with apprehension.

The following day Hitler hosted many members of the German High Command at his Bavarian Chalet 8,000 feet above the town of Berchtesgaden. The Nazi leader received an update on the preparations for invading Russia, on schedule to commence as planned at the end of June, and then attention turned to the air raids of the previous night. Nearly 100 Germans lay dead and a retaliatory attack was required. It was agreed by Hitler and his senior command

Two vets give succour to a little boy's dog after London had been hit in April 1941.

that this would be the last raid before the bulk of the Luftwaffe transferred east. As such it was decided to hurl everything at London.

It was cup final day on Saturday 10 May. Arsenal was playing Preston North End at Wembley and 60,000 fans watched a disappointing 1–1 draw. The game ended a little after 5pm, but few of the spectators were in a rush to go home. Double summer time had been introduced a week earlier and the winding forward of the clocks by two hours kept London bathed in natural light till nearly 10pm.

Elsewhere across the capital people took their seats in the London Palladium to watch Max Miller and Vera Lynn in *Applesauce!* or they applauded the Royal Choral Society performing Elgar's *Dream of Gerontius* at the Queen's Hall in Langham Place. Cinema goers had the choice between *Charlie Chan at the Wax Museum* or *Seven Sinners* starring John Wayne and Marlene Dietrich. People who liked a bet headed to the dogs at New Cross.

When darkness fell so did the temperature. It was a cold, cloudless night, and for the first time since 11 April the moon was full. At 10.30pm No. 80 Wing of the RAF telephoned Fighter Command and informed them that their monitoring unit had detected two German radio beams intersected over West Ham. A few minutes later in Fighter Command's underground filter room, the WAAFs standing around a large map of the English coastline, headphones clamped to their ears and croupiers' rakes clutched in their hands, began pushing dozens of magnetic iron markers across the Channel towards the south coast. The markers were known as 'Hostiles'.

Across London air raid sirens began to howl. In Maida Vale, in the west of the capital, 29-year-old Olivia Smith had spent a tiring day delivering rations to the crews operating the city's barrage balloons. 'The alert sounded sometime around 11pm', she wrote in her diary, 'just as I was on the verge of dropping off to sleep'. Smith curled up under the eiderdown and hoped it was a false alarm.[4]

A service in the ruins of St Mary and Bow church, destroyed on 10 May 1941.

In the American bar of the 500-room Savoy Hotel a group of US war reporters were having a final drink for the road when they heard the siren. Among those present were Quentin Reynolds, recently returned from Plymouth, Ben Robertson of *P.M.*, a New York tabloid, the silver-haired Jamie Macdonald of the *New York Times*, Ed Beattie of the United Press Agency and Larry Rue of the *Chicago Tribune*. 'There's that nasty man', remarked Beattie, as the air raid warning wailed. Reynolds later recalled that 'No one paid any attention to it. The minutes passed and we'd forgotten the siren.'

Sixteen-year-old Joe Richardson was on his way back home when the siren sounded. He'd spent the evening dancing at the Trocadero in Elephant and Castle and was on a tram going down the Walworth Road. 'About halfway down the driver said "right, that's it, I'm stopping here", and he left the tram in the middle of the road.' Richardson jumped off opposite East Lane and found himself criss-crossed by frightened Londoners. 'There was a sense of panic that hadn't been there on other raids', said Richardson. 'People had just had enough of it all and they started running. I didn't believe in running because you're just as likely to run into trouble as you are to run away from it. Anyway, I was 16 and at that age you think everything will be fine.'[5]

A few minutes after 11pm incendiaries clattered onto the east casements of the Tower of London, the first of many thousands to fall on London in the following hours. At midnight a cluster of

Rescue workers clear up the damage caused to Westminster Abbey on the morning of 11 May 1941.

incendiaries landed on the roof of the Queen's Hall, and around the same time the British Museum was hit by a number of firebombs. The museum's director, Sir John Forsdyke, phoned the fire station but it was 45 minutes before eight fire engines arrived. By that time the roof of the Roman Britain room was ablaze and flames were perilously close to the general library.

After the incendiaries came the high explosives and they broke over London like a summer storm in the early hours of 11 May. Bombs fell in the north of the capital, in Purcell Street, Islington, flattening 17 houses and killing eight people; they fell in the south, in Cunard Street, Southwark, leaving 14 dead; they fell in the east, in Coutts Road, Bow, killing half a dozen, and they fell in the west, a stick of high explosives laying waste to Bomore Road, Notting Hill, and seven of its residents.

The Blitz had a way of extracting a person's true character, revealing what lay deep within, the way German bombs did to buildings. At her home in Maida Vale Olivia Smith lay trembling under her eiderdown listening to the devilment outside. 'There was a tremendous loud howling whistle from a falling firebomb', she wrote in her diary. She rushed to the window and saw that some incendiaries had landed in her neighbour's garden.

> So I ran out, shouting to the maids and with some difficulty pulled myself over the wall by means of the branch of an elder tree at the bottom of the garden and ran to deal with it barehanded, fully expecting that one of the maids would come in a moment or two. But this was expecting altogether too much.

The maids were too scared to set foot outside the house so Smith tackled the incendiary alone, shovelling soil over the burning magnesium and then dousing it all with a bucket of water.

SUNDAY PICTORIAL, May 11, 1941.

The Voice of the People

Sunday Pictorial

No. 1,365 TWOPENCE

Special 5 a.m. Edition

MANY NAZI RAIDERS

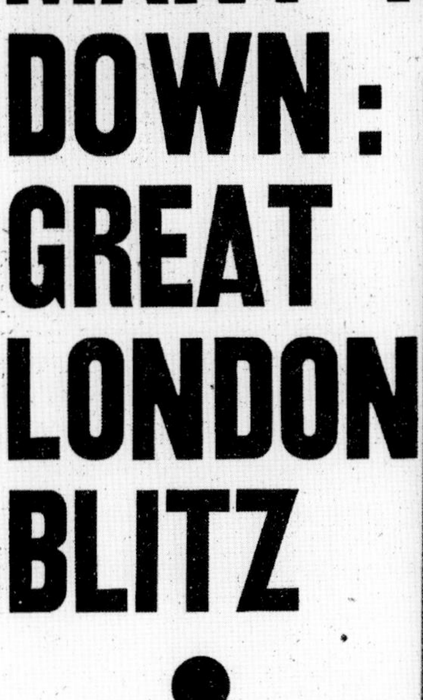

DOWN: GREAT LONDON BLITZ

BATTLES UNDER FULL MOON

NAZI BOMBERS BLITZED LONDON IN BRILLIANT MOONLIGHT LAST NIGHT—AND PAID A HEAVY PRICE. SOON AFTER THE ALERT—IT WAS BEFORE MIDNIGHT—ROOF WATCHERS SAW THE FIRST RAIDER FALL IN A WHIRL OF FLAME ON THE OUTSKIRTS.

"When the bomber crashed there was a heavy anti-aircraft barrage," said one. "The plane was flying very high and suddenly burst into flames—a ball of fire in the sky.

"It took a long time to come down, and when it hit the ground it exploded with a flash that could be seen for miles."

Cannon in the Sky

THE RAID DEVELOPED QUICKLY INTO ONE OF THE HEAVIEST EVER.

Between the bursts of A.A. fire Londoners could hear the sharp crack of machine-guns and the heavier thud of cannon mingling in the whine of planes.

Soon another raider flamed to earth—and another.

THE BLITZ HAD BEEN GOING ONLY A SHORT WHILE WHEN FOUR WERE SEMI-OFFICIALLY REPORTED DOWN, AND AS THE HOURS WENT BY OTHER BOMBERS FOLLOWED BLAZING TO THE GROUND.

Fireblitz and H.E.

Watchers on one roof reported that they had seen twelve planes hurtle down—and the raid was still not over.

Raiders that got through emptied load after load of fire bombs. Down in the streets dim figures hurried everywhere with sandbags and stirrup pumps, putting them out.

They could not tackle all. Fires were started in a number of buildings, and down crashed the high explosives.

These were followed by more incendiaries and more loads of H.E.

Among buildings hit were two hospitals, a warden's post, an A.F.S. post and a club. There were casualties at all these places.

Two famous London churches were also set on fire.

To many people the raiders appeared to dive lower than usual; but the noise of their engines made no difference to anybody who had a ob of work to do.

A.F.S. men and women ambulance and rescue workers and wardens slaved throughout the night to keep in check the fires and to succour the wounded.

Other Towns Raided

Raiders—in smaller numbers—were reported also over Liverpool area and the south-east coast.

It is certain that the number of raiders brought down last night brings the total for the first ten days of this month to more than a hundred, compared with the ninety for the whole of April.

Experts believe that if the average figure of raiders down could be brought to twenty a night, the menace of the night bomber would be broken.

Front cover of the *Daily Mirrors Sunday Pictorial* from 11 May 1941, recording the raids of the previous night.

> Just as I was getting through the last stages of my job a tremendous outburst of noise thundered from the sky. I ran like a hare to the wall … still half-blinded by the brightness of the fire bomb and the awful Blitz noise that filled the air seemed to wind mentally. For what seemed like hours I dithered and fumbled on the wall top, clawing frantically at the twigs that enlaced me and caught in my clothes.[6]

Some of the worst infernos of the night were south of the river. In Elephant and Castle the call went out for an additional 50 fire engines, though the district's superintendent had no idea from where they would come. The vast acres of lock-ups under Waterloo Station were an inferno and flames were seen coming from St Thomas's Hospital. Peckham and Bermondsey were both overwhelmed with the numbers of fires being reported, and if the superintendent had been able to see across the Thames he would have seen that Westminster was also on fire. Crews from Kent and Essex and Surrey began to arrive but by then it was already too late for many of London's most famous buildings.

OPPOSITE: Firefighters tackle a blaze at a church in Marylebone, 10 May 1941.

RIGHT: No lessons today for pupils at Westminster School after the heavy raid of 10 May 1941. From the greatest public schools to the most deprived areas of the East End, no area of London was truly immune from the sustained attacks of the Blitz. However, the damage was significantly worse closer to the industrial areas particularly surrounding the docklands.

The Victoria Tower of Westminster Palace (left), the historic seat of government and part of the historic complex that includes the Houses of Parliament, is just visible through the inferno of 10 May 1941.

The Archbishop of Canterbury, Cosmo Lang, was lucky to escape injury when four high explosives detonated in Lambeth Palace, or perhaps it was divine intervention that caused a brick blast wall to absorb the impact of one of the quartet of bombs. Nevertheless, fires raged unchecked in the palace's library and chapel and in the Lollards' Tower.

In Cheapside the church of St Mary-le-Bow had been reduced to rubble. A church had stood on the site since 1070 and to Cockneys anyone born within the sound of its 12 bells was one of them.

Much of St James' Palace, built by Henry VIII in 1531, was destroyed, as was the British Museum, which had lost its Roman Britain Room, Greek Bronze Room, the Coins and Medal Room and many others. The Old Bailey was a mess, the Queen's Hall was a ruin and the church of St Clement Danes – famous for its 'Oranges and Lemons' song – had burned to the ground.

Even the nation's seat of power was scarred and shattered, though the damage would have been far worse had it not been for the cool courage of the Civil Defence. When Chief Superintendent Charlie McDuell, commanding officer in London's West End, had received reports of a stick of bombs falling on the House of Commons he dispatched Leading Fireman Dave 'Dusty' Millar to investigate and report back to him. Millar sped off towards the Commons, trailed by

Robin Duff, a reporter for the BBC. The pair toured Parliament looking for signs of damage and on entering the Strangers' Gallery, overlooking the Commons Chamber, Millar ran his torch along the rows of green leather and up to the Speaker's Chair. Nothing seemed amiss. He closed the door and then the undetected bomb in the chamber exploded. Millar and Duff were bowled down the passageway by the force of the explosion, after which the pair stumbled out and hurried back to McDuell. Within minutes half a dozen engines were in the Star Courtyard pumping water on to the flaming Chamber above. Millar and Duff volunteered to go back inside the Commons and attack the fire at source. 'Our job was to see that the flames didn't spread across the passage and so towards Big Ben', recalled Millar. They fixed a hose to a hydrant and 'ran it through the door behind the Speaker's Chair into the blazing Chamber'. When that fire was out they worked their way up to the floor above the Chamber to assess the extent of the damage. 'It was burning pretty fiercely and the further wall was alight', said Duff, who described Millar as 'having all the courage you could want'. The fireman began playing water on the fire and soon that was doused.

Walter Elliot, Member of Parliament for Kelvingrove, had spent much of the night dousing the dozens of incendiaries that fell close to his home in Lord North Street. At around 3am he heard that the House of Commons was on fire. He hurried north but found that McDuell had the situation in the Palace of Westminster under

LEFT: Fetters Lane on the night of 10 May 1941.

BELOW: Greenwell took this dramatic photo of the Inner Temple burning in May 1941 from a roof in Fetters Lane.

control. Not so the fires taking hold of the 900-year-old Westminster Hall. Flames were leaping from the roof and threatening to spread inside. The dilemma McDuell faced concerned water: he and his fellow firemen desperately needed to get inside the Hall to fight the seat of the fire but the only way to do so would be to run their hoses from the two steel dams in New Palace Yard and through the Hall's northern door. However, the great oak door was locked, and McDuell didn't want to be responsible for breaking down the door of one of Britain's most venerable buildings. Elliot knew the key to the door was in the key lobby in the House of Commons, but there

Firemen's hoses suck water from the Thames on Sunday 11 May 1941 as the fires continue to rage.

It had been decreed that the church bells of the nation would only ring out when an invasion was imminent. The ancient bells of St Clements, for so long a feature of many children's favourite rhyme, would ring out no more. The raids on 10 May 1940 destroyed the church of St Clement Danes and broke the heart of its rector. The image on the right shows the remains of the devastated church.

wasn't time to fetch it. He asked for the axe that hung from a fireman's webbing belt, and with one mighty blow 'had the great pleasure of laying on to the main doors of Westminster Hall – a combination of conceit and destruction which provided a certain insight into the ecstasy of the iconoclasts'.[7]

Firemen streamed into the Hall and soon the fires were being beaten back. The same wasn't true at Elephant and Castle, where even the arrival of 50 additional pumps appeared to be having little impact in reducing the conflagration. There were now 300 firemen tackling the inferno with water being pumped from the Thames at London Bridge and from an EWS reservoir situated in the Surrey Music Hall, which had been left a shell in an earlier raid. Lampposts buckled in the heat, fire bubbled and peeled from the fire pumps and the men on the hoses had to hunch low, faces near the branch, to gulp down precious lungfuls of air. The Divisional Officer was now on the scene and he ordered 20 of his men to the Music Hall to pump out more water. Hardly had they arrived when a high-explosive bomb dropped on their heads, killing 17 of their number.

A Red Cross van does its rounds, travelling through a London street where pipes have been constructed to provide London's firemen with precious water after the raid of 10 May 1941.

When daylight came and the Germans were gone, Elephant and Castle still burned but not with the untamed fury of a few hours earlier. Elsewhere across the city people emerged from their homes to take stock of the damage. The stationmaster at Waterloo Station had witnessed 16 major incidents and now he was without water, gas and electricity. As he wandered down the tracks assessing the carnage it seemed to be snowing, only the flakes were black. He held out his hands and caught one of the thousands of scraps of burned paper drifting away from the ruins of the London Waste Paper Company warehouse.

The teenage Joe Richardson had passed the raid in a shelter on John Ruskin Street. As dawn broke he walked up the Walworth Road towards Elephant and Castle. He'd thought he'd seen everything in nine months of bombing, but now he was greeted with a sight that stopped him dead. 'I heard this whimpering and turning round I saw this big dog hobbling towards me. His fur was all burned off and his skin was sort of bubbling. It was terrible.' A Home Guard soldier, on duty to prevent looting, raised his rifle and put the dog out of its misery.

Quentin Reynolds and the other members of the American press corps had stayed put in the bar of the Savoy throughout the raid. As seasoned veterans of the Blitz they knew that this attack was unlike any other in its intensity. At 6.30am on Sunday morning Reynolds heard 'the long joyous sound of the siren'. Then he and his peers went out to do their job. 'It was a beautiful day', he wrote in the report he later cabled across the Atlantic.

> A spring sun bathed the city with its warmth but there was a pall of smoke over the city and through it the sun shone blood red. A breeze carried soot from still smoking buildings and your hands and face grew grimy. The firemen unexhausted after a bitter night's work kept at their job methodically. Mobile canteens dashed up and down and uniformed girls served them tea and sandwiches. Air wardens and policemen were searching among ruins hoping that they might find something living under them.[8]

However, it wasn't the countenance of the emergency services that struck Reynolds, it was the attitude of the civilian population that left the deepest impression. During the autumn of 1940 Londoners had 'Taken It' without complaint and merely shrugged their shoulders when asked what they thought of the Blitz. But not on 11 May. 'All that feeling is gone now', wrote Reynolds.

> I walked around the still burning streets of London on Sunday morning. The streets were filled with grim-faced, sullen-looking men and women. They were through taking it. They wanted to give it. Every bomb that the Nazis dropped during the night carried germs with it – germs of hatred. I could feel the hatred rising from the ruins infecting everyone. Tight-lipped men and women stared at the debris of treasured landmarks and you could feel the hatred of Nazi Barbarism emanating from them. This war is too important to be fought by Generals – it is being fought by the people.

Five hundred and seven German aircraft had set out on Saturday night to bomb London. Fourteen were shot down by RAF fighters but that was of little comfort to London and its people. The Luftwaffe had dropped 711 tons of high-explosive bombs on the capital during the six-and-a-half-hour raid, including 77 parachute mines and seven of the 1,800kg 'Satan' bombs. Ninety thousand incendiaries had also been unfurled over London, though to those on the ground it seemed like a lot more.

In total 11,000 homes had been damaged beyond repair and nearly 13,000 people were now homeless. They at least were alive, unlike the 1,436 men, women and children who had been killed. No previous raid had exacted such a heavy human price. Two thousand more were seriously wounded. A month later the tally increased by one with the death of the Reverend William Pennington-Bickford, rector of St Clement Danes. His wife said he'd died of a broken heart, caused by watching his church burn down on 10 May.

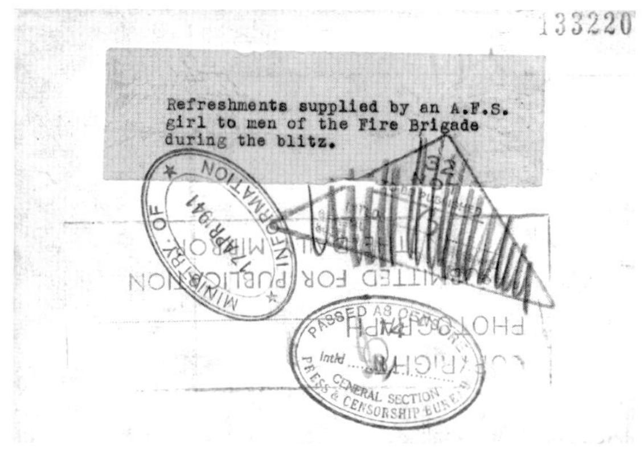

Two images from the *Daily Mirror*'s archive showing the censor stamp at work. These photos, both from early 1941, carry their original captions. The right hand side of the image below shows where the censor has marked part of the image as unsuitable for printing in the paper. Neither image was allowed to be printed.

CHAPTER NINE

V IS FOR VENGEANCE: 1944 AND 1945

"They seem to be rockets which drop from the stratosphere. You may be out peaceably walking and one drops. Nice prospect!"

Vere Hodgson, diarist and London resident

SIX WEEKS AFTER THE GREAT RAID on London the German war machine attacked Russia. Winston Churchill was at Chequers when the invasion began on 21 June. John Colville, his private secretary, woke him with the news, which 'produced a smile of satisfaction' on the Prime Minister's sleepy face.

In London and other British cities and towns, the realisation that the German war machine was now directing its fury at Russia caused similar reactions, but the levity was only skin-deep. Behind the collective smile lay the deep trauma induced by ten months of sustained bombing, much of it indiscriminate. Forty three thousand Britons were dead, the youngest an 11-hour-old baby, and the oldest a Chelsea Pensioner aged 100. More than 500 people weren't even afforded the dignity of a funeral, blown to unrecognisable bits as they were.

OPPOSITE: An elderly couple in Newcastle salvage what they can after a raid in 1943.

RIGHT: One of the rare attacks on the capital in 1942 occurred here at Blackfriars Bridge on 22 February after a hit-and-run raid.

LEFT: The Luftwaffe launched a 'Little Blitz' against Britain in early 1944, which claimed the lives of this London woman and 1,555 others.

OPPOSITE: One of the first V-1 bombs to hit London landed here in Kentish Town on 19 June 1944.

In London 1,150,000 houses had been damaged by German bombs and it was estimated that one in six people had been homeless for a day or more. In towns and cities across Britain, the scale of devastation was equally numbing. Nearly one of every four houses in Plymouth was damaged during their Blitz and in Hull only 6,000 homes out of 93,000 remained unscathed. In 1939 Britain had boasted 13,000,000 houses; after the Luftwaffe passed through, that figure had been reduced by 200,000.

Even after the German attack on Russia, there were intermittent small-scale raids on Britain. Birmingham was hit in July and 40 bombers struck Manchester in October, while Hull and South Shields suffered short, sharp attacks. By the start of 1942 the RAF had not only introduced a new night fighter – the Mosquito – superior even to the vaunted Beaufighter in its capabilities but Bomber Command, under its new chief, Arthur Harris, had also improved its navigational system. In March the RAF bombed the industrial town of Essen and the port of Lubeck, inflicting considerable damage and enraging Hitler. Reprisals followed, breaking the almost year-long peace enjoyed by Britons.

The Luftwaffe attacks that ensued were nicknamed the *Baedeker* raids after the guidebooks found in the pocket of every

"The distant hum, getting louder and louder, growing into a roar and then a deafening rattle as it passed overhead. Sometimes the rattle would diminish as the flying bomb continued on its dead-straight flaming course towards London. But sometimes it would stop abruptly as the engine cut out. I would hold my breath and count – one, two, three, four, five. Somewhere there was an explosion … somewhere there was tragedy."

Cyril Oakley

A dog stands guard outside a house in Kentish Town destroyed by a V-1 flying rocket in June 1944 and seems more reluctant to leave the ruined house than its owner, see page 164.

seasoned tourist. Inside the towns and cities vital to the British war effort, the Germans sought retribution by attacking some of the nation's most treasured tourist destinations, where ground defence was far weaker. One of the first to suffer was Exeter, attacked on 24 April 1942, and in the months that followed York, Canterbury, Norwich, Bath, Poole, Weston-Super-Mare, Canterbury and Cowes were all targeted. By the end of the year 3,236 people had been killed in the *Baedeker* raids and another 4,000 had been seriously wounded.

1943 began ominously for Londoners when 118 German bombers attacked the capital on 17 January, the first major raid since May 1941. Two months later there was another heavy attack on London, a raid that resulted in the loss of 178 lives in a single incident. A crowd of people descending the steps of Bethnal Green Underground panicked at the sound of a nearby explosion and, according to the investigating authorities, the stairs were 'converted from a corridor into a charnel-house in from ten to fifteen seconds'.

Sporadic attacks continued for the rest of 1943 with Newcastle, Grimsby, Cheltenham, Cardiff, Sunderland, Ipswich, Plymouth, Hull and Great Yarmouth all bombed. Casualties were lower than in 1942 – 2,372 people dead and 3,450 wounded.

The New Year began as the old one had, with London on the receiving end of Luftwaffe hostility once more. However, 1944 commenced not with one single heavy raid but with what came to be called the 'Little Blitz'. The attacks were brief, usually lasting only one brutal, bewildering hour, but the effect on Londoners concerned the authorities: 'The population are more jittery than they were in the old days', noted Wing Commander Eric Hodsoll, the Inspector General of Air Raid Precautions.

> Probably to a lot of contributory factors such as belief that we had air superiority and therefore no more attacks to fear; lack of stamina, and so on. There were no signs of panic, but the people seemed more helpless and more dependent on the Civil Defence services than they were in the old days.[1]

By the end of May 1944 the air raids over Britain had claimed 1,556 lives, most of them Londoners. Yet the damage to the Luftwaffe had also been grievous, thanks to the ground defences and the efficiency of the RAF fighters, far more effective than they had been in 1940. Three hundred German aircraft were shot down, a staggering 60 per cent of the force that had begun the Little Blitz bombing campaign in January 1944. It was estimated that for every five British civilians killed, the Luftwaffe lost four of its aircrew. Germany would be unable to sustain such losses if it wished to continue terrorising the British population, but its High Command knew that wouldn't be necessary. They were about to unleash their secret weapon.

THE V-1

At 4.08am on Tuesday 13 June 1944 two members of the Royal Observer Corps were at their post at Dymchurch, on the Kent coast, when they saw a strange object streaking through the sky, flames shooting from its rear and making 'a noise like a Model T-Ford going up a hill'. Immediately they telephoned a warning to their command post at Maidstone – whatever it was, it was heading their way. At 4.13am the object arrowed into the ground and exploded with appalling ferocity on heathland at Swanscombe, a couple of miles east of Dartford. The *Vergeltungswaffen* campaign had begun.

The object making the noise like a Model T-Ford was in fact a *Vergeltungswaffe-1* (V-1) flying bomb. The British came to call it a 'doodlebug' – because it doodled across the sky – continuing their tradition of trivialising the Luftwaffe's most heinous weapons, from 'breadbasket' incendiaries to 'Fritz' high explosives. But there was nothing trivial about a V-1 flying bomb. From the ground it looked like a light aircraft with a wing span of nearly 18 feet and measuring 25 feet from top to tail. It was constructed from sheet steel and plywood, and was powered by a 600-pound jet engine giving it a cruising speed of around 400 miles per hour. When a V-1 hit the ground its 1,870-pound warhead detonated with devastating consequences for anyone in close proximity.

Minutes after the explosion at Swanscombe, there were similar eruptions in Cuckfield, West Sussex, and Borough Green in Kent. No one was killed in the countryside, but the bomb that reached London killed six people in Bethnal Green, including a 19-year-old mother and her eight-month-old baby.

The British had been aware that Germany was producing a secret weapon, thanks to the courage of the Polish Resistance, who alerted them to tests being conducted on the Baltic coast. There was a meeting in Whitehall the day after the opening salvo in which Lord Cherwell, the Prime Minister's scientific advisor, smugly declared: 'The mountain hath roared and brought forth a mouse.'

Five days later, at 9am on Sunday 18 June, the first V-1 bomb landed on Westminster, in Rutherford Street, killing ten and injuring 62. John Brasier, who was a child during the war, recalled this attack:

OPPOSITE LEFT: Charlie Boorman and Brian Walters, aged nine and ten, look out for V-1 doodlebugs from their improvised schoolroom in Otham village, Kent.

BELOW: Doodlebugs, as V-1s were nicknamed, killed approximately 6,000 people in total throughout southern England. Here firefighters rush to put out the fires from a V-1.

BELOW LEFT: A V-1 'doodling' its way to Hampstead, London, in June 1944.

Rescuers ferry the wounded to hospital minutes after a V-1 had landed in Aldwych, shortly after lunchtime on 30 June 1944, killing 48 people who had been enjoying their lunch in the June sunshine.

> One Sunday morning in 1944, I was doing a Sunday paper round when I heard a noise which I later understood to be a V-1 doodlebug. I ran into a side of a house and pressed myself against the wall. Dogs were barking – I had no idea what it was. I had no idea that it was a pilotless vehicle with a bomb in it. It was a cigar-shaped thing with a fin and a flame belching out of the back and a terrible humming noise. To see it so low, literally a hundred feet up in the air – I'll never forget it as long as I live.[2]

Smoke from the incident was still visible two hours later as worshippers entered the Guards' Chapel attached to Wellington Barracks, in Birdcage Walk, just east of Buckingham Palace. Twenty minutes into the service a V-1 dived through the roof of the chapel and exploded. Auxiliary fireman William Sansom recalled that when he arrived 'the scene in its subsiding dust looked vast and boxlike, impenetrable; sloping masses of the grey walls and roof shut in the wounded: the doors were blocked, the roof crammed down; it was

DOWNING A DOODLEBUG

WHEN THE FIRST concentrated V-1 attack was launched against London on the night of 15–16 June out of a total of 144 missiles that reached the English coast seven were shot down by British fighters. Downing a doodlebug became an increasingly popular pastime for RAF pilots in the summer of 1944 and the mainstay of British defence against such rocket attacks. The RAF concluded that the Hawker Tempest was the best choice as an interceptor thanks to its speed and 20mm cannon. It was incredibly dangerous for the pilots because if they fired at too close a range the cannon could detonate the V-1's one-ton warhead and destroy themselves in the process. In late June, British pilots also discovered that shooting down the V-1s was not always necessary. Instead they accidentally discovered that if they could fly alongside the V-1 they could tip it over by banking their aircraft. The V-1's limited guidance system could not cope with a change in direction and it would plummet to the ground. The fact that the speed of the V-1 was invariably slower than its maximum, particularly as it neared its target, meant that the Tempest flying at a low altitude, and to a lesser extent later models of the Spitfire, could catch them. The most successful pilot was 24-year-old Squadron Leader Joseph Berry, DFC and two bars, of 501 squadron. Flying first a Spitfire IX and then a Hawker Tempest, Barry shot down 60 V-1 flying bombs before he was killed in a sortie over northern Germany in early October 1944. Shortly before his death Berry described chasing flying bombs in a radio broadcast, of which the following is the transcript:

> There is a new kind of battle going on in the skies over London – Spitfires versus the German Flying Bombs. These deadly missiles which have been nicknamed 'Doodle Bugs' are just another attempt by Hitler to try to bring this nation to its knees. But, just as happened in the Battle of Britain, I believe our fighters will prove to be too good, and in fact we've already knocked one thousand of them out of the skies before they have been able to inflict any damage on the capital city.
>
> There are lots of stories being told about the bravery of the pilots in tackling these Flying Bombs. Only the other day I saw an old Cockney sorting through the rubble of what had once been his home – hit by one of the bombs – and yet he could still look upwards as a plane flew overhead and smile, 'It's them young fellas in those Spitfires what are saving London!'
>
> And recently I heard a report from the south of England about a chase between three of our fighters and a Doodle Bug. Apparently it was heading in over the coast in the direction of an anti-aircraft battery, but the planes were so close the gunners were afraid of opening up in case they hit one of our chaps. The men and women of the gun-site heard the fighters' guns and then saw the bomb begin to falter. Horrified, they saw it was going to plunge right onto them – and yet still they could do nothing.
>
> But at this precise moment, one of the fighters raced level with the now erratic missile and 'formatting' and 'flipping' it with a wing tip, turned it off course. The bomb crashed about 250 yards from the gun position and well clear of any houses. Did everyone sigh with relief!
>
> Mind you, I can say from personal experience that the Doodle Bug doesn't go down easily. It will take a lot of punishment, and you have to aim at the propulsion unit – that's the long stove-pipe, as we call it, on the tail. If your range and aim are dead on, you can see pieces flying off the stove-pipe. The big white flame at the end goes out, and down goes the bomb. Sometimes it dives straight to earth, but at other times it goes crazy and gives a wizard display of aerobatics before finally crashing. Sometimes the bomb explodes in mid-air and the flash is so blinding that you cannot see a thing for about ten seconds. If this happens, you hope to be the right way up when you are able to see again, because the explosion often throws the fighter about and sometimes even turns it upside down.[3]

Squadron Leader Joseph Berry. (Courtesy of Norman Franks)

Rescue workers assess the damage in Aldwych after a V-1 landed on 30 June 1944.

difficult to find any entrance. But there was one – behind the altar'. Of the 260-strong congregation, 119 were killed and 102 were seriously injured. Sansom thought it a miracle that anyone escaped.

In the first few days of the V-1s, people frequently mistook them for aircraft on fire. One child remembered looking up at one with his mother. 'I hope the poor pilot gets down safely', she said, seconds later the bomb nosedived into London. Often the engine cut out before the V-1 began its descent. That was the moment people came to dread, what many described as the 'deafening silence', as if the V-1 were pausing while searching for a suitable prey. 'The doodlebug was a terrible thing', remembered Una Quibell, a munitions worker in Hayes, Middlesex. 'It looked like a dagger with flames coming out one end. While the engine was going you were OK, but when it stopped you had better take cover.'

Kent became known as Hellfire Corner because of the number of V-1s that dropped on the county as they failed to reach their intended target of London. The noise of the doodlebugs never left Cyril Oakley from Gravesend:

There is no weak link.

The end approached. Hitler launched his flying-bombs in swarms on battered South-eastern England. But London could still take it.

LEFT and BELOW: Two cartoonists' reactions to the flying bombs threat. The cartoon below makes reference to the V3 which had indeed been constructed near Calais but was never put into use due to design flaws.

> The distant hum, getting louder and louder, growing into a roar and then a deafening rattle as it passed overhead. Sometimes the rattle would diminish as the flying bomb continued on its dead-straight flaming course towards London. But sometimes it would stop abruptly as the engine cut out. I would hold my breath and count – one, two, three, four, five. Somewhere there was an explosion … somewhere there was tragedy.[4]

Other people seemed less concerned. Vere Hodgson saw her first doodlebug on Friday 7 July as she returned to her flat in Holland Park. First she heard a 'thrum-thrum', but when she looked skywards she could see nothing. A platinum blonde on the other side of the road broke off from reading a letter and glanced up, then she shouted across to Hodgson 'Can you see it?' Hodgson said she couldn't. 'Come over here', said the blonde. 'And there, between the clouds, sure enough right over our heads, was a horrible black thing', wrote Hodgson in her diary that evening. 'It gave me a turn. The platinum blonde went on her way, unmoved, still reading her letter.'

When the V-1s came over Britain there was a sense of powerlessness, as Terrence McEwan explained:

"Ah, Prof. Schnitzel, if only we could make that one!"

This set of three photos was taken in the immediate aftermath of a V-1 bomb that exploded in Roseberry Avenue, Clerkenwell, on 6 July 1944. It was the deafening silence that occurred when the doodlebug's engine cut out that people feared most. As William Sansom noted, doodlebugs rarely penetrated the ground but caused extensive damage at street level.

> You'd hear the V-1 cut out and when it didn't hit you, your attitude was, 'Oh good, I'm all right'. It was a very selfish attitude we all had. I suppose one blocked out imagination in those days. On one occasion when we were in the shelter, we heard a V-1 cut out and my mother put a blanket over our heads to stop it hitting us. I'm not sure it would have helped much, but we never thought these weapons would turn the war in the German favour. It didn't ever dawn on me that we would lose.[5]

The government issued instructions on how to guard against the new threat, advice that the *London Evening Standard* reproduced on its front page of 16 June:

> The Ministry of Home Security offers the following advice to the public:
> When the engine of the pilotless engine stops, and the lights at the end of the machine are seen to go out, it may mean that the explosion will soon follow, perhaps in five to 15 seconds. So take refuge from blast: even those indoors should keep out of the way of blast and use the most solid protection immediately available.

A disparity between the V-1 campaign and the Blitz of 1940–41 was the timing. The latter had been a nocturnal event for the most part, but the Germans liked to launch their doodlebugs between 8am and 9am, to catch the morning rush-hour, and again around noon as office girls took an hour for lunch in the summer sun. One bomb came down on Aldwych at lunchtime on Friday 30 June, wreaking havoc among the office workers sunning themselves outside. 'The bomb impacted on a row of buses', remembered Cecille Daly, who worked nearby, 'and when the dust lifted, there was a scene of terrible slaughter – pavements were littered with the dead and wounded, and on the road were the twisted, unrecognisable frames of a line of buses. The sunbathing girls had been blown to eternity.'

Another difference between the V-1s and the high-explosive bombs of the Luftwaffe was in the structural devastation caused. The blast damage of a V-1 was extensive with flying glass being the greatest danger. On the other hand, unlike HE bombs, the doodlebugs hardly ever penetrated the surface and so the broken

This group of young and old Londoners don't look too frightened by the V-1 flying bombs as they gawp at the damage caused by one in June 1944.

water mains, ruptured gas and severed electricity cables so prevalent during the Blitz were not a factor. However, the human damage was just as grave. Between 13 June and 1 September 1944 (when the V-1's launch pads in France were overrun by Allied forces advancing from Normandy), approximately 6,000 people in London and the Home Counties were killed by doodlebugs. The worst single incident was the destruction of the Guards' Chapel, but there were also horrific scenes at Sloane Court in Chelsea, where 74 people died, on Lewisham High Street, where 58 people died, and the carnage in Aldywch that resulted in the deaths of 48.

THE V-2

On Friday 1 September Vere Hodgson wrote in her diary: 'Marvellously quiet day and night. Our capture of the Fly Bomb coast is telling immediately.' Two days later Londoners marked the fifth anniversary of the war with quiet optimism that this would be the last year of conflict. The V-1s had all but stopped (the Germans launched a few V-1s from specially adapted aircraft up until January 1945) and Allied forces were quickening their pace east with Brussels and Antwerp within their grasp. Then on the evening of 8 September

This series of images show Montford Place in Kensington not long after a V-1 had landed on 8 July 1944, and again a few hours later. Rescuers sift through the rubble in the desperate search for survivors which continued throughout the day and into the following night.

Neither trees nor buildings survived when a V-1 hit this part of Kensington on 23 July 1944.

something queer occurred in London: 'At a quarter to seven a terrific explosion rent the air, followed by a low rumble', Hodgson told her diary. 'I nearly leapt out of my skin. No Warning on. So it could not be the new secret weapon. Perhaps it was an explosion at a munitions factory, or a bomb of long delayed action.'

William Sansom heard it too, describing it as a 'double thunder-clap followed by the noise of a remote and aerial express train'. It also shook the walls of the Air Ministry, causing Dr R. V. Jones of Scientific Intelligence to turn to a colleague and say: 'That's the first one.'

There were more mysterious explosions in the days that followed, but the only official proclamation on what they might be was an oblique reference to 'gas main explosions'. Londoners laughed grimly. 'We're being attacked by flying gas mains', remarked one.

The 'gas main' explosion at Chiswick on 8 September was followed by similar incidents in Epping, in Southend and in Crockenhall, Kent. Then early in the morning of Tuesday 12 September, a gas main blew in Kew Gardens. 'I had been fast asleep', wrote Vere Hodgson.

BELOW: A V-2 missile nearly ready for launch. The missiles were towed into place with the use of a trailer, but here, all that remains is the launch pad and the missile. Courtesy of NARA

LEFT: A London double-decker bus bears grim testament to the destructive power of a V-1 flying bomb.

RIGHT: A fairly intact V-1 found near an airfield in northern France. This was the standard type used in the V-1 campaign against England during the later years of the Blitz. Courtesy of NARA

V-ROCKETS

THE V-1 FLYING BOMB had the technical designation of Fieseler Fi 103 but was also referred to in German as *Vergeltungswaffe* (Retaliation) 1 hence its contraction to the V-1. It was the most widely used guided missile of the Second World War and the world's first successful cruise missile. Developed by the Luftwaffe it was an unmanned bomb powered by a pulse jet engine and it was the buzz created by this pulsing and the way that it doodled across the sky that earned it the nickname of 'buzz bomb' or 'doodlebug' amongst British civilians. It was capable of a top speed of 400 miles per hour at a range of 150 miles although its quite simple, and certainly imperfect, autopilot guidance system did mean that quite a few were lost over the English Channel before ever reaching their target. Just as importantly, it was easy to manufacture and practical to operate and as a result was ultimately responsible for the deaths of tens of thousands of civilian casualties not only in London, but also throughout Britain as well as other European cities. Allied intelligence was not unaware of the development of this secret weapon and had learned from French and Polish resistance of the construction of unusual bases throughout Normandy and the Pas de Calais and tests on the Baltic coast by the summer of 1943. The Allies launched a concentrated bombing campaign, Operation *Crossbow*, throughout the rest of the year, which did succeed in delaying the launch of V-1 rocket attacks on London. On 16 May 1944 Hitler issued an order that the missile attack against the British capital would need to begin by mid-June. The D-Day landings and concentrated Allied bombing campaign that accompanied the landings caused some disruptions but the first V-1s were officially launched at 11pm on 12 June. This first wave of attacks was not particularly successful but on the night of the 15–16 June 1944 over 244 missiles were fired, of which 144 reached the English coast and 73 fell on London. British aerial defences immediately swung into action against these so-called 'doodlebugs' relying on anti-aircraft guns, the balloon barrage and, increasingly, fighter interception. V-1 attacks reached their peak in the August but the Allied advances and the loss of launch sites meant that the threat gradually reduced. As German pilot Ernst Eberling explained: 'Because there were no launch sites left in France and Belguim, the V-1 rockets were struggling to reach central London.'[6] The development of the V-1 had revolutionised warfare and both the Americans and the Soviets attempted to develop their own V-1 missile programme before the end of the war.

The second German 'retaliation' weapon was the V-2, or A4 long-range ballistic missile. The V-2 was the culmination of years of pioneering work by German aeronautical engineers for the German Army that had first begun in the 1930s. Inspired by the potential for greater range and payloads that liquid fuel could offer, the development process literally took off once the Nazis came to power. However, the first test missile did not fly until 1942 and the entire development programme, although revolutionary, was expensive and plagued by technical failings. Indeed, although the V-1 was actually developed after the V-2 it was quicker to enter operational service. The first V-2 attack was launched against Paris on 8 September 1944, with attacks against London quickly following later that same day. Much faster than the V-1, with speeds over 1,780 miles per hour and a range of over 200 miles, it was a phenomenal weapon capable of huge destruction and impervious to attacks by fighters or anti-aircraft guns. However, it was hamstrung by its cost to produce which meant that it was never available in the same numbers as the V-1 and once the launch sites were lost to the advancing Allies in early 1945 it could no longer pose a threat to the British public. The V-2 would have a huge impact on the development of ballistic missiles after the war but it could not alter the outcome of the war itself. Its true worth in German eyes was as a retaliation weapon as the name implied, wrecking havoc on London just as Allied bombers intensified their campaigns against German cities.

There was no Warning. I felt sure it was no Gas Works exploding, as we thought when we heard it on Friday. It was something the Germans were sending over! It is the great topic of conversation as soon as people meet. But neither radio nor newspapers speak. But we feel if many more come the truth must be told. Rumour says this last fell on a motor factory near Kew. Many were killed. It is all hush-hush. They seem to be Rockets which drop from the stratosphere. You may be out peaceably walking and one drops. Nice prospect!

Hodgson was right. It wasn't a gas works exploding, it was something the Germans were sending over, it was a *Vergeltungswaffe* (V-2) rocket, fired from the Dutch coast. Each rocket weighed 13 tons, a ton of which was high explosive, travelled at over 1,780 miles per hour and descended from its ceiling of 328,000 feet at four times the speed of sound. A new age of warfare had dawned.

The doodlebugs were pretty frightening, but the V-2s were terrifying. Perhaps we were tired by that point in the war, but we were much more scared than when the bombs were raining down on us during the Blitz. I was longing for the end by then.[7]

BELOW AND LEFT: Churchill inspects damage caused by a V-1 flying bomb that fell on Westminster in July 1944.

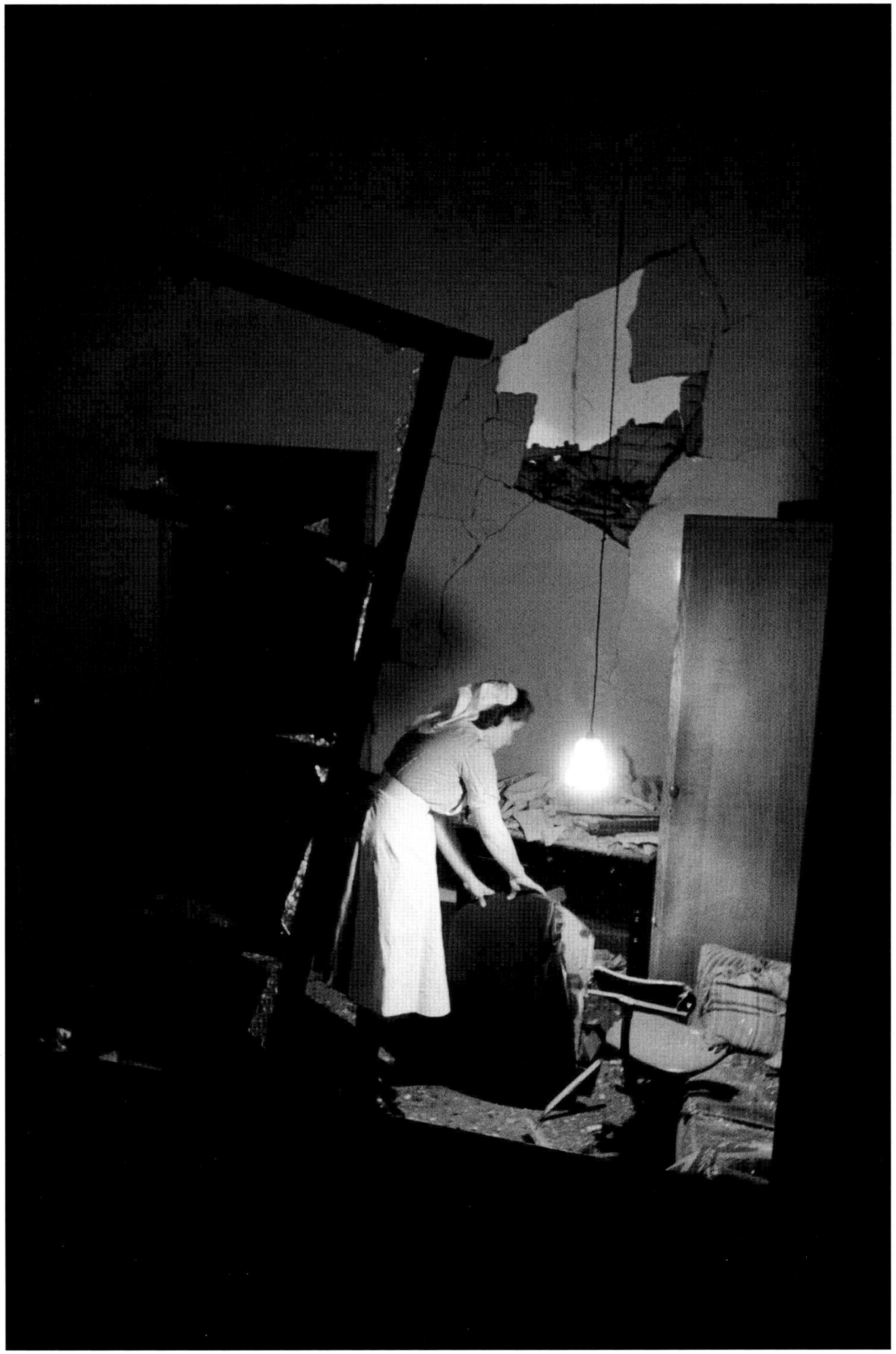

Business as usual for this nurse at the Royal Free Hospital despite the damage caused by a V-1.

Smoke billows up from Great Eastern Street in Islington following the detonation of a V-1 on 26 July 1944.

This series of four photos shows a group of London children being rescued after a V-1 landed on their school in July 1944.

Greenwell captures the moment a V-1 explodes from the roof of the *Daily Mirror* offices.

The first V-2 to fall killed three people in Chiswick, all of whom died without terror, having not known what hit them. Immediately, Churchill ordered a news blackout, not to shield the truth from his people but to deny the rockets' range plotters from honing their aim. So Londoners were left to speculate whether the explosion was another of Hitler's secret weapons. The speculation ceased on 17 September when a row of terraced houses in Lewisham exploded, killing 14 people, including five members of the Shin family, from three-year-old Beatrice to 67-year-old Louisa.

It wasn't until 10 November that the British government finally conceded that the country was under attack from V-2 rockets, an announcement prompted by a German broadcast claiming that London had been 'devastated' by the new weapon. 'For the last few weeks the enemy has been using his new weapon, the long-range rocket, and a number have landed at widely scattered points in this country', declared Churchill in a statement to the Commons. 'In all, the casualties and damage have so far not been heavy, though I am sure the House will wish me to express my sympathy with the victims of this as

LEFT: A V-1 explodes in central London during the morning rush hour.

TOP: 'A scene of terrible slaughter', was how one Londoner described the aftermath of a V-1 attack. This flying bomb exploded at lunchtime on 1 August 1944.

ABOVE: Policemen and rescue workers lead stunned survivors to safety after a V-rocket attack.

OPPOSITE TOP: The destruction caused by the first V-2 to land is clear to see. It landed in Chiswick, London, and was initially passed off by the government as a gas mains explosion.

OPPOSITE RIGHT: George Greenwell, *Mirror* photojournalist and auxiliary fireman, captures the grim determination of one of the exhausted firemen who helped douse a fire caused by a V-2 in Shooters Hill, London in the dying days of the war.

with other attacks.' The next day the Prime Minister's comments were reported in all the newspapers in more dramatic prose, the *Daily Herald* describing a 'comet that dives from 70 miles … the most indiscriminate weapon of this or any other war. It is a sinister, eerie form of war.'

Churchill hadn't been downplaying the malignancy of the V-2s when he announced the damage caused as less than anticipated. Though they continued to drop on London, and as far afield as East Anglia, throughout November, the rockets weren't as terrifying as first feared. It was hard to fear something you couldn't see. Unlike doodlebugs with their flaming rears and diving noses, 'the V-2s were just a sort of bang and the floor rocked a bit', recalled Rosamond Boddy, a London office girl. 'If you heard the bang you knew you were all right. You didn't hear anything before so you couldn't spend you whole life wondering if you were going to hear a bang, so one tried not to think about anything until they went off.'[8]

Nonetheless, Londoners were dying in clusters – nine at Peckham, 30 at Deptford, 33 at Wandsworth, 18 at Poplar, 25 at Greenwich – right up until the 251st V-2 hit the capital on Saturday 25 November. On that occasion people died in their scores. The rocket fell at 12.26pm just behind Woolworth's and the Co-Op in New Cross Road. One of the first emergency workers on the scene was Lewis Blake, who described what he saw in his book *Bolts from the Blue*: 'Tumbled masonry completely blocked the A2 and everywhere

RIGHT: The funeral of two London firemen killed by a V-1.

TOP RIGHT: Rescue workers sort Blitz debris into giant cauldrons following another V-1 rocket attack, while one of their colleagues comforts a stray cat (far right).

BOTTOM RIGHT: This Londoner was just one of the 60,595 people killed by enemy air attacks during the course of the war. Such a high loss of life amongst civilians during wartime had never before been experienced by Britain.

lay ankle deep in broken glass … scores of dazed and blood-covered victims moaned on the pavements, or ran hysterically they knew not where. Others were silent and motionless.'

One hundred and sixty bodies were pulled from the rubble, though the death toll was estimated to be 171. Eleven people known to have been shopping in the area at the time were never found, presumed liquidated, including two young mothers who had popped into Woolworth's for a cup of tea pushing their prams.

The rocket that destroyed a large part of New Cross was one of 1,300 V-2s launched at London from September 1944 to March 1945, although only 517 reached the capital. They killed 2,724 people. Stray V-2s reached as far afield as Bedford and Horsham. The very last V-2 to hit London did so on the afternoon of Monday 27 March, exploding in Kynaston Road in Orpington, just as Ivy Millichamp began to prepare the evening supper in her kitchen. The 34-year-old was the only fatality. A fortnight later, on 9 April, Vere Hodgson wrote in her diary: 'No more bombs for more than a week. No one knows what it means to us to go to bed in peace, and not take leave of all our possessions, and wonder if we shall wake up in pieces with the roof collapsing on our heads, unless they have lived with it.'

LEFT: At first the government tried to pass off the detonations caused by V-2s as exploding gas mains; however few people believed the official line when the damage was as great as here.

TOP AND ABOVE: A London factory is reduced to rubble by a V-2 rocket. However, there are smiles all around among these factory workers who survived the attack.

Residents in Bounds Green Road, Southgate, examine the remains of a V-2 after it landed on 16 September 1944.

One rescuer likened the devastation caused by V-weapons to a First World War battlefield and the comparison is justified after a V-2 exploded here in Tottenham.

This V-2 came down in Tewkesbury Road, just off the Seven Sisters Road, in January 1945.

Not much remains of this lead paint factory in Islington after a V-2 exploded in January 1945.

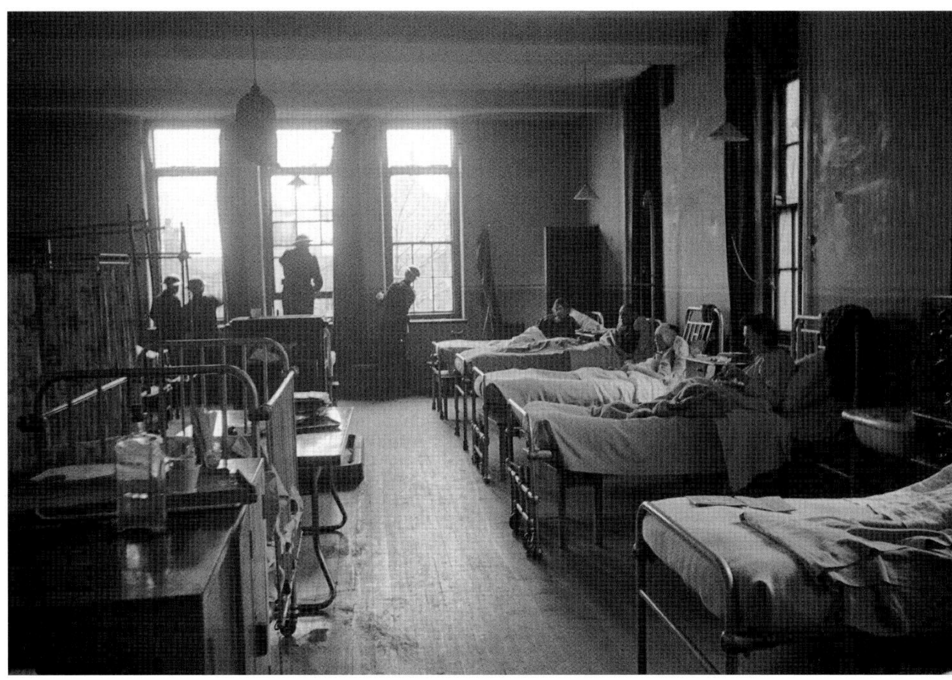

Patients in Bethnal Green hospital try to ignore the commotion caused by a V-2 landing nearby.

CONCLUSION

"… do not despair, do not yield to violence and tyranny, march straightforward and die if need be unconquered."

Anonymous, quoted by Winston Churchill, 8 May 1945

IVY MILLICHAMP WAS THE LAST of 60,595 civilians killed in Great Britain as a result of enemy action during the Second World War. A further 86,182 suffered serious injuries, many life-changing, and 150,833 were classified as slightly injured. However, they were just the physical wounds. The mental suffering caused by nearly six years of bombing affected millions. Yet despite the terror, many survivors consider themselves enriched, not impoverished, by the Blitz. As Tom Winter said of his experiences as a teenage boy in Bermondsey: 'I think I'm lucky to have lived through a time in history when people on the whole were good, decent and much more socially conscious of their fellow man.'[1]

It was this spirit Winston Churchill encapsulated when he addressed the nation on Tuesday 8 May 1945:

> The lights went out and the bombs came down. But every man, woman and child in the country had no thought of quitting the struggle. London can take it. So we came back after long months from the jaws of death, out of the mouth of hell, while all the world wondered. When shall the reputation and faith of this generation of English men and women fail? I say that in the long years to come not only will the people of this island but of the world, wherever the bird of freedom chirps in human hearts, look back to what we've done and they will say 'do not despair, do not yield to violence and tyranny, march straightforward and die if need be unconquered.'

Not for the first time Churchill had sacrificed exactness for eloquence. Not every man, woman and child in the country had stood up to the Blitz with a stiff upper lip and a steely eyed look. Thousands fled the cities for the countryside, abandoning their poorer neighbours to their fate. Some of those who stayed looted and stole, exploiting the misery of the bombed. Very few people, be they in London, Liverpool or Glasgow, would have willingly espoused a battle cry of 'march straightforward and die'.

Yet those Britons who lived through the eye of the Luftwaffe storm displayed their own brand of gallantry. Not the battlefield kind, the dash up the landing beach or the charge at the machine-gun nest. Rather it was defensive courage – stubborn, resilient and bloody-minded. Pounded by bombs day and night, week after week, unable to fight back, Britain's civilians did the only thing they could, they went about their business. And it was the manner in which they carried on as usual that set them apart: with defiance, dignity and that indefatigable good humour typified by the sign that appeared in the shattered shop front of a London draper's the morning after a heavy raid – 'Göring may break our windows but he can't break our hearts'.

OPPOSITE: St Paul's survived both the Blitz of 1940–1 and the 'Little Blitz' of the V-rocket attacks to come through the war relatively unscathed. The same could not be said of other parts of London or indeed any other major city in Britain.

NOTES

INTRODUCTION

1. Churchill, Winston, *Their Finest Hour*, Volume 2, Mariner Books (1986)

CHAPTER ONE

1. Eric Hill, IWM Sound 12673
2. All Sansom quotes taken from William Sansom, *The Blitz: Westminster at War*, Oxford Paperbacks; New Ed edition (1990)
3. Author interview and quoted in Gavin Mortimer, *The Longest Night: Voices from the Blitz*, Weidenfeld & Nicolson (2005)
4. Letter to author from Lillian Patient 2004
5. Walter Blanchard, IWM Sound 19906, quoted in Joshua Levine, *Forgotten Voices of the Blitz and the Battle for Britain*, Ebury Press (2007), p.280
6. Quoted in Alfred Price, *Blitz on Britain 1939–45*, Purnell Books (1977)
7. Author interview with Iris Grant 2010
8. Sir Aylmer Firebrace, *Front Line*, HMSO (1942)
9. Bernard Kops, *The World is a Wedding*, MacGibbon and Kee (1963)
10. Doreen E. Idle, *The War over West Ham*, Faber and Faber Limited, (1943)
11. George Unwin, IWM Sound 11544
12. Kathleen Clayden, IWM Sound 12429, quoted in *Forgotten Voices of the Blitz and the Battle for Britain*, p.281
13. Author interview with May Richards
14. Sir Frederick Pile, *Ack-ack. Britain's defence against air attack during the Second World War*, G.G. Harrap (1949)
15. William Gray, IWM Sound 11478, quoted in *Forgotten Voices of the Blitz and the Battle for Britain*, p.319
16. Cajus Bekker, *The Luftwaffe Diaries: The German Air Force in World War II*, Macdonald (1967)
17. Combat report quoted in Sansom, *The Blitz: Westminster at war*

CHAPTER TWO

1. Quoted in Alfred Price, *Blitz on Britain 1939–45*, Purnell Books (1977)
2. Quoted in Gavin Mortimer, *The Longest Night*, Weidenfeld & Nicolson (2005)
3. All Corville quotes taken from John Corville, *The Fringes of Power: Downing Street Diaries 1939–40*, Weidenfeld and Nicolson (2004)
4. All Vere Hodgson quotes taken from V. Hodgson and J. Hartley, *Few Eggs and No Oranges: The Diaries of Vere Hodgson 1940–45*, Dobson Books Ltd (1976)
5. Walter Marshall, IWM Sound 23849, quoted in Joshua Levine, *Forgotten Voices of the Blitz and the Battle for Britain*, Ebury Press (2007), p.325
6. Hugh Varah, IWM Sound 14783
7. Ibid.
8. Ballard Berkeley, IWM Sound 5340
9. Erik Sommers, IWM Sound 9629, quoted in *Forgotten Voices of the Blitz and the Battle for Britain*, p.309
10. Flight-Lieutenant John Cunningham, IWM Sound 19913
11. Quoted in *Forgotten Voices of the Blitz and the Battle for Britain*, p.315

CHAPTER THREE

1. Author interview with Joe Richardson
2. Thomas Parkinson, IWM Sound 21566
3. Ruth Tanner, IWM Sound 15291, quoted in *Forgotten Voices of the Blitz and the Battle for Britain*, p.353
4. Teresa Wilkinson, IWM Sound 21596
5. All quotes attributed to Vera Brittain are taken from her memoirs *England's Hour*, Futura Publications (1981)
6. All quotes attributed to Constantine Fitzgibbon are taken from his memoir *The Blitz*, Macdonald (1970)
7. Quoted in *Forgotten Voices of the Blitz and the Battle for Britain*, p.349
8. Joan Varley, IWM Sound 28454, quoted in *Forgotten Voices of the Blitz and the Battle for Britain*, p.408
9. Quoted in Gavin Mortimer, *The Longest Night*, Weidenfeld & Nicolson (2005)
10. Sylvia Clark, IWM Sound 20305, quoted in *Forgotten Voices of the Blitz and the Battle for Britain*, p.433
11. Alfred Senchell, IWM Sound 5344
12. Marie Agazarian, IWM Sound 9579, quoted in *Forgotten Voices of the Blitz and the Battle for Britain*, p.409
13. Joan Varley, IWM Sound 28454
14. Quoted in Mortimer, *The Longest Night*
15. James Oates, IWM Sound 19784
16. Author interview with Bobbie Tanner

CHAPTER FOUR

1. Winston Churchill, *Their Finest Hour*, Volume 2, Mariner Books (1986)
2. *Midlands Daily Telegraph*, Blitz diary, *Mirror* archives, London
3. Thomas Cunningham-Boothe, IWM Sound 19913
4. Cajus Bekker, *The Luftwaffe Diaries: The German Air Force in World War II*, Macdonald (1967)
5. Peter Townsend, *Duel in the Dark*, Arrow Books (1986)
6. Guy Gibson, *The Enemy Coast Ahead*, Royal Air Force Museum (1946)
7. Dilwyn Evans, IWM Sound 20792, quoted in Joshua Levine, *Forgotten Voices of the Blitz and the Battle for Britain*, Ebury Press (2007), p.391
8. *Daily Mirror*, 21 November 1940, *Mirror* archives, London

CHAPTER FIVE

1. Eric Hill, IWM Sound 12673
2. Albert Prior, IWM Sound 5347, quoted in Joshua Levine, *Forgotten Voices of the Blitz and the Battle for Britain*, Ebury Press (2007), p.411
3. BBC radio interview 1941, quoted in Constantine Fitzgibbon, *The Blitz*, Macdonald (1970)
4. Walter Marshall, IWM Sound 23849
5. Mary Warschauer, IWM Sound 16762, quoted in *Forgotten Voices of the Blitz and the Battle for Britain*, p.399
6. Ernie Pyle, *Ernie Pyle in England*; Robert M. McBride; Later Printing edition (1945)
7. Quoted in Fitzgibbon, *The Blitz*
8. Sharp, BBC radio interview 1941, quoted in Fitzgibbon, *The Blitz*
9. Mason, BBC radio interview 1941, quoted in Fitzgibbon, *The Blitz*.
10. Lewis, BBC radio interview 1941, quoted in Fitzgibbon, *The Blitz*
11. Ibid.
12. Stanley Barron, IWM Sound 8877, quoted in *Forgotten Voices of the Blitz and the Battle for Britain*, p.398

CHAPTER SIX

1. Swansea Museum archives
2. All quotes attributed to Harry Beckingham taken from an interview with the author
3. Quoted in Constantine Fitzgibbon, *The Blitz*, Macdonald (1970)
4. Hugh Varah, IWM Sound 14783, quoted in Joshua Levine, *Forgotten Voices of the Blitz and the Battle for Britain*, Ebury Press (2007), p.365
5. Ibid.
6. Ruth Wittman, IWM Sound 10345, quoted in *Forgotten Voices of the Blitz and the Battle for Britain*, pp.400–401
7. Mrs Blair-Hickman, IWM Sound 2302
8. Ballard Berkeley, IWM Sound 5340
9. Ballard Berkeley, IWM Sound 5340

CHAPTER SEVEN

1. *Daily Mirror*, 22 March 1941
2. Quentin Reynolds, *Only the Stars are Neutral*, Random House (1942)
3. Gibson, Guy, *The Enemy Coast Ahead,* Royal Air Force Museum (1946)
4. Anthony Cruickshank, letter to BBC Liverpool, 2003

CHAPTER EIGHT

1. Hansard HC Deb 2 April 1941, Volume 370 cc982–3
2. Quoted in Constantine Fitzgibbon, *The Blitz*, Macdonald (1970)
3. Tony Cox, letter to the author
4. Quoted in Gavin Mortimer, *The Longest Night*, Weidenfeld & Nicolson (2005)
5. All quotes attributed to Joe Richardson taken from author interview
6. Quoted in Mortimer, *The Longest Night*
7. Ibid.
8. Quentin Reynolds, *Only the Stars are Neutral*, Random House (1942)

CHAPTER NINE

1. Alfred Price, *Blitz on Britain 1939–45*, Purnell Books (1977)
2. John Brasier, IWM Sound 6064, quoted in Max Arthur, *Forgotten Voices of the Second World War*, Ebury Press (2004), p.369
3. BBC radio interview quoted in Peter Haining (compiler), *The Spitfire Log*, Souvenir Press (1985)
4. Bob Ogley, *Doodlebugs and Rockets*, Froglets Publication (1992)
5. Terrence McEwan, IWM Sound 12846, quoted in *Forgotten Voices of the Second World War*, p.370
6. Ernst Eberling, IWM Sound 11389, quoted in *Forgotten Voices of the Second World War*, p.372
7. Myrtle Solomon, IWM Sound 8486, quoted in *Forgotten Voices of the Second World War*, p.372
8. Rosamond Boddy, interview with author

CONCLUSION

1. Tom Winter, interview with author

FURTHER READING

Arthur, Max, *Forgotten Voices of the Second World War*, Ebury Press (2004)

August, Evelyn, *The Black-out Book*, Osprey Publishing (2009)

de la Bedoyere, Guy, *Home Front*, Shire Publications (2002)

Bekker, Cajus, *The Luftwaffe Diaries: The German Air Force in World War II*, Macdonald (1967)

Blake, Lewis, *Bolts from the Blue*, self-published (1990)

Brittain, Vera, *England's Hour*, Futura Publications (1981)

Brown, Mike, *Evacuees of the Second World War*, Shire Publications (2009)

Brown, Mike, *Wartime Childhood*, Shire Publications (2009)

Churchill, Winston, *Their Finest Hour*, Volume 2, Mariner Books (1986)

Colville, John, *The Fringes of Power: Downing Street Diaries 1939–October 1941*, Hodder and Stoughton (1985)

Cossey, Bob, *A Tiger's Tale: The Story of John Freeborn*, J&KH Publishing (2002)

Doyle, Peter, *ARP and Civil Defence in the Second World War*, Shire Publications (2010)

Doyle, Petter, *The Blitz*, Shire Publications (2010)

Evans, Paul and Doyle, Peter, *The 1940s Home*, Shire Publications (2009)

Firebrace, Sir Aylmer, *Front Line*, HMSO (1942)

Fitzgibbon, Constantine, *The Blitz*, Macdonald (1970)

Fountain, Nigel (ed.), *The Battle of Britain and the Blitz*, Michael O'Mara (2002)

Gibson, Guy, *The Enemy Coast Ahead*, Royal Air Force Museum (1946)

Haining, Peter (compiler), *The Spitfire Log*, Souvenir Press (1985)

Hodgson, Vere & Hartley, Jenny, *Few Eggs and No Oranges: The Diaries of Vere Hodgson 1940–45*, Persephone Books (1999)

Idle, Doreen E., *The War over West Ham*, Faber and Faber Limited (1943)

Kops, Bernard, *The World is a Wedding*, MacGibbon and Kee (1963)

Levine, Joshua, *Forgotten Voices of the Blitz and the Battle for Britain*, Ebury Press (2007)

Mitchell, Jaqueline (compiler), *Blitz Spirit*, Osprey Publishing (2010)

Moore, Kate, *The Battle of Britain*, Osprey Publishing (2010)

Mortimer, Gavin, *The Longest Night*, Weidenfeld & Nicolson (2005)

Ogley, Bob, *Doodlebugs and Rockets*, Froglets Publication (1992)

Pile, Sir Frederick, *Ack-ack. Britain's defence against air attack during the Second World War*, G.G. Harrap (1949)

Price, Alfred, *Blitz on Britain 1939–45*, Purnell Books (1977)

Pyle, Ernie, *Ernie Pyle in England*, Robert M. McBridge; Later Printing edition (1945)

Ramsey, Winston G. (ed.), *The Blitz: Then and Now*, Volume 2, Battle of Britain Prints International Ltd (1988)

Reynolds, Quentin, *Only the Stars are Neutral*, Random House (1942)

Sansom, William, *The Blitz: Westminster at War*, Oxford Paperbacks; New Ed edition (1990)

Storey, Neil R., *The Home Guard*, Shire Publications (2010)

Thomas, Chris, *Typhoon and Tempest Aces of World War 2*, Aircraft of the Aces 27, Osprey Publishing (1999)

Townsend, Peter, *Duel in the Dark*, Arrow Books (1986)

Zaloga, Steven J., *V-1 Flying Bomb 1942–52: Hitler's infamous 'doodlebug'*, Osprey Publishing, (2005)

Zaloga, Steven J., *V-2 Ballistic Missile 1942–52*, Osprey Publishing, (2003)

UNPUBLISHED SOURCES

Beckingham, Harry interview with author, 2004
Boddy, Rosamond, interview with author
Cox, Tony, letter to author, 2004
Cruickshank, Anthony, letter to BBC Liverpool, 2003
Curry, Florence, interview with author, 2004
Grant, Iris, author interview, 2010
Hill, Eric, interview with author
Oakley, Cyril, interview with author
Patient, Lillian, letter to author, 2004
Richards, May, letter to author, 2004
Richardson, Joe, interview with author, 2004
Shaw, Gladys, interview with author, 2004
Tanner, Bobbie, interview with author, 2004
Winter, Tom, interview with author, 2004

IWM SOUND ARCHIVES

Agazarian, Marie, IWM Sound 9579
Barron, Stanley, IWM Sound 8877
Berkeley, Ballard, IWM Sound 5340
Blair-Hickman, Mrs, IWM Sound 5340
Blanchard, Walter, IWM Sound 19906
Clark, Sylvia, IWM Sound 20305
Clayden, Kathleen, IWM Sound 12429
Cunningham, Flight-Lieutenant John, IWM Sound 5373
Cunningham-Boothe, Thomas, IWM Sound 19913
Eberling, Ernst, IWM Sound 11389
Evans, Dilwyn, IWM Sound 20792
Gray, William, IWM Sound 11478
Hill, Eric, IWM Sound 12673
Marshall, Walter, IWM Sound 23849
McEwan, Terrence, IWM Sound 12846
Oates, James, IWM Sound 19784
Parkinson, Thomas, IWM Sound 21556
Prior, Albert, IWM Sound 5347
Senchell, Alfred, IWM Sound 5344
Solomon, Myrtle, IWM Sound 8486
Sommers, Erik, IWM Sound 9629
Tanner, Ruth, IWM Sound 15291
Unwin, George, IWM Sound 11544
Varah, Hugh, IWM Sound 14783
Varley, Joan, IWM Sound 28454
Warschauer, Mary, IWM Sound 16762
Wilkinson, Teresa, IWM Sound 21596
Wittman, Ruth, IWM Sound 10345

NEWSPAPERS, MAGAZINES, JOURNALS AND ARCHIVES

BBC Liverpool
Clydebank Press
The Coventry Evening Telegraph
Daily Herald
The Daily Mirror
Diary from *Mirror* archive
London Evening Standard
Midland Daily Telegraph
Ministry of Home Security handbook
The New Yorker
The Sunday Mirror
Swansea Museum archive
Westminster and Pimlico News

APPENDICES

Appendix 1

CIVILIAN CASUALTIES – MINISTRY OF HOME SECURITY STATISTICS (Compiled from Police and Medical Reports)
Source: Civil Defence, O'Brien, HMSO, Official War History Series

	KILLED			ADMITTED TO HOSPITAL (seriously injured)		
	London	**Elsewhere**	**Total**	**London**	**Elsewhere**	**Total**
September–December 1940	13,596	10,171	23,767	18,378	12,151	30,529
1941	6,487	13,431	19,918	7,641	13,524	21,165
1942	27	3,209	3,236	52	4,096	4,148
1943	542	1,830	2,327	989	2,461	3,450
1944	7,533	942	8,475	19,611	2,378	21,989
January–May 1945	1,705	155	1,860	3,836	387	4,223
Northern Ireland		967	967		678	678
Total	29,890	30,705	60,595	50,507	35,675	86,182

Note: In addition 150,833 civilians were slightly injured.

Appendix 2

CIVILIAN CASUALTIES BY BOMBING AND VARIOUS FORMS OF LONG RANGE BOMBARDMENT
Source: *The Defence of the United Kingdom*, Collier, HMSO, Official War History Series

	Killed	**Seriously Injured**	**Total**
Bombing	51,509	61,423	112,932
Flying bombs	6,148	17,981	24,165
Rockets	2,754	6,523	9,277
Cross-Channel guns	148	255	403
Total	60,595	86,182	146,777

Note: Of these 146,777 casualties, 80,397 occurred in the London Civil Defence Region and 66,380 elsewhere. Casualties to service personnel are not included.

INDEX

References to illustrations are shown in **bold**. Locations relate to London unless otherwise stated.